Home Plans Designed with
SOUTHERN CHARM

the
Garlinghouse
company

HELPING TO BUILD DREAMS SINCE **1907**

Home Plans Designed with
SOUTHERN CHARM

Published by
The Garlinghouse Company

CEO
D. Jarret Magbee

Editorial/Sales Director
Bruce Arant

Contributing Writer
Carol Shea

Graphic Design Consultant
Pamela Stant

Production Assistant
Jessica Salazar

Accounting Manager
Monika Jackson

Customer Service
Jeremy Priest

Designer Relations
Rick Miller

Fulfillment Operations
Daniel Fuentes

For Home Plan Orders in United States
4125 Lafayette Center Drive, Suite 100
Chantilly, Va 20151
800-235-5700

Plan #68186, pages 122-123
Photo courtesy of the Designer

On the Cover:
Plan #97756, page 72
Photo courtesy of the Designer

CONTENTS

Home Plans

Throughout this book you'll discover a rich selection of refined designs that are most popular in today's South. Architectural styles include Traditional Southern, Historic, Coastal, Mediterranean, Southern Country and European. Ranging from nearly 3,000 sq. ft., to over 6,000 sq. ft., these well-appointed home plans offer amenities and design characteristics most often associated with more affluent lifestyles. For the location of designs within a specific square footage range, please refer to the Home Plan Index on page 238.

Southern Style

The "look" of Southern homes has evolved from an eclectic blend of historic architectural styles and design elements. Our special features on Southern Style provide glimpses at the history and evolution of many of the design elements considered to typify Southern architecture.

Photography © istockphoto.com

41

Details & Services

Near the back of the book, we've provided information on a variety of topics that will hopefully be of help. If you have questions that require further explanation, however, please feel free to call our knowledgeable customer service staff at 800-235-5700.

Photo courtesy of The Designer

188

Home Plans Designed with
SOUTHERN CHARM

Southern Charm. It's a simple phrase that defines the complex character of an entire culture.

For the past four centuries, the fabric of America's South has been woven together from its rich heritage and fascinating history. It's been both blessed with prosperity and cursed with an inordinate amount of bloodshed and heartache.

41

203

Forged from both good times and bad, the South of today reflects a society that is refined and dignified, yet relaxed and hospitable.

For most of us, the phrase "Southern Charm" brings to mind a wide range of picturesque images: Sweet tea, sipped within the shade of a covered front porch. Stately pillars adorning the façade of historic Antebellum mansions. The perfume of Magnolia blossoms in the warm Spring breeze. Genteel gatherings on elegant, sprawling verandas. Backyard barbeques beneath moss-shrouded, ancient Oaks. Whether sophisticated or casual, these reflections of Southern culture maintain their lure of undeniable charm.

130

23

tured designs generally range between 3,000 and 6,000 square feet and offer the accoutrements one would expect to find in higher-end homes. Furthermore, the collection's larger designs are presented over two pages, to help

Architecturally speaking, the South is perhaps the most diverse and richly influenced region of the United States. Throughout the years, the design of Southern homes has been inspired by classical European elements and equally so by the region's oppressive summertime climate. The blend of these influences over time has established a veritable garden of design styles, each one distinctly "Southern."

It was with the diverse "flavors" of Southern architecture that this book was prepared. *Home Plans Designed with Southern Charm – Refined Designs of the South* offers a carefully selected collection of over 150 well-appointed home designs, most popular in the South. With a focus toward more affluent lifestyles, the fea-

159

you more easily study the homes' floor plans and special features.

In addition to providing a superb selection of refined Southern designs, this book will give you reason to pause at several brief vignettes titled **Southern Style**, which we've placed throughout the following pages. These informative presentations offer enlightening insights on a variety of design elements typically associated with Southern architecture. Topics include Covered Porches, Greek Pillars, Elaborate Friezes, Grand Staircases and more – each with an overview of the design element's origin, evolution and contribution to the "look" of the South.

It's with a warm Southern greeting that we welcome you to this book and we genuinely hope that within this presentation of home plans you'll find a design that meets your specific needs and speaks to your heart. Although these designs embody the genteel look of the South, they will, of course, feel at home wherever they're built.

56

23

176

As always, please feel free to talk with us if you wish to learn more about any of these home designs. Our well-trained customer service representatives are here to answer your questions at **800-235-5700**. Additionally, you can view thousands of additional home plans in a wide range of sizes and styles by visiting us on the web at **www.familyhomeplans.com**. Whether you're ordering home plans for your next new home, or just have some questions, we hope to hear from you soon – and to offer you a bit of Southern Charm.

Photo Courtesy of Carolina Lanterns

221

72

Photo Courtesy of The Designer

35

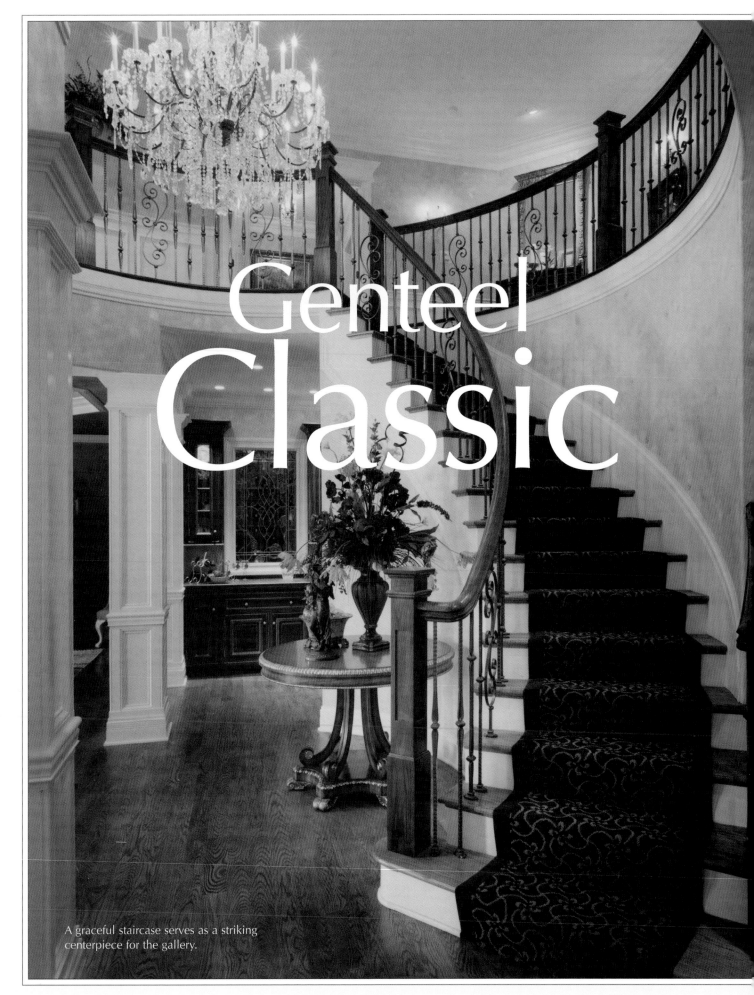

Genteel
Classic

A graceful staircase serves as a striking
centerpiece for the gallery.

This home, as shown, may differ from the original design.

With its stately pillars, sweeping staircase and sprawling outdoor living space, this gracious home imparts the classic spirit of Southern luxury. First impressions inside reveal formal rooms flanking the foyer, and beyond, a gallery area adorned by the graceful sweep of a staircase. The living room, music room and octagonal library flow together as one exquisite space in which to relax and entertain. Further inside, an expansive hearth room opens to the kitchen and breakfast area for more casual living. The well-appointed master suite is separated from the secondary bedrooms, which all access private baths and reside on the second and lower levels. The upstairs guest bedroom receives special attention with enhanced amenities. The lower level is strictly designed for fun.

RIGHT: Views to the outside surround the octagonal library, which opens adjacent to the music room.

A sizeable island in the kitchen provides an abundance of workspace and accommodates more casual dining.

A view from the foyer into the living room, music room and library beyond.

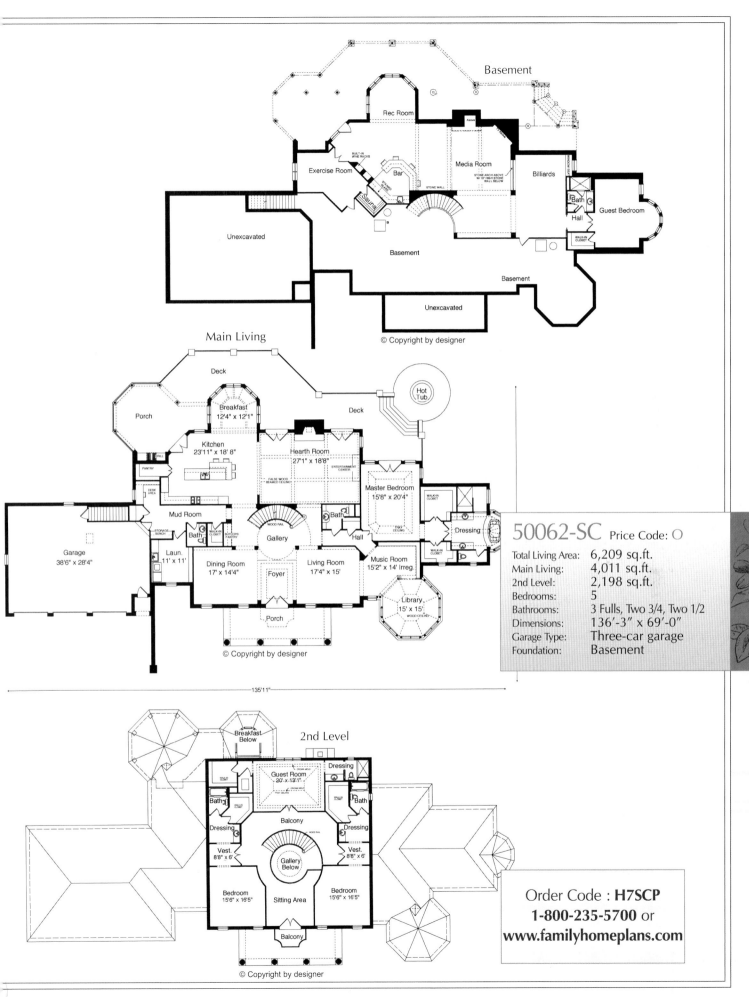

Basement

Rec Room

Media Room

Billiards

Exercise Room

Bar

Sauna

Bath

Hall

Guest Bedroom

Unexcavated

Basement

Basement

Unexcavated

© Copyright by designer

Main Living

Deck

Breakfast
12'4" x 12'1"

Deck

Hot Tub

Porch

Kitchen
23'11" x 18' 8"

Hearth Room
27'1" x 18'8"

Master Bedroom
15'8" x 20'4"

Pantry

Dressing

Desk Area

Mud Room

Bath

Gallery

Bath

Hall

Music Room
15'2" x 14' Irreg.

Garage
38'6" x 28'4"

Laun.
11' x 11'

Dining Room
17' x 14'4"

Foyer

Living Room
17'4" x 15'

Library
15' x 15'

Porch

© Copyright by designer

135'11"

50062-SC Price Code: O

Total Living Area:	6,209 sq.ft.
Main Living:	4,011 sq.ft.
2nd Level:	2,198 sq.ft.
Bedrooms:	5
Bathrooms:	3 Fulls, Two 3/4, Two 1/2
Dimensions:	136'-3" x 69'-0"
Garage Type:	Three-car garage
Foundation:	Basement

2nd Level

Breakfast Below

Guest Room
20' x 13'1"

Dressing

Bath

Dressing

Balcony

Bath

Dressing

Vest.
8'8" x 6'

Gallery Below

Vest.
8'8" x 6'

Bedroom
15'6" x 16'5"

Sitting Area

Bedroom
15'6" x 16'5"

Balcony

© Copyright by designer

Order Code : **H7SCP**
1-800-235-5700 or
www.familyhomeplans.com

61025-SC Price Code: L

Total Living Area : 4,155 sq.ft.
Main Living : 2,952 sq.ft.
2nd Level : 1,203 sq.ft.
Bedrooms : 5
Bathrooms : 3.5
Dimensions : 68'-8" x 76'-0"
Garage Type : Three-car garage
Foundation : Basement, Slab, Crawlspace

Uniquely designed main-level dormers add character to a spacious game room and office at the rear of this home. Sensible accoutrements include a sizeable laundry center and walk-in pantry just off the kitchen.

Order Code : **H7SCP**
1-800-235-5700 or
www.familyhomeplans.com

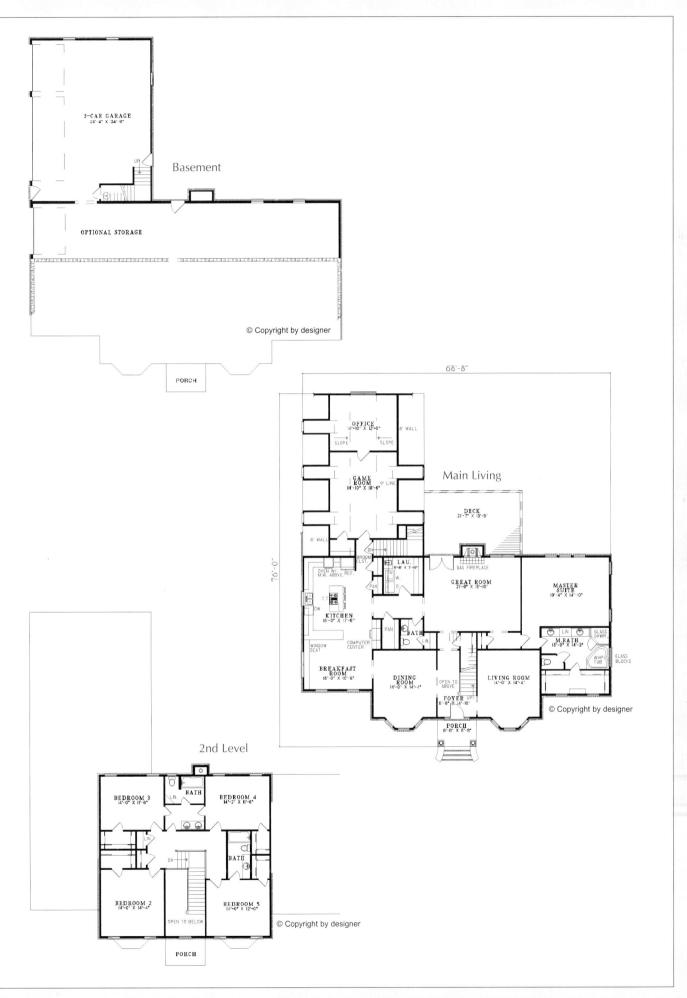

Basement

3-CAR GARAGE
26'-4" X 34'-8"

UP

OPTIONAL STORAGE

© Copyright by designer

PORCH

68'-8"

Main Living

OFFICE
14'-10" X 12'-0"

6' WALL

SLOPE   SLOPE

GAME ROOM
14'-10" X 18'-6"

9' LINE

DECK
21'-7" X 13'-9"

6' WALL

DN

BROOM CLST.

LAU.
8'-8" X 7'-0"

GAS FIREPLACE

GREAT ROOM
21'-8" X 18'-10"

MASTER SUITE
19'-4" X 14'-10"

76'-0"

OVEN W/ M.W. ABOVE REF.

W.
D

PAN

C.T.

KITCHEN
16'-0" X 17'-8"

BATH

LIN

PAN

M.BATH
16'-0" X 14'-2"

LIN   GLASS SHWR

GLASS BLOCKS

WHP TUB

WINDOW SEAT

COMPUTER CENTER

BREAKFAST ROOM
16'-0" X 10'-8"

DINING ROOM
14'-0" X 14'-6"

OPEN TO ABOVE

LIVING ROOM
14'-0" X 14'-4"

FOYER
8'-8" X 14'-10"

UP

PORCH
8'-8" X 5'-8"

© Copyright by designer

2nd Level

BEDROOM 3
14'-0" X 11'-6"

LIN

BATH

BEDROOM 4
14'-2" X 11'-6"

LIN

DN

BATH

BEDROOM 2
14'-0" X 14'-4"

OPEN TO BELOW

BEDROOM 5
14'-0" X 12'-0"

© Copyright by designer

PORCH

50020-SC Price Code: I

Total Living Area : 3,366 sq.ft.
Main Living : 1,759 sq.ft.
2nd Level : 1,607 sq.ft.
Bedrooms : 4
Bathrooms : 4
Dimensions : 69'-8" x 56'-8"
Garage Type : Three-car garage
Foundation : Basement

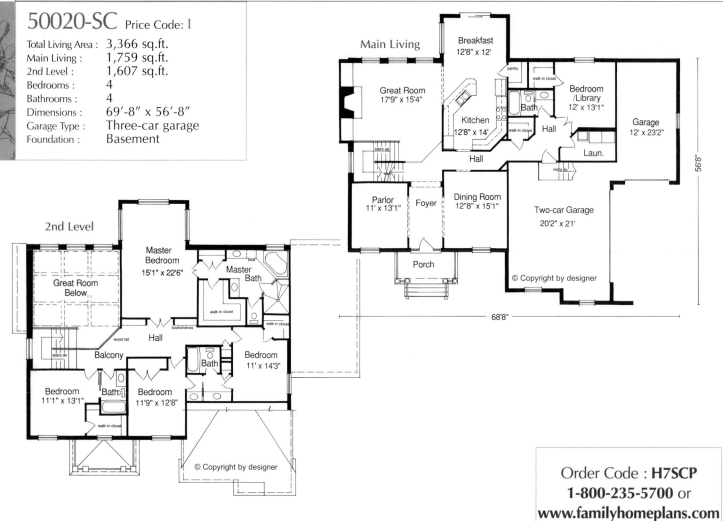

Main Living

Breakfast 12'8" x 12'

pantry

walk-in closet

Great Room 17'9" x 15'4"

Bedroom /Library 12' x 13'1"

Bath

Kitchen 12'8" x 14'

walk-in closet

Hall

Garage 12' x 23'2"

stairs up

Hall

Laun.

Hall

stairs dn

Parlor 11' x 13'1"

Foyer

Dining Room 12'8" x 15'1"

Two-car Garage 20'2" x 21'

Porch

© Copyright by designer

56'8"

68'8"

2nd Level

Great Room Below

Master Bedroom 15'1" x 22'6"

Master Bath

walk-in closet

bookshelves

walk-in closet

stairs dn

wood rail

Hall

Balcony

Bath

Bedroom 11' x 14'3"

Bedroom 11'1" x 13'1"

Bath

Bedroom 11'9" x 12'8"

walk-in closet

© Copyright by designer

Main Living

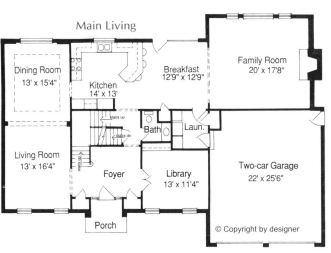

Dining Room
13' x 15'4"

Kitchen
14' x 13'

Breakfast
12'9" x 12'9"

Family Room
20' x 17'8"

stairs up

Bath

Laun.

stairs dn

Living Room
13' x 16'4"

Foyer

Library
13' x 11'4"

Two-car Garage
22' x 25'6"

Porch

© Copyright by designer

97704-SC Price Code: I

Total Living Area :	3,296 sq.ft.
Main Living :	1,800 sq.ft.
2nd Level :	1,496 sq.ft.
Bedrooms :	4
Bathrooms :	2.5
Dimensions :	64'-0" x 44'-10"
Garage Type :	Two-car garage
Foundation :	Basement

2nd Level

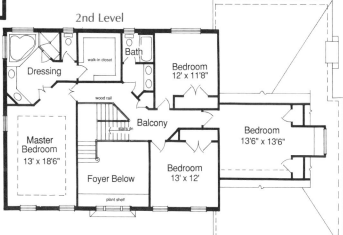

Dressing

walk-in closet

Bath

Bedroom
12' x 11'8"

wood rail

Balcony

stairs dn

Master
Bedroom
13' x 18'6"

Foyer Below

Bedroom
13' x 12'

Bedroom
13'6" x 13'6"

plant shelf

© Copyright by designer

82126-SC Price Code: K

Total Living Area : 3,978 sq.ft.
Main Living : 2,500 sq.ft.
2nd Level : 1,478 sq.ft.
Bedrooms : 5
Bathrooms : 3.5
Dimensions : 73'-10" x 61'-2"
Garage Type : Three-car garage
Foundation : Basement*, Slab,
Crawlspace

Main Living

73'-10"

GRILLING PORCH
24'-0" X 10'-0"

MASTER SUITE
17'-0" X 18'-8"
10' BOXED CEILING

M. BATH
17'-6" X 22'-0"

GLASS BLOCKS
WHP TUB
GLASS SHWR

GREAT ROOM
17'-4" X 27'-2"

BREAKFAST/HEARTH ROOM
10'-10" X 20'-2"

8' COLUMNS

KITCHEN
12'-8" X 17'-2"

STORAGE
15'-0" X 9'-8"

REF.

OVENS

OPTIONAL BASEMENT STAIRS

61'-2"

LAU.
9'-4" X 9'-0"

PAN.

3-CAR GARAGE
21'-2" X 32'-0"

HOBBY ROOM
9'-6" X 9'-0"

DINING RM.
13'-0" X 16'-0"

FOYER
12'-4" X 13'-4"
OPEN TO ABOVE

STUDY
11'-0" X 15'-0"

PORTICO
9'-0" X 6'-0"

8' COLUMNS

© Copyright by designer

2nd Level

10' BOXED CEILING BELOW

MEDIA ROOM / BEDROOM 5
13'-0" X 16'-2"

BATH
10'-0"

BEDROOM 4
13'-4" X 15'-1"

ATTIC STORAGE

8' WALL

LIN.
LIN.

LIN.

BONUS ROOM
18'-8" X 10'-8"

COMPUTER CENTER

BATH
12'-3" X 8'-0"

DN

R.A.

8' LINE

6' WALL

BEDROOM 2
13'-0" X 16'-6"

DN

BEDROOM 3
13'-4" X 13'-6"

4' WALL

BONUS ROOM
12'-0" X 24'-0"

OPEN TO BELOW

© Copyright by designer

50108-SC Price Code: L

Total Living Area : 4,222 sq.ft.
Main Living : 3,008 sq.ft.
2nd Level : 1,214 sq.ft.
Bedrooms : 4
Bathrooms : 3.5
Dimensions : 93'-0" x 75'-0"
Garage Type : Three-car garage
Foundation : Walkout Basement

Order Code : **H7SCP**
1-800-235-5700 or
www.familyhomeplans.com

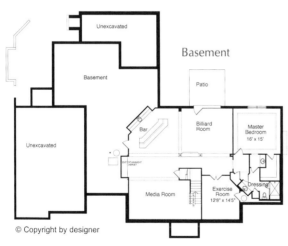

Basement

Unexcavated

Basement

Unexcavated

Patio

Bar

Billiard Room

Master Bedroom
16' x 15'

Media Room

Exercise Room
12'8" x 14'5"

Dressing

© Copyright by designer

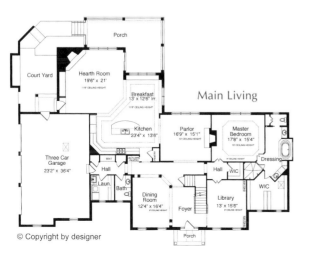

Main Living

Porch

Court Yard

Hearth Room
19'6" x 21'

Breakfast
13' x 12'6" Irr.

Kitchen
23'4" x 13'6"

Parlor
16'9" x 15'1"

Master Bedroom
17'8" x 15'4"

Three Car Garage
23'2" x 36'4"

Hall

Laun.

Bath

Dining Room
12'4" x 16'4"

Foyer

Library
13' x 15'6"

Hall

WIC

WIC

Dressing

Porch

© Copyright by designer

2nd Level

Bedroom
17'1" x 15'6"

Bedroom
13' x 14'8"

Foyer Below

Bedroom
13' x 14'8"

Hall

Bath

© Copyright by designer

This home, as shown, may differ from the original design.

An irresistible gazebo and screened porch take their places on either side of a rear deck, expanding the options for outdoor entertaining. Inside, a bank of tall windows brightens the formal dining room.

92671-SC Price Code: I

Total Living Area :	3,445 sq.ft.
Main Living :	1,666 sq.ft.
2nd Level :	1,779 sq.ft.
Bedrooms :	4
Bathrooms :	3.5
Dimensions :	71'-8" x 38'-10"
Garage Type :	Three-car garage
Foundation :	Basement

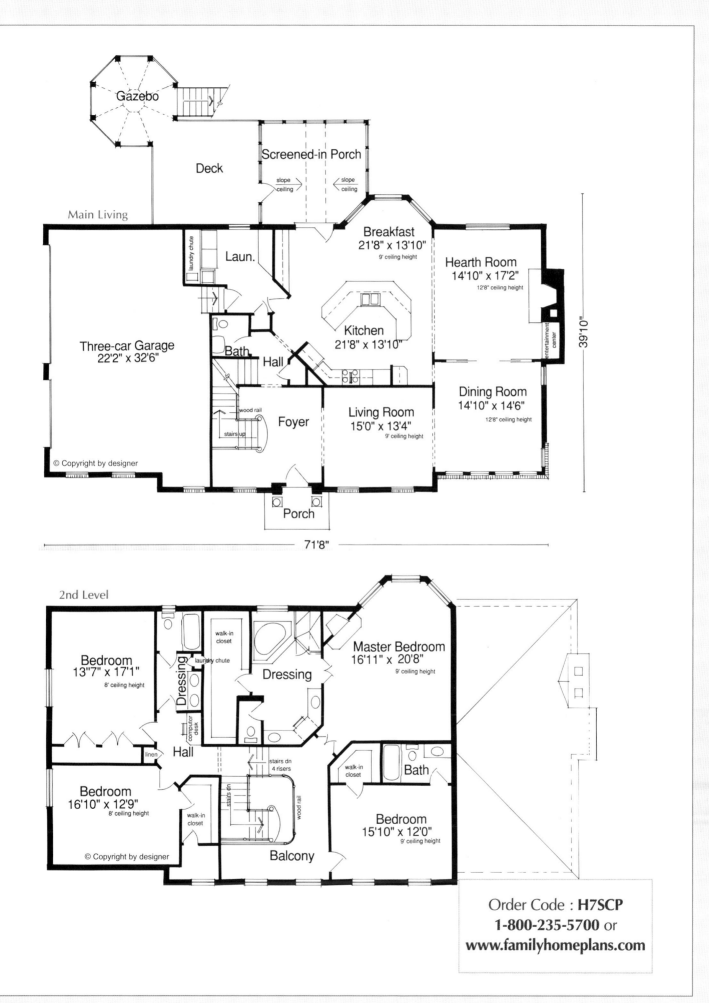

Gazebo

Deck

Screened-in Porch

slope ceiling   slope ceiling

Main Living

Laun.

laundry chute

Breakfast
21'8" x 13'10"
9' ceiling height

Hearth Room
14'10" x 17'2"
12'8" ceiling height

entertainment center

Kitchen
21'8" x 13'10"

Three-car Garage
22'2" x 32'6"

Bath

Hall

Dining Room
14'10" x 14'6"
12'8" ceiling height

wood rail

Foyer

stairs up

Living Room
15'0" x 13'4"
9' ceiling height

© Copyright by designer

Porch

39'10"

71'8"

2nd Level

Bedroom
13"7" x 17'1"
8' ceiling height

Dressing

walk-in closet

laundry chute

Dressing

Master Bedroom
16'11" x 20'8"
9' ceiling height

computer desk

linen

Hall

Bedroom
16'10" x 12'9"
8' ceiling height

walk-in closet

stairs dn
4 risers

stairs dn

wood rail

walk-in closet

Bath

Bedroom
15'10" x 12'0"
9' ceiling height

© Copyright by designer

Balcony

Order Code : **H7SCP**
1-800-235-5700 or
www.familyhomeplans.com

63073-SC Price Code: L

Total Living Area :	4,094 sq.ft.
Main Living :	3,079 sq.ft.
2nd Level :	1,015 sq.ft.
Bedrooms :	4
Bathrooms :	4.5
Dimensions :	88'-4" x 79'-4"
Garage Type :	Three-car garage
Foundation :	Slab

A rear-loading garage preserves the historic appearance of this design's front elevation. The main level entertains guests with an open layout inside and a covered patio showcased as an outdoor centerpiece. There is even a sunken wine cellar just off the foyer.

Order Code : **H7SCP**
1-800-235-5700 or
www.familyhomeplans.com

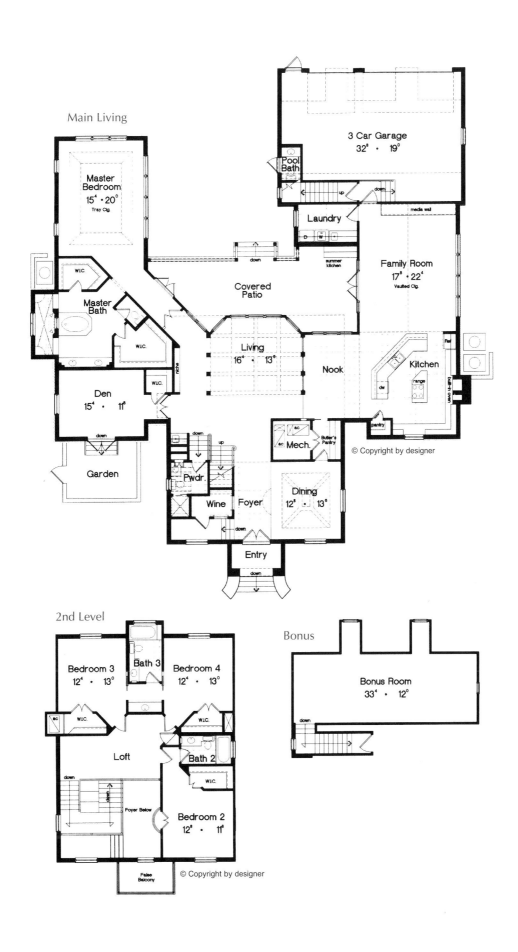

Main Living

Master
Bedroom
15⁴ · 20⁰
Tray Clg.

3 Car Garage
32⁸ · 19⁰

Pool
Bath

W.I.C.

Master
Bath

Laundry

W.I.C.

Covered
Patio

Family Room
17⁸ · 22⁴
Vaulted Clg.

summer
kitchen

niche

Living
16⁴ · 13⁰

Nook

Kitchen

W.I.C.

Den
15⁴ · 11⁸

range

dw

pantry

Garden

down

up

Pwdr.

Mech.

Butler's
Pantry

© Copyright by designer

Wine

Foyer

Dining
12⁸ · 13⁸

Entry

down

2nd Level

Bonus

Bedroom 3
12⁴ · 13⁰

Bath 3

Bedroom 4
12⁴ · 13⁰

Bonus Room
33⁴ · 12⁰

W.I.C.

W.I.C.

down

Loft

Bath 2

down

W.I.C.

Foyer Below

Bedroom 2
12⁸ · 11⁸

False
Balcony

© Copyright by designer

97717-SC Price Code: I

Total Living Area :	3,311 sq.ft.
Main Living :	1,670 sq.ft.
2nd Level :	1,641 sq.ft.
Bedrooms :	4
Bathrooms :	3.5
Dimensions :	60'-0" x 45'-6"
Garage Type :	Three-car garage
Foundation :	Basement

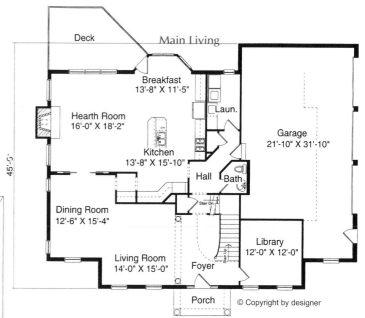

Deck

Main Living

Breakfast
13'-8" X 11'-5"

Laun.

Hearth Room
16'-0" X 18'-2"

Garage
21'-10" X 31'-10"

Kitchen
13'-8" X 15'-10"

45'-5"

Hall

Bath

Dining Room
12'-6" X 15'-4"

Stair Dn.

Living Room
14'-0" X 15'-0"

Library
12'-0" X 12'-0"

Foyer

Porch

© Copyright by designer

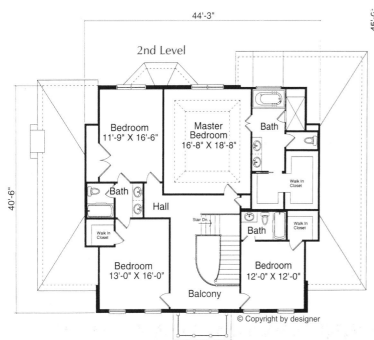

44'-3"

2nd Level

Bedroom
11'-9" X 16'-6"

Master
Bedroom
16'-8" X 18'-8"

Bath

40'-6"

Bath

Walk In
Closet

Hall

Walk In
Closet

Stair Dn.

Bath

Walk In
Closet

Walk In
Closet

Bedroom
13'-0" X 16'-0"

Bedroom
12'-0" X 12'-0"

Balcony

© Copyright by designer

Order Code : **H7SCP**
1-800-235-5700 or
www.family homeplans.com

Southern Style
Balconies

Balconies are a common architectural feature of Southern Antebellum homes. Often tied to a specific home style, balconies adorn many types of Southern homes, including Georgian, Italianate, and Classic Revival styles. Balconies were typically supported by decorative corbels or brackets, or by columns that framed a lower covered porch or portico. The overall design of the home determined the specific look of the balcony, but usually classic details were favored. Railings were constructed of wood and typically contained turned balusters.

Most of the balconies on Southern homes served little functional use for members of the household. However, one practical aspect of the balcony may have been that it allowed for greater movement of air inside the upper story of a home, as the doors that opened to it often were louvered. The sweltering heat of the summer months would have made this a welcome feature. Regardless, the primary purpose of a balcony on a Southern Antebellum home would have been for aesthetic appeal and showmanship.

Because balconies do not protrude out of a building, but are merely an extension of the upper floor of a home, they do expand a room's capabilities, and offer a respite from the confines a home's interior. It's possible that on many warm evenings, Southerners escaped to balconies to cool off or to experience a change of scenery.

Photography © istockphoto.com

65910-SC Price Code: I

Total Living Area :	3,499 sq.ft.
Main Living :	2,008 sq.ft.
2nd Level :	1,491 sq.ft.
Bedrooms :	4
Bathrooms :	3.5
Dimensions :	68'-0" x 84'-0"
Garage Type :	Two-car garage
Foundation :	Basement, Slab, Crawlspace

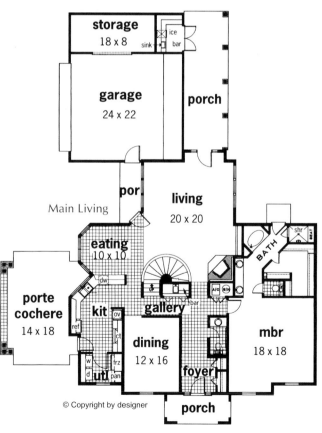

storage
18 x 8

garage
24 x 22

porch

por

Main Living

living
20 x 20

eating
10 x 10

porte cochere
14 x 18

kit

gallery

BATH

dining
12 x 16

mbr
18 x 18

utl

foyer

porch

© Copyright by designer

2nd Level

open to lower level

game room
13 x 19

br 4
11 x 12

handrail

balcony

hall

kit

br 2
16 x 15

br 3
17 x 14

dress

balcony
6 x 14

© Copyright by designer

Order Code : **H7SCP**
1-800-235-5700 or
www.familyhomeplans.com

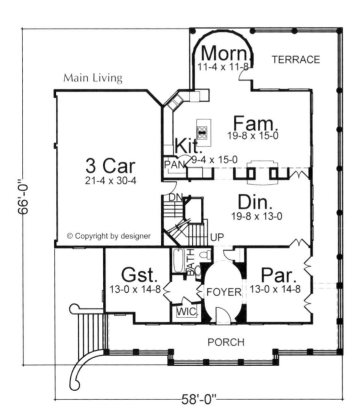

98251-SC Price Code: J

Total Living Area :	3,688 sq.ft.
Main Living :	1,681 sq.ft.
2nd Level :	2,007 sq.ft.
Bedrooms :	5
Bathrooms :	4.5
Dimensions :	58'-0" x 66'-0"
Garage Type :	Three-car garage
Foundation :	Walkout Basement

Main Living

Morn
11-4 x 11-8

TERRACE

Fam.
19-8 x 15-0

Kit.
9-4 x 15-0

PAN

3 Car
21-4 30-4

© Copyright by designer

DN

Din.
19-8 x 13-0

UP

BATH

Gst.
13-0 x 14-8

WIC.

FOYER

Par.
13-0 x 14-8

PORCH

66'-0"

58'-0"

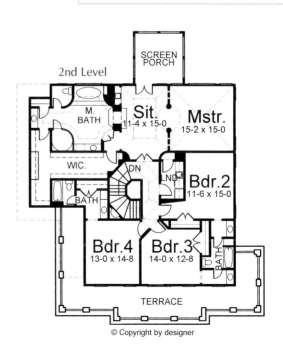

SCREEN
PORCH

2nd Level

M. BATH

Sit.
11-4 x 15-0

Mstr.
15-2 x 15-0

WIC.

DN

LND

Bdr.2
11-6 x 15-0

BATH

Bdr.4
13-0 x 14-8

Bdr.3
14-0 x 12-8

BATH

TERRACE

© Copyright by designer

62020-SC Price Code: K

Total Living Area : 3,955 sq.ft.
Main Living : 2,782 sq.ft.
2nd Level : 1,173 sq.ft.
Bedrooms : 5
Bathrooms : 4
Dimensions : 82'-0" x 58'-10"
Garage Type : Three-car garage
Foundation : Basement, Slab, Crawlspace

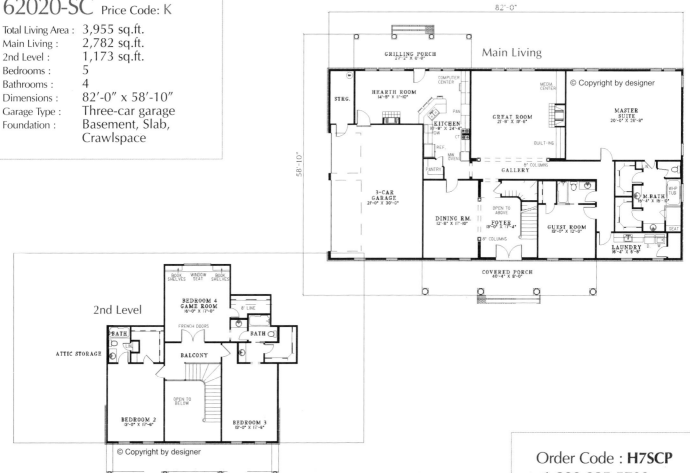

© Copyright by designer

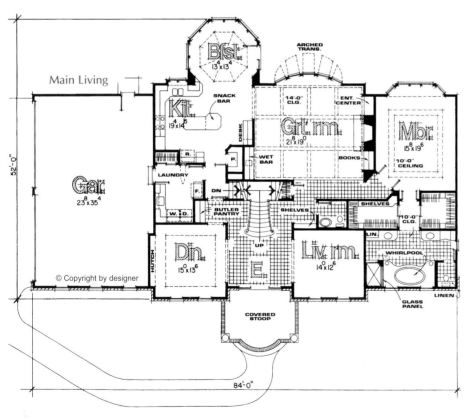

Main Living

- Gar. 23⁸ x 35⁴
- Bfst. 13⁴ x 13⁴
- Kit. 19⁴ x 14⁵
- SNACK BAR
- LAUNDRY
- W. D.
- BUTLER PANTRY
- Dn. 15⁰ x 13⁶
- HUTCH
- DESK
- P.
- R.
- F.
- DN
- Grt. rm. 21 x 19⁰
- 14'-0" CLG.
- ARCHED TRANS.
- ENT. CENTER
- WET BAR
- BOOKS
- Mbr. 15⁸ x 19⁶
- 10'-0" CEILING
- SHELVES
- UP
- Liv. rm. 14⁰ x 12⁶
- SHELVES
- WHIRLPOOL
- LIN.
- 10'-0" CLG.
- LINEN
- GLASS PANEL
- COVERED STOOP

© Copyright by designer

84'-0"

52'-0"

97459-SC Price Code: I

Total Living Area :	3,473 sq.ft.
Main Living :	2,500 sq.ft.
2nd Level :	973 sq.ft.
Bedrooms :	4
Bathrooms :	3.5
Dimensions :	84'-0" x 52'-0"
Garage Type :	Four-car garage
Foundation :	Basement

2nd Level

- Br. 11⁸ x 14²
- CLOTHES CHUTE IN LIN.
- DN
- DN
- Br. 14⁰ x 13⁶
- OPEN TO BELOW
- Br. 14⁰ x 13¹
- TRANSOMS

© Copyright by designer

Order Code : **H7SCP**
1-800-235-5700 or
www.familyhomeplans.com

65615-SC Price Code: N

Total Living Area :	5,474 sq.ft.
Main Living :	4,193 sq.ft.
2nd Level :	1,281 sq.ft.
Bedrooms :	4
Bathrooms :	5
Dimensions :	94'-0" x 71'-0"
Garage Type :	Three-car garage
Foundation :	Slab

A dramatic sweeping staircase is the centerpiece of the spacious foyer, drawing eyes upward to the soaring ceiling above. In the master suite, a sitting room adjacent to the bedroom offers ample space to curl up with a good book in front of the fireplace.

Order Code : **H7SCP**
1-800-235-5700 or
www.familyhomeplans.com

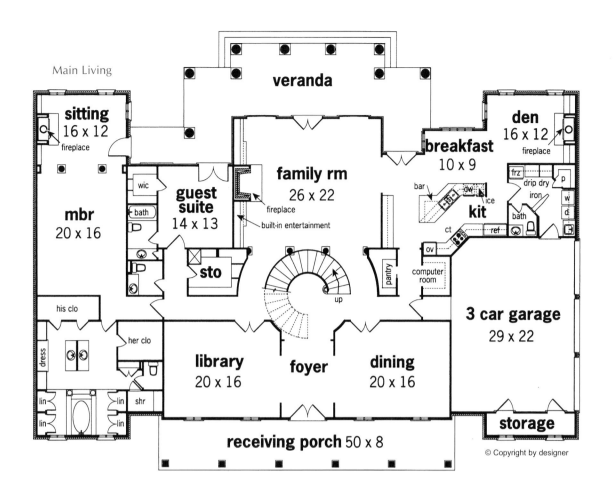

Main Living

veranda

sitting
16 x 12
fireplace

den
16 x 12
fireplace

wic

breakfast
10 x 9

frz drip dry

iron

family rm
26 x 22

fireplace

built-in entertainment

bar

dw

ice

kit

p

w

d

bath

mbr
20 x 16

bath

guest suite
14 x 13

sto

ct

ref

ov

computer room

his clo

her clo

dress

library
20 x 16

foyer

up

pantry

dining
20 x 16

3 car garage
29 x 22

lin

shr

lin

lin

receiving porch 50 x 8

storage

© Copyright by designer

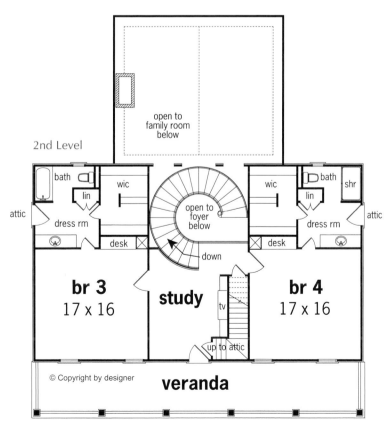

2nd Level

open to family room below

attic

bath

lin

wic

wic

lin

bath

shr

dress rm

desk

open to foyer below

desk

dress rm

attic

br 3
17 x 16

study

tv

down

br 4
17 x 16

up to attic

© Copyright by designer

veranda

62012-SC Price Code: H

Total Living Area : 3,060 sq.ft.
Main Living : 1,564 sq.ft.
2nd Level : 1,496 sq.ft.
Bedrooms : 3
Bathrooms : 4
Dimensions : 58'-0" x 48'-0"
Garage Type : Two-car garage
Foundation : Basement, Slab, Crawlspace

Basement

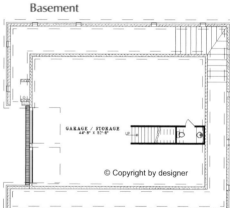

GARAGE / STORAGE
44'-8" X 32'-8"

© Copyright by designer

Main Living

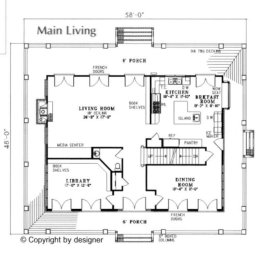

58'-0"

48'-0"

8' PORCH

FRENCH DOORS

LIVING ROOM
10' CEILING
26'-8" X 17'-8"

KITCHEN
18'-4" X 17'-10"

BRKFAST ROOM
8'-2" X 8'-10"

BOOK SHELVES

ISLAND

MEDIA CENTER

REF

PANTRY

ICE MAKER

BOOK SHELVES

UP

LIBRARY
17'-0" X 12'-8"

DINING ROOM
18'-4" X 17'-0"

FRENCH DOORS

6' PORCH

© Copyright by designer

2nd Level

8' BALCONY

BATH

MASTER SUITE
20'-0" X 17'-8"

BEDROOM 2
17'-2" X 13'-6"

ATTIC FAN

M.BATH
14'-0" X 15'-4"

BEDROOM 3
15'-0" X 15'-4"

LAU.

BATH

6' BALCONY

© Copyright by designer

62256-SC Price Code: H

Total Living Area :	3,130 sq.ft.
Main Living :	1,600 sq.ft.
2nd Level :	1,530 sq.ft.
Bedrooms :	3
Bathrooms :	3.5
Dimensions :	60'-2" x 60'-2"
Foundation :	Crawlspace, Slab

Main Living

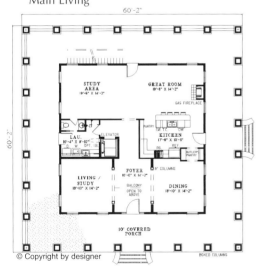

60'-2"

STUDY AREA
19'-6" X 14'-2"

GREAT ROOM
19'-6" X 14'-2"

GAS FIREPLACE

LAU.
10'-4" X 9'-10"

ELEVATOR

KITCHEN
17'-6" X 10'-0"

PANTRY

BUTLER'S PANTRY

LIVING / STUDY
18'-0" X 14'-2"

FOYER
10'-0" X 14'-2"

8" COLUMNS

DINING
18'-10" X 14'-2"

BALCONY OPEN TO ABOVE

10' COVERED PORCH

BOXED COLUMNS

© Copyright by designer

2nd Level

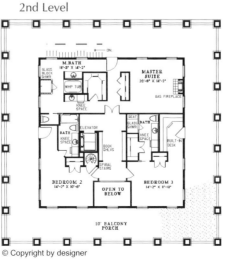

M.BATH
18'-3" X 14'-2"

GLASS BLOCK SHWR

MASTER SUITE
20'-6" X 14'-3"

GAS FIREPLACE

WHP TUB

KNEE SPACE

SEAT

GLASS SHWR

BATH

BATH

KNEE SPACE

ELEVATOR

BOOK SHLVS

SPIRAL STAIRS

KNEE SPACE

BUILT-IN DESK

BEDROOM 2
14'-2" X 10'-8"

OPEN TO BELOW

BEDROOM 3
14'-2" X 11'-10"

10' BALCONY PORCH

© Copyright by designer

3rd Level

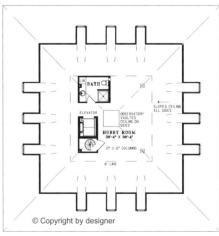

LIN

BATH

SLOPED CEILING ALL SIDES

ELEVATOR

OBSERVATORY VAULTED CEILING ON SIDES

HOBBY ROOM
39'-4" X 39'-4"

12" X 12" COLUMNS

8" LINE

© Copyright by designer

63166-SC Price Code: L

Total Living Area :	4,106 sq.ft.
Main Living :	2,755 sq.ft.
2nd Level :	1,351 sq.ft.
Bedrooms :	5
Bathrooms :	4
Dimensions :	75'-0" x 93'-0"
Garage Type :	Three-car garage
Foundation :	Slab

A summer kitchen and sprawling covered rear patio create the perfect setting for a backyard pool and spa. Formal entertaining is comfortably accommodated with a generously sized dining room and living room with built-in bar.

Order Code : **H7SCP**
1-800-235-5700 or
www.familyhomeplans.com

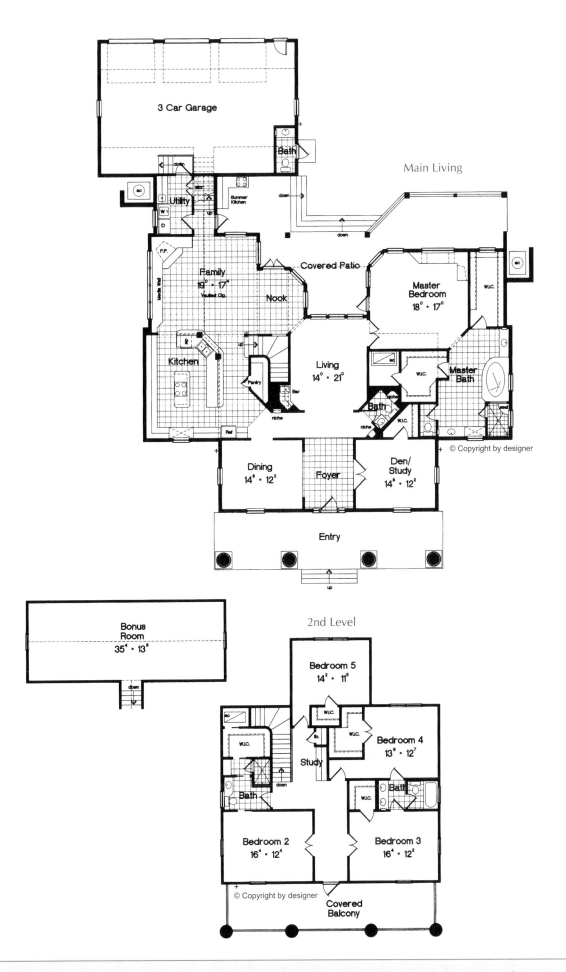

3 Car Garage

Bath

Main Living

Utility

Summer Kitchen

F.P.

Family
19⁰ · 17⁴
Vaulted Clg.

Covered Patio

Master
Bedroom
18⁰ · 17⁰

W.I.C.

Nook

Kitchen

Living
14⁰ · 21⁰

W.I.C.

Master
Bath

Pantry

Bar

Bath

niche

niche

W.I.C.

niche

W.I.C.

Ref

© Copyright by designer

Dining
14⁸ · 12²

Foyer

Den/
Study
14⁸ · 12²

Entry

up

Bonus
Room
35⁴ · 13⁸

2nd Level

down

Bedroom 5
14² · 11⁵

W.I.C.

W.I.C.

W.I.C.

Bedroom 4
13⁸ · 12⁷

Study

Bath

Bath

W.I.C.

Bedroom 2
16⁴ · 12²

Bedroom 3
16⁴ · 12²

© Copyright by designer

Covered
Balcony

99437-SC Price Code: H

Total Living Area : 3,235 sq.ft.
Main Living : 1,717 sq.ft.
2nd Level : 1,518 sq.ft.
Bedrooms : 4
Bathrooms : 3.5
Dimensions : 78'-0" x 42'-0"
Garage Type : Three-car garage
Foundation : Basement, Slab*,
Crawlspace*

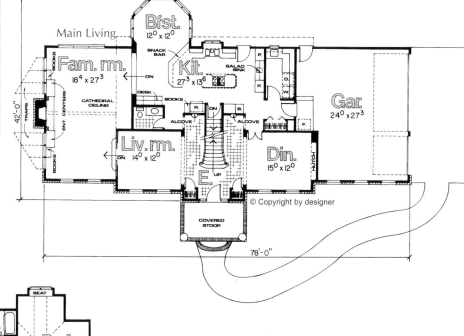

Main Living

Bfst.
12⁰ x 12⁰

Fam. rm.
18⁴ x 27³

SNACK BAR

Kit.
27³ x 13⁶

SALAD SINK

Gar.
24⁰ x 27³

CATHEDRAL CEILING

DESK
BOOKS

Liv. rm.
14⁰ x 12⁰

ALCOVE   ALCOVE

Din.
15⁰ x 12⁰

HUTCH

UP

COVERED STOOP

© Copyright by designer

78'-0"

42'-0"

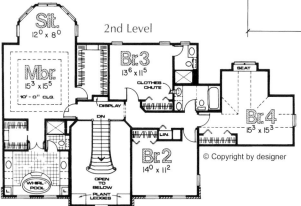

Sit.
12⁰ x 8⁰

2nd Level

Mbr.
15³ x 15⁵
10'-0" CLG.

Br. 3
13⁶ x 11⁵

CLOTHES CHUTE

SEAT

DISPLAY

DN

Br. 4
15³ x 15³

WHIRL POOL

OPEN TO BELOW

PLANT LEDGES

Br. 2
14⁰ x 11²

LIN.

© Copyright by designer

This home, as shown, may differ from the original design.

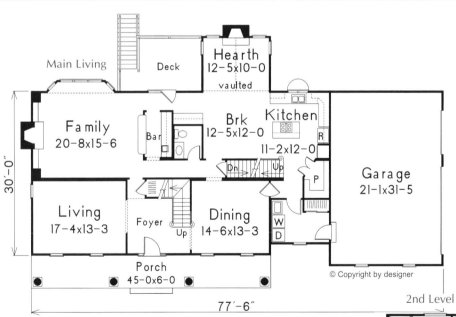

Main Living

Deck

Hearth
12-5x10-0
vaulted

Family
20-8x15-6

Brk
12-5x12-0

Kitchen
11-2x12-0

Bar

30'-0"

Living
17-4x13-3

Foyer
Up

Dn   Up

P

Garage
21-1x31-5

Dining
14-6x13-3

W
D

Porch
45-0x6-0

© Copyright by designer

77'-6"

2nd Level

MBr
17-4x14-1

open to foyer

Dn

Br 4
12-0x12-0

Br 3
12-0x12-0

L

Dn

Br 2
14-6x13-6

© Copyright by designer

87304-SC Price Code: H

Total Living Area : 3,216 sq.ft.
Main Living : 1,834 sq.ft.
2nd Level : 1,382 sq.ft.
Bedrooms : 4
Bathrooms : 4.5
Dimensions : 77'-6" x 30'-0"
Garage Type : Three-car garage
Foundation : Walkout Basement

Order Code : **H7SCP**
1-800-235-5700 or
www.familyhomeplans.com

63219-SC Price Code: H

Total Living Area :	3,183 sq.ft.
Main Living :	2,782 sq.ft.
2nd Level :	401 sq.ft.
Bedrooms :	3
Bathrooms :	4
Dimensions :	65'-0" x 88'-3"
Garage Type :	Two-car garage
Foundation :	Slab

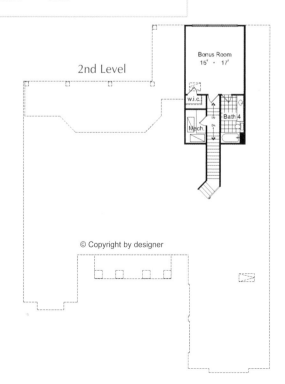

2nd Level

Bonus Room
15⁰ · 17⁷

w.i.c.

Bath 4

Mech.

© Copyright by designer

Main Living

Covered Patio

Gathering
19² · 19²

Breakfast

Bedroom 3
12⁷ · 11⁸

Master Suite
23⁰ · 13⁷

Bath 3

Living Room
13⁰ · 17⁰

Kitchen
13⁰ · 11⁰

Family

Bath 2

w.i.c. w.i.c.

Office
11⁰ · 13⁰

Foyer

Dining
11⁰ · 11⁰

Bedroom 2
15⁰ · 12⁰

Utility

M. Bath

Covered Entry

2 Car Garage
20¹⁰ · 25⁰

© Copyright by designer

92219-SC Price Code: I

Total Living Area : 3,335 sq.ft.
Main Living : 2,432 sq.ft.
2nd Level : 903 sq.ft.
Bedrooms : 4
Bathrooms : 3.5
Dimensions : 90'-0" x 45'-4"
Garage Type : Three-car garage
Foundation : Slab, Basement, Crawlspace

Main Living

Pool

90' - 0"

45' - 4"

Gar
22x23

Covered Patio

Covered Patio

Cathedral Clg.

FamilyRm
18x22

Kit

Brkfst
10x15

MstrBed
15x21

Pwdr

GolfCart
Stor.
15x20

Rear Entry

15x15

12' Vaulted Clg.

Util

Entertainment
Center

Plant Ledge

WorkShop

FmlDin
13x15

Bar
LivRm/
Parlor
15x17

Sloping Clg.

To Basement

UP

21'Clg.

Ent

Covered
Por

© Copyright by designer

2nd Level

Bed#4
13x11

Sloping Clg.

10'Clg.

Balcony

Bed#3
13x14

DN

21'Clg.

Ent Below

Bed#2
15x11

© Copyright by designer

Order Code : **H7SCP**
1-800-235-5700 or
www.familyhomeplans.com

65614-SC Price Code: L

Total Living Area : 4,242 sq.ft.
Main Living : 3,439 sq.ft.
2nd Level : 803 sq.ft.
Bedrooms : 4
Bathrooms : 5.5
Dimensions : 95'-0" x 90'-0"
Garage Type : Two-car garage
Foundation : Slab

Poolside entertaining is easy and elegant with the veranda's outdoor grill and bar. The interior's crowning jewel is found in the upper level's stylish balcony and library, which overlooks the living room.

Order Code : **H7SCP**
1-800-235-5700 or
www.familyhomeplans.com

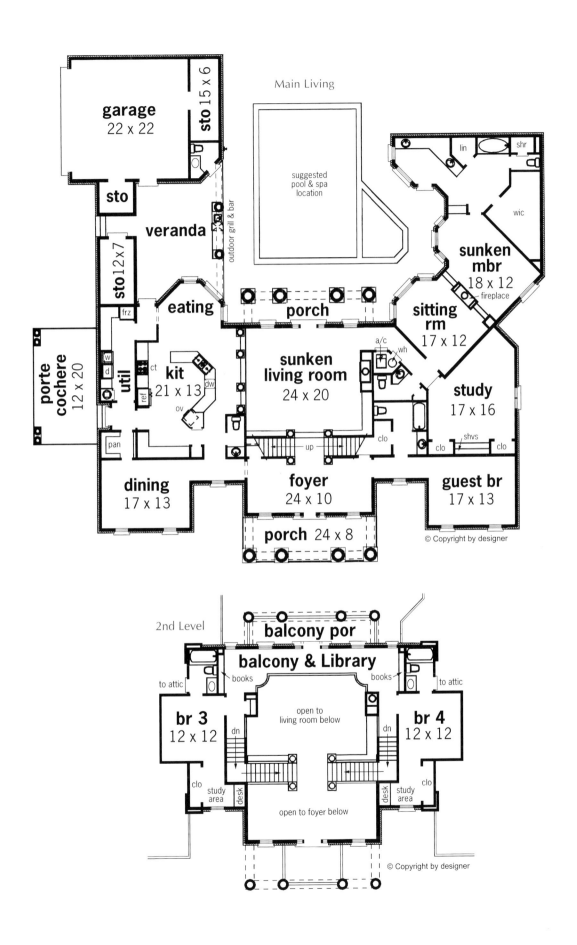

garage
22 x 22

sto 15 x 6

Main Living

suggested
pool & spa
location

lin

shr

sto

outdoor grill & bar

veranda

sto 12 x 7

wic

frz

eating

porch

sunken
mbr
18 x 12

fireplace

sitting
rm
17 x 12

porte
cochere
12 x 20

util

w

d

kit
21 x 13

ref

ct

dw

ov

pan

a/c

wh

sunken
living room
24 x 20

study
17 x 16

clo

shvs

dining
17 x 13

up

clo

foyer
24 x 10

clo

clo

guest br
17 x 13

© Copyright by designer

porch 24 x 8

2nd Level

balcony por

balcony & Library

to attic

books

books

to attic

br 3
12 x 12

open to
living room below

dn

dn

br 4
12 x 12

clo

study
area

desk

open to foyer below

desk

study
area

clo

© Copyright by designer

65908-SC Price Code: I

Total Living Area :	3,284 sq.ft.
Main Living :	2,655 sq.ft.
2nd Level :	629 sq.ft.
Bedrooms :	4
Bathrooms :	4
Dimensions :	74'-0" x 78'-0"
Garage Type :	Two-car garage
Foundation :	Basement, Slab, Crawlspace

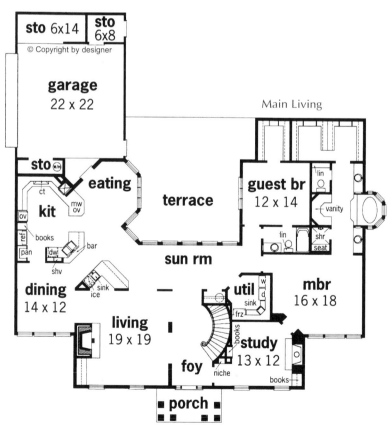

Main Living

- sto 6x14
- sto 6x8
- © Copyright by designer
- garage 22 x 22
- sto
- eating
- terrace
- guest br 12 x 14
- vanity
- kit
- books
- sun rm
- shr seat
- dining 14 x 12
- bar
- util
- mbr 16 x 18
- living 19 x 19
- study 13 x 12
- foy
- niche
- books
- porch

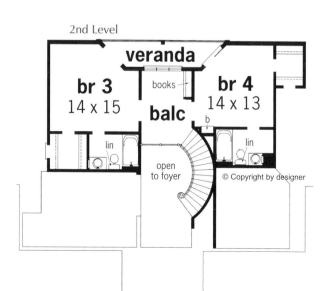

2nd Level

- veranda
- br 3 14 x 15
- books
- br 4 14 x 13
- balc
- open to foyer
- © Copyright by designer

Southern Style
Greek Columns

Quintessential features of the Southern plantation home, columns were a status symbol on the homes of Southern society's well-to-do. Their wide use—transcending specific house styles—reveals the Southern aristocrat's love for classical architecture. They started appearing in the vernacular soon after Anglo-Americans moved into the area around the time of the Louisiana Purchase in 1803. While they can be found on many styles of houses, they really came into favor when Greek Revival architecture became popular in the 1830s. The Greek Revival style finds its roots in the ancient temples of Greece with their triangular pediments and fluted columns. The style took hold as the United States struggled to severe ties with Great Britain and Europe in the early 1800s. Ancient Greece came to embody the spirit of independence driving the early republic. The style was made popular with the building of Thomas Jefferson's Monticello home and University of Virginia campus buildings and it soon spread farther south. The classical names for the various types of columns include Doric, Tuscan, Ionic, Corinthian, and Composite. Each style has its roots in ancient Greece or Rome and all five styles can be found among surviving antebellum homes.

Besides serving an aesthetic function, columns also proved their worth in durability and practicality. In many Greek Revival, Georgian, and Classical Revival homes, columns supported the roof over a portico or a porch. These sloping roofs provided areas of continuous shade during the hot and muggy times of year. A decorative strip called a frieze was often located just above the capital, or upper portion of the column. The symbolic colonnade, sometimes found lining the facade, added to the symmetry of the homes, which usually featured evenly spaced windows and a central door.

Photography © istockphoto.com

87305-SC Price Code: H

Total Living Area : 3,144 sq.ft.
Main Living : 1,724 sq.ft.
2nd Level : 1,420 sq.ft.
Bedrooms : 4
Bathrooms : 3.5
Dimensions : 77'-6" x 30'-0"
Garage Type : Three-car garage
Foundation : Basement

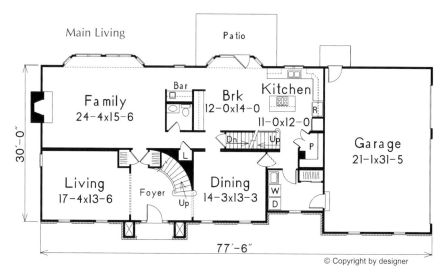

Main Living

Patio

Family
24-4x15-6

Bar

Brk
12-0x14-0

Kitchen

R

Dn   Up

P

Garage
21-1x31-5

Living
17-4x13-6

Foyer   Up

Dining
14-3x13-3

W
D

30'-0"

77'-6"

© Copyright by designer

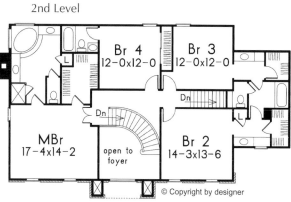

2nd Level

Br 4
12-0x12-0

Br 3
12-0x12-0

L

Dn

MBr
17-4x14-2

Dn   open to foyer

Br 2
14-3x13-6

L

© Copyright by designer

87316-SC Price Code: I

Total Living Area :	3,420 sq.ft.
Main Living :	1,894 sq.ft.
2nd Level :	1,526 sq.ft.
Bedrooms :	4
Bathrooms :	3.5
Dimensions :	80'-0" x 52'-0"
Garage Type :	Three-car garage
Foundation :	Crawlspace, Walkout Basement

Main Living

80'-0"

52'-0"

Deck

Hearth
14-0x17-8
vaulted

Gallery

Kit
17-5x13-8

Brk

Family
18-0x18-10

Living
14-0x12-0

Foyer

Dining
14-0x12-0

OVEN
R
Up
P
W
D

Dn
Up

Garage
29-4x21-4

© Copyright by designer

Porch

2nd Level

Br 2
14-0x12-0

Br 3
12-9x13-4

MBr
14-0x15-7

Dn
L
Dn

Br 4
11-8x12-0

Foyer

L

Porch

© Copyright by designer

Order Code : **H7SCP**
1-800-235-5700 or
www.familyhomeplans.com

44086-SC Price Code: N

Total Living Area :	5,010 sq.ft.
Main Living :	3,268 sq.ft.
2nd Level :	1,742 sq.ft.
Bedrooms :	5
Bathrooms :	5
Dimensions :	102'-0" x 87'-0"
Garage Type :	Four-car garage
Foundation :	Basement, Slab*, Crawlspace*

Five spacious bedrooms easily accommodate a growing family.
Each has a walk-in closet and access to a bath. To the rear of the home, a covered deck complete with fireplace, invites gatherings to the outside – even on chilly nights.

Order Code : **H7SCP**
1-800-235-5700 or
www.familyhomeplans.com

Main Living

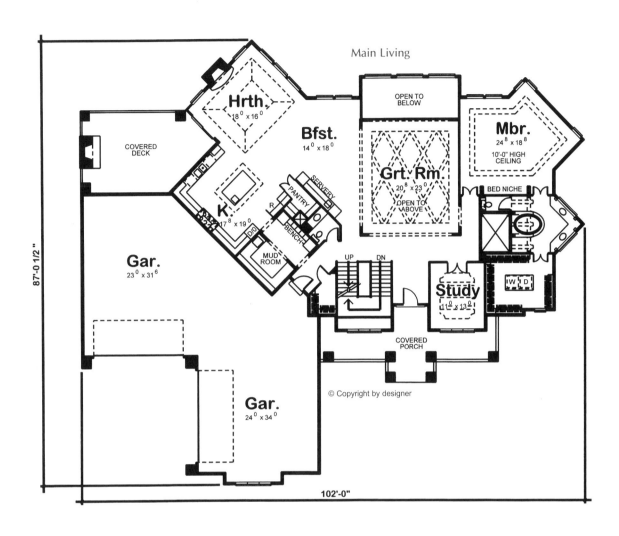

COVERED DECK

Hrth.
$18^0 \times 16^0$

Bfst.
$14^0 \times 18^0$

OPEN TO BELOW

Mbr.
$24^8 \times 18^8$
10'-0" HIGH CEILING

SERVERY

PANTRY

R

BENCH

K.
$17^8 \times 19^0$

Grt. Rm.
$20^8 \times 23^0$
OPEN TO ABOVE

BED NICHE

MUD ROOM

UP   DN

Gar.
$23^0 \times 31^6$

Study
$11^0 \times 13^0$

W D

Gar.
$24^0 \times 34^0$

COVERED PORCH

87'-0 1/2"

102'-0"

2nd Level

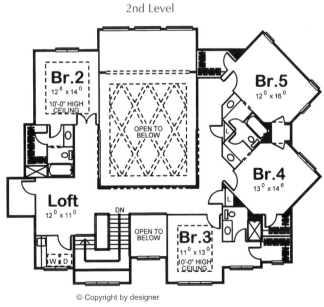

Br.2
$12^8 \times 14^0$
10'-0" HIGH CEILING

OPEN TO BELOW

Br.5
$12^0 \times 16^0$

Br.4
$13^0 \times 14^6$

Loft
$12^0 \times 11^0$

DN

W D

OPEN TO BELOW

Br.3
$11^0 \times 13^0$
10'-0" HIGH CEILING

69008-SC Price Code: K

Total Living Area : 3,850 sq.ft.
Main Living : 2,306 sq.ft.
2nd Level : 1,544 sq.ft.
Bedrooms : 5
Bathrooms : 3.5
Dimensions : 80'-8" x 51'-8"
Garage Type : Three-car garage
Foundation : Basement

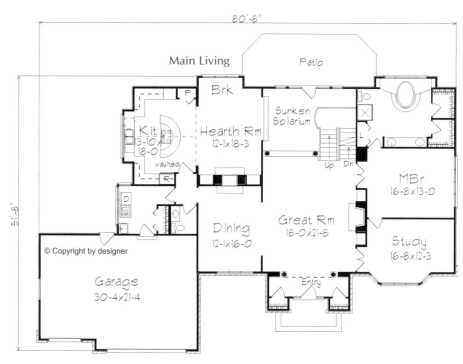

Main Living

80'-8"

51'-8"

Patio

Brk

Kit
13-10x
18-0

vaulted

Hearth Rm
12-1x18-3

Sunken
Solarium

Up   Dn

MBr
16-8x13-0

© Copyright by designer

Dining
12-1x16-0

Great Rm
18-0x21-8

Study
16-8x12-3

Garage
30-4x21-4

Entry

2nd Level

Br 5
12-1x14-3

Sunken
Solarium
Below

Dn

Br 2
13-11x15-9

Loft

Br 4
12-1x12-0

Library
15-8x9-8

Br 3
15-5x12-0

open to below   © Copyright by designer

This home, as shown, may differ from the original design.

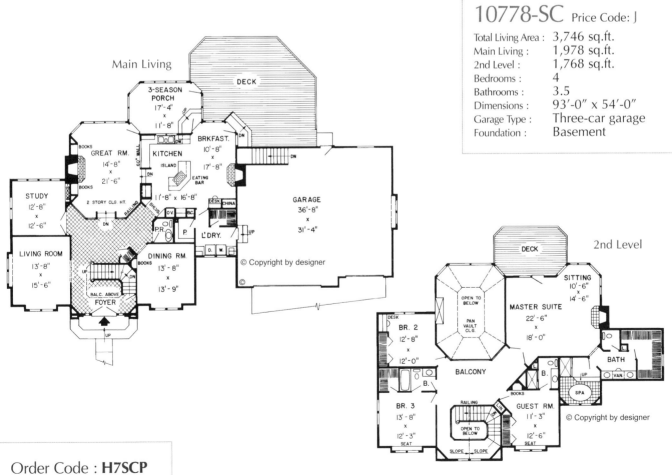

Main Living

DECK

3-SEASON PORCH
17'-4"
x
11'-8"

BRKFAST.
10'-8"
x
17'-8"

KITCHEN

ISLAND

EATING BAR

11'-8" x 16'-8"

GREAT RM.
14'-8"
x
21'-6"

BOOKS

BOOKS

2 STORY CLG. HT.

STUDY
12'-8"
x
12'-6"

GARAGE
36'-8"
x
31'-4"

DESK   CHINA

O.V.

P.R.   P.

L'DRY.

D   W

LIVING ROOM
13'-8"
x
15'-6"

DINING RM.
13'-8"
x
13'-9"

BOOKS

BALC. ABOVE

FOYER

UP

© Copyright by designer

10778-SC Price Code: J

Total Living Area :	3,746 sq.ft.
Main Living :	1,978 sq.ft.
2nd Level :	1,768 sq.ft.
Bedrooms :	4
Bathrooms :	3.5
Dimensions :	93'-0" x 54'-0"
Garage Type :	Three-car garage
Foundation :	Basement

2nd Level

DECK

SITTING
10'-6"
x
14'-6"

MASTER SUITE
22'-6"
x
18'-0"

OPEN TO BELOW

PAN VAULT CLG.

DESK

BR. 2
12'-8"
x
12'-0"

BALCONY

BATH

VAN.

SPA

BOOKS

BR. 3
13'-8"
x
12'-3"

RAILING

OPEN TO BELOW

GUEST RM.
11'-3"
x
12'-6"

SEAT   SEAT

SLOPE   SLOPE

© Copyright by designer

24978-SC Price Code: L

Total Living Area : 4,207 sq.ft.
Main Living : 2,764 sq.ft.
2nd Level : 1,443 sq.ft.
Bedrooms : 5
Bathrooms : 6
Dimensions : 84'-0" x 62'-0"
Garage Type : Three-car garage
Foundation : Basement, Slab, Crawlspace

Appreciation for the finer things in life is reflected in this design's gallery area, a tasteful interlude between the entry and sunken living room. Upstairs, each of the secondary bedrooms enjoys the privacy of its own full bath.

Order Code : **H7SCP**
1-800-235-5700 or
www.familyhomeplans.com

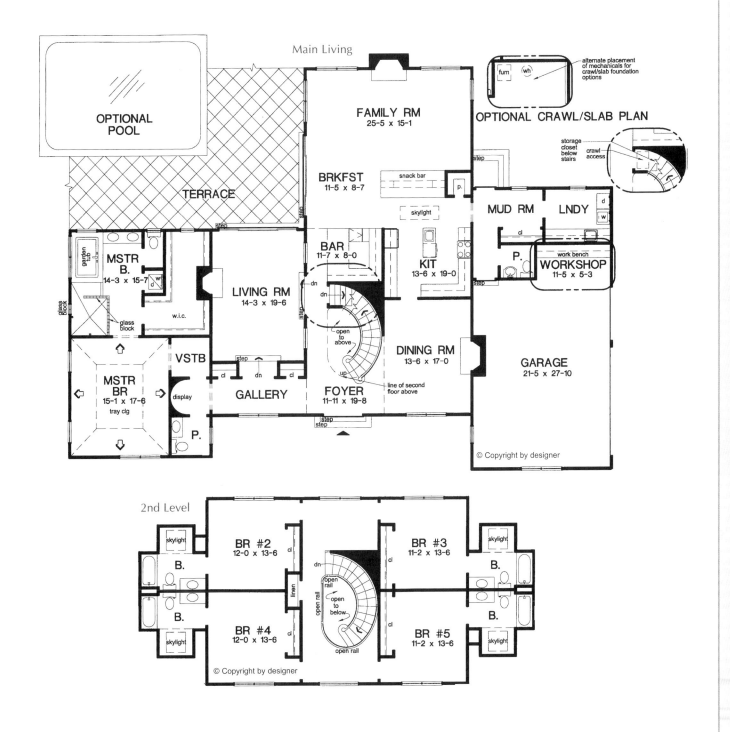

Main Living

OPTIONAL POOL

FAMILY RM
25-5 x 15-1

alternate placement
of mechanicals for
crawl/slab foundation
options

OPTIONAL CRAWL/SLAB PLAN

furn   wh

TERRACE

BRKFST
11-5 x 8-7

snack bar

skylight

storage
closet
below
stairs

crawl
access

MUD RM   LNDY

d
w

BAR
11-7 x 8-0

KIT
13-6 x 19-0

work bench
WORKSHOP
11-5 x 5-3

garden
tub

MSTR
B.
14-3 x 15-7

w/
d

LIVING RM
14-3 x 19-6

dn

dn

open
to
above

P.

glass
block

glass
block

w.i.c.

up

DINING RM
13-6 x 17-0

GARAGE
21-5 x 27-10

MSTR
BR
15-1 x 17-6

tray clg

VSTB

display

P.

step

dn

cl   cl

GALLERY

FOYER
11-11 x 19-8

line of second
floor above

step
step

© Copyright by designer

2nd Level

skylight

BR #2
12-0 x 13-6

cl

B.

dn
open
rail

open rail

open
to
below

cl

BR #3
11-2 x 13-6

B.

skylight

linen

B.

BR #4
12-0 x 13-6

cl

open rail

cl

BR #5
11-2 x 13-6

B.

skylight

skylight

© Copyright by designer

92237-SC Price Code: K

Total Living Area :	3,783 sq.ft.
Main Living :	2,804 sq.ft.
2nd Level :	979 sq.ft.
Bedrooms :	4
Bathrooms :	3.5
Dimensions :	98'-0" x 45'-10"
Garage Type :	Three-car garage
Foundation :	Slab, Basement

Main Living

© Copyright by designer

2nd Level

© Copyright by designer

99462-SC Price Code: K

Total Living Area : 3,950 sq.ft.
Main Living : 2,839 sq.ft.
2nd Level : 1,111 sq.ft.
Bedrooms : 4
Bathrooms : 4.5
Dimensions : 95'-9" x 70'-2"
Garage Type : Three-car garage
Foundation : Basement, Slab*, Crawlspace*

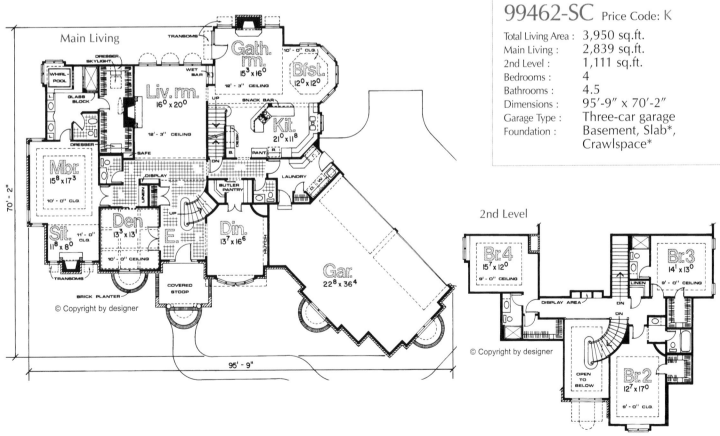

Main Living

TRANSOMS

DRESSER SKYLIGHT

WHIRL POOL

GLASS BLOCK

DRESSER

Liv. rm.
16⁰ x 20⁰

12'-3" CEILING

SAFE

WET BAR

Gath. rm.
15³ x 16⁰

12'-3" CEILING

10'-0" CLG.

Bfst.
12⁰ x 12⁰

SNACK BAR

Kit.
21⁰ x 11⁸

UP

DN

PANT.

Mbr.
15⁸ x 17³

10'-0" CLG.

DISPLAY

LINEN

BUTLER PANTRY

LAUNDRY

Sit.
11⁸ x 8⁰

Den
13³ x 13¹

11'-0" CLG.

UP

Din.
13⁷ x 16⁶

HUTCH

Gar.
22⁸ x 36⁴

10'-0" CEILING

TRANSOMS

BRICK PLANTER

COVERED STOOP

© Copyright by designer

70' - 2"

95' - 9"

2nd Level

Br. 4
15⁷ x 12⁰

9'-0" CEILING

Br. 3
14¹ x 13⁰

9'-0" CEILING

LINEN

DISPLAY AREA

DN

DN

OPEN TO BELOW

Br. 2
12⁷ x 17⁰

9'-0" CLG.

© Copyright by designer

Order Code : **H7SCP**
1-800-235-5700 or
www.familyhomeplans.com

Home Plans Designed with Southern Charm

51

53776-SC Price Code: M

Total Living Area :	4,574 sq.ft.
Main Living :	2,563 sq.ft.
2nd Level :	2,011 sq.ft.
Bedrooms :	4
Bathrooms :	4
Dimensions :	85'-0" x 57'-3"
Garage Type :	Three-car garage
Foundation :	Crawlspace

A trio of French entry doors provide a suitably formal introduction that carries through to the interior's elegant entrance hall. The upper level offers more casual spaces with three secondary bedrooms, a media room and a generously sized bonus room.

Order Code : **H7SCP**
1-800-235-5700 or
www.familyhomeplans.com

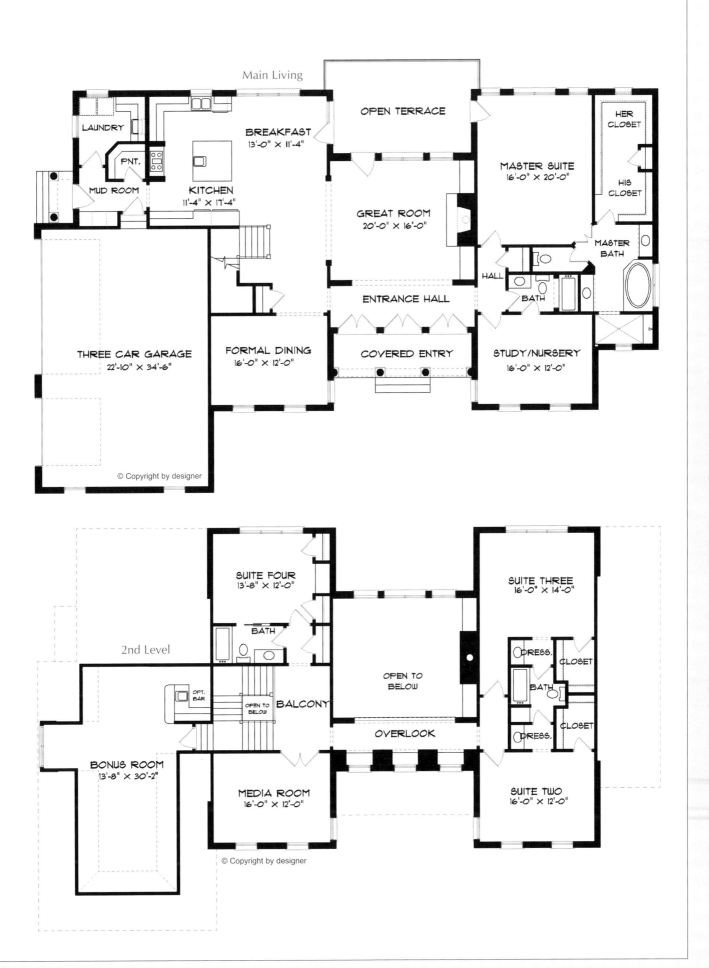

Main Living

LAUNDRY

PNT.

MUD ROOM

KITCHEN
11'-4" × 17'-4"

BREAKFAST
13'-0" × 11'-4"

OPEN TERRACE

GREAT ROOM
20'-0" × 16'-0"

MASTER SUITE
16'-0" × 20'-0"

HER CLOSET

HIS CLOSET

MASTER BATH

HALL

BATH

THREE CAR GARAGE
22'-10" × 34'-6"

FORMAL DINING
16'-0" × 12'-0"

ENTRANCE HALL

COVERED ENTRY

STUDY/NURSERY
16'-0" × 12'-0"

© Copyright by designer

2nd Level

SUITE FOUR
13'-8" × 12'-0"

BATH

OPT. BAR

OPEN TO BELOW

BALCONY

SUITE THREE
16'-0" × 14'-0"

DRESS.

CLOSET

BATH

DRESS.

CLOSET

BONUS ROOM
13'-8" × 30'-2"

MEDIA ROOM
16'-0" × 12'-0"

OVERLOOK

SUITE TWO
16'-0" × 12'-0"

© Copyright by designer

24969-SC   Price Code: H

Total Living Area : 3,122 sq.ft.
Main Living : 2,014 sq.ft.
2nd Level : 1,108 sq.ft.
Bedrooms : 4
Bathrooms : 3.5
Dimensions : 73'-0" x 59'-4"
Garage Type : Three-car garage
Foundation : Slab, Basement, Crawlspace

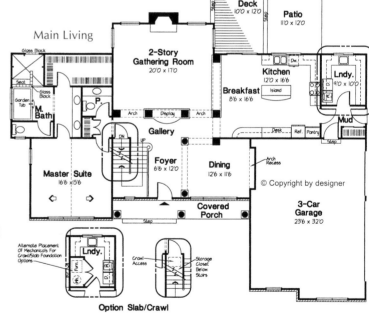

Main Living

2-Story Gathering Room
20'0 x 17'0

Glass Block

Seat

Garden Tub

M. Bath

Glass Block

Kitchen
12'0 x 16'6

Deck
10'0 x 12'0

Patio
11'0 x 12'0

Breakfast
8'6 x 16'6

Island

Lndy.
4'0 x 10'0

Mud

Gallery

Display

Arch

Arch

Ref. Pantry

DN   UP

Foyer
6'6 x 12'0

Dining
12'6 x 11'6

Arch Recess

Master Suite
16'6 x15'6

Covered Porch

3-Car Garage
23'6 x 32'0

Step

© Copyright by designer

Alternate Placement Of Mechanicals For Crawl/Slab Foundation Options

Lndy.

Furn.

Crawl Access

Storage Closet Below Stairs

Option Slab/Crawl

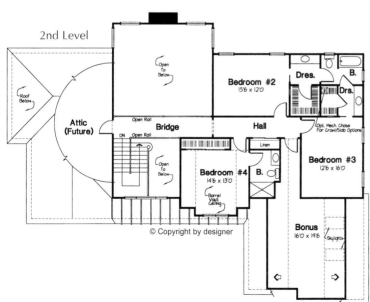

2nd Level

Roof Below

Attic (Future)

Open To Below

Open Rail   Bridge   Open Rail   Hall

Bedroom #2
15'6 x 12'0

Dres.

Drs.

B.

Opt. Mech. Chase For Crawl/Slab Options

DN

Open To Below

Linen

Bedroom #4
14'6 x 13'0

B.

Bedroom #3
12'6 x 16'0

Barrel Vault Ceiling

Bonus
16'0 x 19'6

Skylights

© Copyright by designer

65472-SC Price Code: I

Total Living Area : 3,251 sq.ft.
Main Living : 1,536 sq.ft.
2nd Level : 1,715 sq.ft.
Bedrooms : 4
Bathrooms : 4
Dimensions : 54'-0" x 43'-0"
Garage Type : Two-car garage
Foundation : Walkout Basement

Main Living

2-CAR GARAGE
22-0 X 20-0

16-8 X 13-0

13-2 X 13-4

15-0 X 7-0

14-8 X 11-0

16-8 X 17-4

© Copyright by designer

2nd Level

14-2 X 14-0

16-4 X 11-10

16-8 X 17-10

14-8 X 11-10

© Copyright by designer

This home, as shown, may differ from the original design.

A striking gazebo on the front of this design

provides a powerful first impression to passersby. Even more impressive, is the experience of relaxing beneath its trayed ceiling. Inside the home, a sunroom/breakfast room competes for status as a favorite living space.

96882-SC Price Code: N

Total Living Area :	5,003 sq.ft.
Main Living :	3,062 sq.ft.
2nd Level :	1,941 sq.ft.
Bedrooms :	5
Bathrooms :	3.5
Dimensions :	87'-6" x 74'-8"
Garage Type :	Three-car garage
Foundation :	Basement, Crawlspace, Slab

rear view

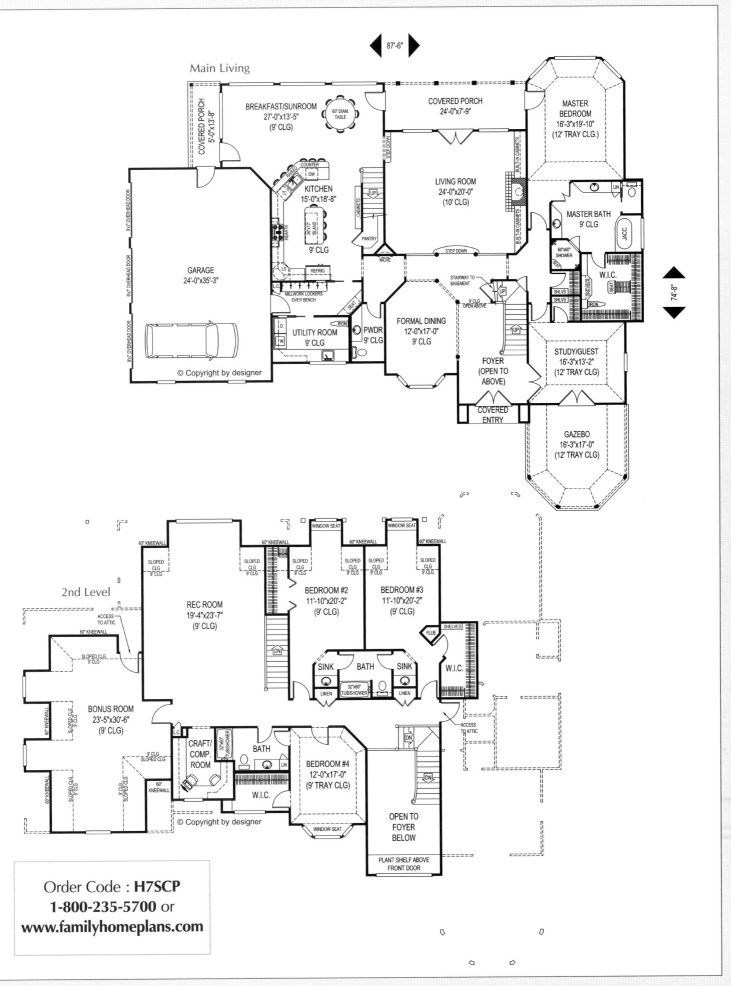

Main Living

87'-6"

COVERED PORCH
5'-0"x13'-8"

BREAKFAST/SUNROOM
27'-0"x13'-5"
(9' CLG)

60" DIAM.
TABLE

COVERED PORCH
24'-0"x7'-9"

MASTER BEDROOM
16'-3"x19'-10"
(12' TRAY CLG.)

COUNTER
DW
TC

KITCHEN
15'-0"x18'-8"

36"x72"
ISLAND

9' CLG

PANTRY

LIVING ROOM
24'-0"x20'-0"
(10' CLG)

STEP DOWN

NICHE

STEP DOWN

BUILT-IN CABINETS

MASTER BATH
9' CLG

60"x60"
SHOWER

JACC.

LIN

W.I.C.

SHLVS
SHLVS

DRESSER

SEAT

IRON

GARAGE
24'-0"x35'-3"

9'x7' OVERHEAD DOOR

9'x7' OVERHEAD DOOR

9'x7' OVERHEAD DOOR

9'x7' OVERHEAD DOOR

HEARTH

REFRIG

LS

L.C.

MILLWORK LOCKERS
OVER BENCH

SEAT

IRON

UTILITY ROOM
9' CLG

D

W

PWDR
9' CLG

FORMAL DINING
12'-0"x17'-0"
9' CLG

STAIRWAY TO
BASEMENT

9' CLG
OPEN ABOVE

UP

UP

FOYER
(OPEN TO
ABOVE)

STUDY/GUEST
16'-3"x13'-2"
(12' TRAY CLG)

74'-8"

© Copyright by designer

COVERED
ENTRY

GAZEBO
16'-3"x17'-0"
(12' TRAY CLG)

2nd Level

60" KNEEWALL

SLOPED
CLG
9' CLG

60" KNEEWALL

WINDOW SEAT

60" KNEEWALL

WINDOW SEAT

60" KNEEWALL

ACCESS
TO ATTIC

60" KNEEWALL

SLOPED CLG
9' CLG

REC ROOM
19'-4"x23'-7"
(9' CLG)

SLOPED
CLG
9' CLG

SLOPED
CLG
9' CLG

BEDROOM #2
11'-10"x20'-2"
(9' CLG)

SLOPED
CLG
9' CLG

SLOPED
CLG
9' CLG

BEDROOM #3
11'-10"x20'-2"
(9' CLG)

SLOPED
CLG
9' CLG

FLUE

SHELVES

DN

60" KNEEWALL

BONUS ROOM
23'-5"x30'-6"
(9' CLG)

SLOPED CLG
9' CLG

SLOPED CLG
9' CLG

SINK

BATH

SINK

LINEN

32"x60"
TUB/SHOWER

LINEN

W.I.C.

ACCESS
TO ATTIC

L.C.

CRAFT/
COMP.
ROOM

32"x60"
TUB/SHOWER

BATH

LIN

W.I.C.

BEDROOM #4
12'-0"x17'-0"
(9' TRAY CLG)

DN

DN

9' CLG
SLOPED CLG

9' CLG
SLOPED CLG

60"
KNEEWALL

© Copyright by designer

WINDOW SEAT

OPEN TO
FOYER
BELOW

PLANT SHELF ABOVE
FRONT DOOR

Order Code : **H7SCP**
1-800-235-5700 or
www.familyhomeplans.com

99440-SC Price Code: L

Total Living Area : 4,228 sq.ft.
Main Living : 2,688 sq.ft.
2nd Level : 1,540 sq.ft.
Bedrooms : 4
Bathrooms : 3.5
Dimensions : 84'-3" x 80'-1"
Garage Type : Three-car garage
Foundation : Basement*, Slab

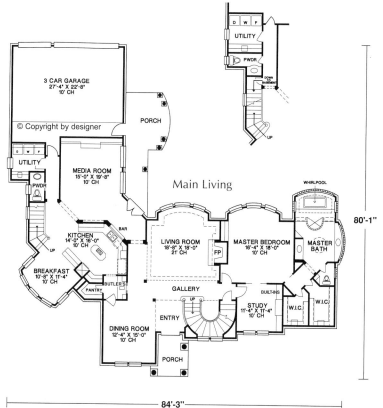

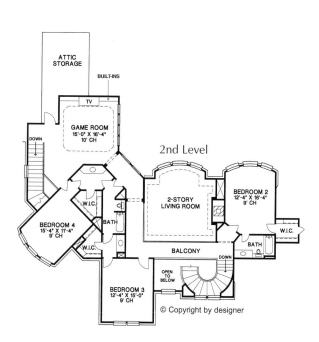

∽ Home Plans Designed with Southern Charm ∾

This home, as shown, may differ from the original design.

Photo Courtesy of The Designer

92623-SC Price Code: F

Total Living Area :	2,653 sq.ft.
Main Living :	1,365 sq.ft.
2nd Level :	1,288 sq.ft.
Bedrooms :	4
Bathrooms :	2.5
Dimensions :	61'-0" x 37'-6"
Garage Type :	Two-car garage
Foundation :	Basement

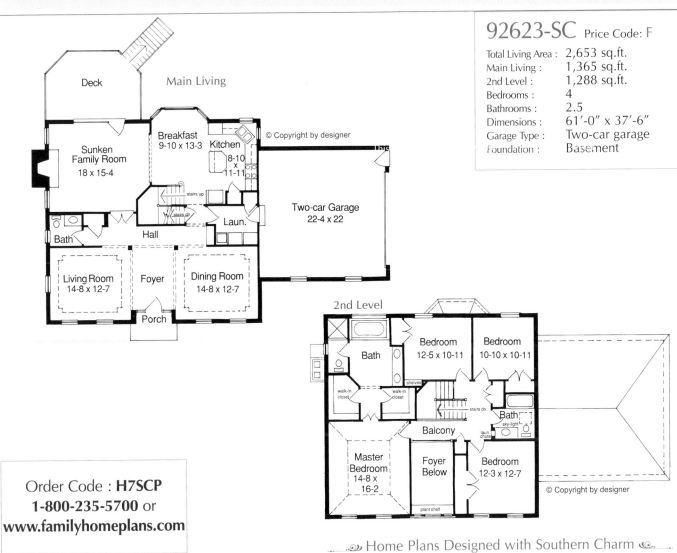

Main Living

Deck

Sunken Family Room 18 x 15-4

Breakfast 9-10 x 13-3

Kitchen 8-10 x 11-11

© Copyright by designer

stairs up
stairs dn

Laun.

Two-car Garage 22-4 x 22

Bath

Hall

Living Room 14-8 x 12-7

Foyer

Dining Room 14-8 x 12-7

Porch

2nd Level

Bath

Bedroom 12-5 x 10-11

Bedroom 10-10 x 10-11

walk-in closet

walk-in closet

shelves

stairs dn

Bath

sky-light

laun. chute

Master Bedroom 14-8 x 16-2

Foyer Below

Balcony

Bedroom 12-3 x 12-7

plant shelf

© Copyright by designer

Home Plans Designed with Southern Charm

65912-SC Price Code: J

Total Living Area : 3,623 sq.ft.
Main Living : 3,623 sq.ft.
Bedrooms : 3
Bathrooms : 3.5
Dimensions : 98'-0" x 80'-0"
Garage Type : Two-car garage
Foundation : Basement, Slab,
Crawlspace

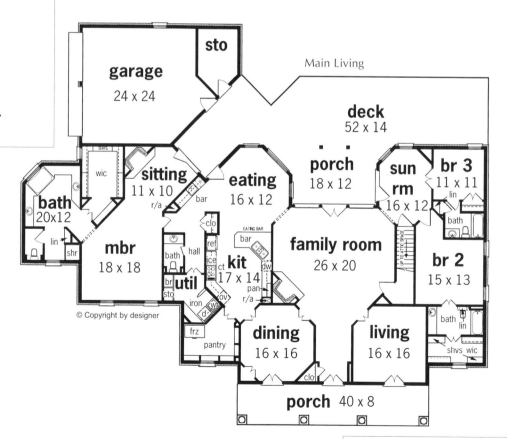

garage
24 x 24

sto

Main Living

deck
52 x 14

sitting
11 x 10

eating
16 x 12

porch
18 x 12

sun
rm
16 x 12

br 3
11 x 11

bath
20x12

mbr
18 x 18

bath
util

kit
17 x 14

family room
26 x 20

br 2
15 x 13

© Copyright by designer

pantry

dining
16 x 16

living
16 x 16

bath

porch 40 x 8

Southern Style
Palladian Windows

Photo Courtesy of The Pella Corporation

Regardless of their obvious differences, many of the great architectural house styles of the Antebellum South—Federal, Greek Revival, Classical Revival, coastal Tidewater—feature a unifying thread that that indelibly links them together. That thread is the work of Italian Renaissance architect Andrea Palladio. Even though this 16th Century architect worked solely in Veneto, and Venice, Italy, his design style influenced architecture throughout Europe and North America from the 16th Century to modern times. Many 17th Century European architects studying in Italy were influenced by his work and brought his ideals to their regions, adapting his principles to suit their locales. As Americans looked to Europe for influential design ideas, elements of his work began popping up in early American architecture, as well.

His work primarily was based on mathematical proportions and modeled after classical Greek and Roman forms. Ancient Roman temples particularly influenced his work. Arches are prominent in his buildings, as are porticos, pediments, loggias, columns, and pilasters. These elements became prominent in North American classical and colonial architectural styles by the 18th Century. Southern Greek Revival homes, with their classical pediments, columns, and porticos were heavily influenced by Palladio's work.

One of the architect's signature elements is the Palladian or Venetian window. The Palladian window consists of three parts: an arched center section and two flanking side sections. The window figures largely in his work, and it became a hallmark of his early career. In Antebellum architecture, Palladian windows are found in many house styles, including Classical Revival, Colonial Revival, Federal and Georgian. Federal house styles, for example, often feature a Palladian window in the center of the second story.

What's most remarkable about Palladio and his now-famous window is that five centuries later, his work is still influencing the classical-style and neo-eclectic home designs of today.

Photography © istockphoto.com

99408-SC Price Code: L

Total Living Area :	4,139 sq.ft.
Main Living :	2,489 sq.ft.
2nd Level :	1,650 sq.ft.
Bedrooms :	4
Bathrooms :	3.5
Dimensions :	72'-8" x 77'-0"
Garage Type :	Three-car garage
Foundation :	Basement*, Slab

Ascending the staircase, a mid-level landing grants entry to a semi-secluded study, brightened by a bay of tall windows. On the second level, all upstairs bedrooms enjoy close proximity to a spacious game room and sun deck.

Order Code : **H7SCP**
1-800-235-5700 or
www.familyhomeplans.com

Basement

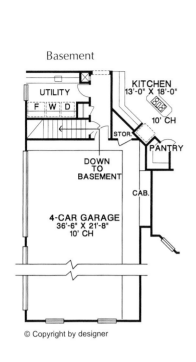

KITCHEN
13'-0" X 18'-0"
10' CH

UTILITY

F W D

STOR.

PANTRY

DOWN TO BASEMENT

CAB.

4-CAR GARAGE
36'-6" X 21'-8"
10' CH

© Copyright by designer

Main Living

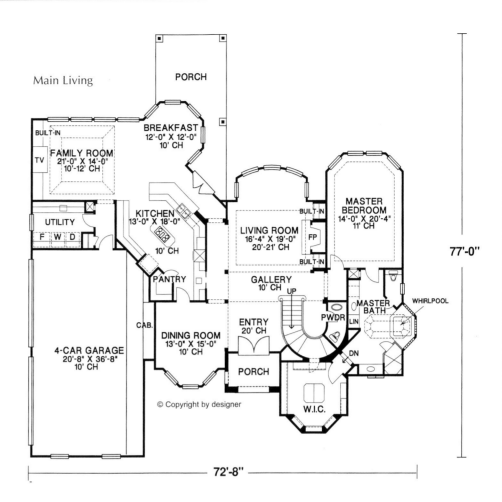

PORCH

BREAKFAST
12'-0" X 12'-0"
10' CH

BUILT-IN

TV

FAMILY ROOM
21'-0" X 14'-0"
10'-12' CH

UTILITY

F W D

KITCHEN
13'-0" X 18'-0"
10' CH

PANTRY

CAB.

4-CAR GARAGE
20'-8" X 36'-8"
10' CH

DINING ROOM
13'-0" X 15'-0"
10' CH

ENTRY
20' CH

PORCH

BUILT-IN

LIVING ROOM
16'-4" X 19'-0"
20'-21' CH

FP

BUILT-IN

GALLERY
10' CH

UP

PWDR

LIN

MASTER BEDROOM
14'-0" X 20'-4"
11' CH

MASTER BATH

WHIRLPOOL

DN

W.I.C.

© Copyright by designer

77'-0"

72'-8"

2nd Level

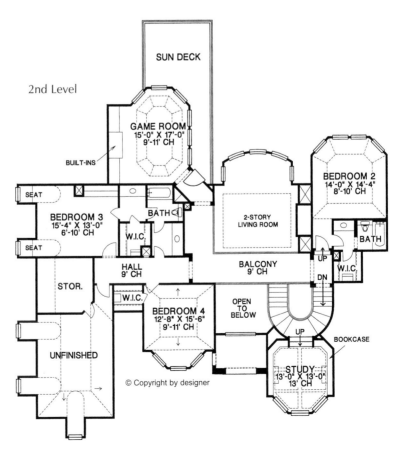

SUN DECK

GAME ROOM
15'-0" X 17'-0"
9'-11' CH

BUILT-INS

SEAT

BEDROOM 3
15'-4" X 13'-0"
6'-10' CH

SEAT

BATH

W.I.C.

2-STORY LIVING ROOM

BEDROOM 2
14'-0" X 14'-4"
8'-10' CH

BATH

W.I.C.

STOR.

HALL
9' CH

W.I.C.

BALCONY
9' CH

UP

DN

UNFINISHED

BEDROOM 4
12'-8" X 15'-6"
9'-11' CH

OPEN TO BELOW

UP

BOOKCASE

STUDY
13'-0" X 13'-0"
13' CH

© Copyright by designer

67845-SC Price Code: K

Total Living Area :	3,863 sq.ft.
Main Living :	2,474 sq.ft.
2nd Level :	1,389 sq.ft.
Bedrooms :	4
Bathrooms :	3.5
Dimensions :	76'-0" x 81'-0"
Garage Type :	Three-car garage
Foundation :	Basement*, Slab

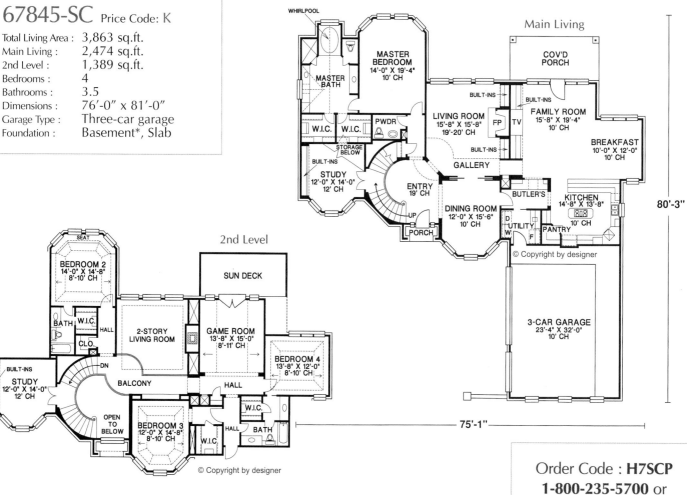

Main Living

WHIRLPOOL

MASTER BEDROOM
14'-0" X 19'-4"
10' CH

MASTER BATH

W.I.C. W.I.C.

PWDR

STORAGE BELOW

BUILT-INS

STUDY
12'-0" X 14'-0"
12' CH

ENTRY
19' CH

UP

PORCH

DINING ROOM
12'-0" X 15'-6"
10' CH

COV'D PORCH

BUILT-INS BUILT-INS

LIVING ROOM
15'-8" X 15'-8"
19'-20" CH

FP TV

BUILT-INS

GALLERY

BUTLER'S

UTILITY

D W

F

PANTRY

FAMILY ROOM
15'-8" X 19'-4"
10' CH

BREAKFAST
10'-0" X 12'-0"
10' CH

KITCHEN
14'-8" X 13'-8"
10' CH

© Copyright by designer

3-CAR GARAGE
23'-4" X 32'-0"
10' CH

80'-3"

75'-1"

2nd Level

SEAT

BEDROOM 2
14'-0" X 14'-8"
8'-10' CH

BATH W.I.C.

HALL

CLO.

BUILT-INS

STUDY
12'-0" X 14'-0"
12' CH

DN

OPEN TO BELOW

BALCONY

2-STORY LIVING ROOM

SUN DECK

GAME ROOM
13'-8" X 15'-0"
8'-11' CH

HALL

BEDROOM 3
12'-0" X 14'-8"
8'-10' CH

W.I.C.

HALL

BATH

BEDROOM 4
13'-8" X 12'-0"
8'-10' CH

W.I.C.

© Copyright by designer

Order Code : **H7SCP**
1-800-235-5700 or
www.familyhomeplans.com

76129-SC Price Code : G

Total Living Area : 2,934 sq.ft.
Main Living : 1,943 sq.ft.
2nd Level : 991 sq.ft.
Bedrooms : 4
Bathrooms : 3.5
Dimensions : 56'-8" x 52'-0"
Garage Type : Two-car garage
Foundation : Slab

Main Living

20-0 X 15-8

11-4 X 10-8

13-0 X 15-0

11-4 X 12-0

10-8 X 12-4

9-4 X 11-0

© Copyright by designer

2-CAR GARAGE
21-4 X 22-4

12-8 X 15-0

2nd Level

12-0 X 12-0

11-4 X 10-0

12-0 X 12-0

© Copyright by designer

A free-flowing connection between the kitchen and great room is enhanced by open views to an octagonal outdoor living area, complete with fireplace. Above the garage, a bonus room anticipates use as a studio, hobby room or secluded get-away space.

87401-SC Price Code: L

Total Living Area :	4,195 sq.ft.
Main Living :	3,603 sq.ft.
2nd Level :	592 sq.ft.
Bedrooms :	4
Bathrooms :	3
Dimensions :	86'-0" x 87'-0"
Garage Type :	Three-car garage
Foundation :	Crawlspace

rear view

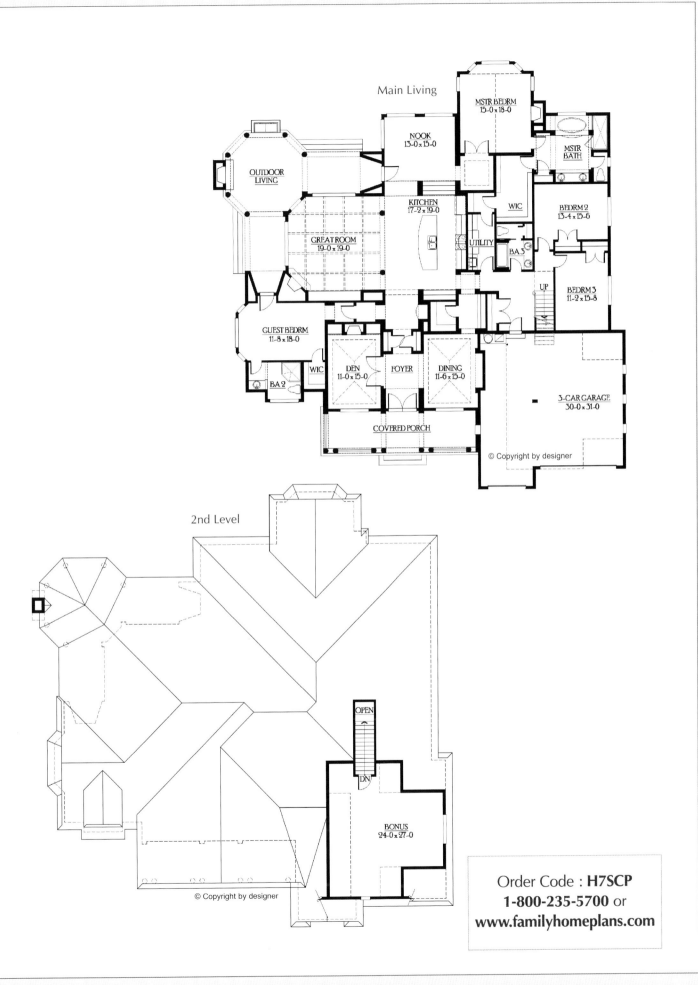

Main Living

OUTDOOR LIVING

NOOK
13-0 x 15-0

MSTR BEDRM
15-0 x 18-0

MSTR BATH

KITCHEN
17-2 x 19-0

WIC

BEDRM 2
13-4 x 15-6

GREAT ROOM
19-0 x 19-0

UTILITY

BA 3

UP

BEDRM 3
11-2 x 15-8

GUEST BEDRM
11-8 x 18-0

WIC

DEN
11-0 x 15-0

FOYER

DINING
11-6 x 15-0

3-CAR GARAGE
30-0 x 31-0

BA 2

COVERED PORCH

© Copyright by designer

2nd Level

OPEN

DN

BONUS
24-0 x 27-0

© Copyright by designer

Order Code : **H7SCP**
1-800-235-5700 or
www.familyhomeplans.com

This home, as shown, may differ from the original design.

24803-SC Price Code: K

Total Living Area :	3,947 sq.ft.
Basement :	1,533 sq.ft.
Main Living :	2,414 sq.ft.
Bedrooms :	4
Bathrooms :	2.5
Dimensions :	82'-0" x 62'-0"
Garage Type :	Three-car garage
Foundation :	Basement

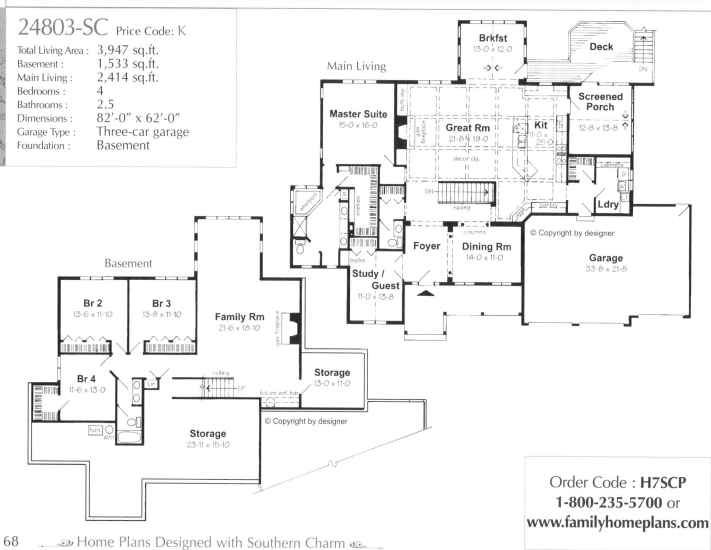

Main Living

Brkfst
13-0 x 12-0

Deck

DN

Master Suite
15-0 x 16-0

built-ins

gas fireplace

Great Rm
21-8 x 19-0

Kit
11-0 x 25-0

Screened Porch
12-8 x 13-8

decor clg.

whirlpool

shelves

DN

railing

pantry

Ldry

LT

© Copyright by designer

books

Foyer

columns

Dining Rm
14-0 x 11-0

Garage
33-8 x 21-8

Study / Guest
11-0 x 13-8

Basement

Br 2
13-6 x 11-10

Br 3
13-8 x 11-10

Family Rm
21-6 x 18-10

gas fireplace

Storage
13-0 x 11-0

Br 4
11-6 x 13-0

Lin

railing

UP

future wet bar

© Copyright by designer

furn.

W/H

Storage
23-11 x 15-10

Order Code : **H7SCP**
1-800-235-5700 or
www.familyhomeplans.com

This home, as shown, may differ from the original design.

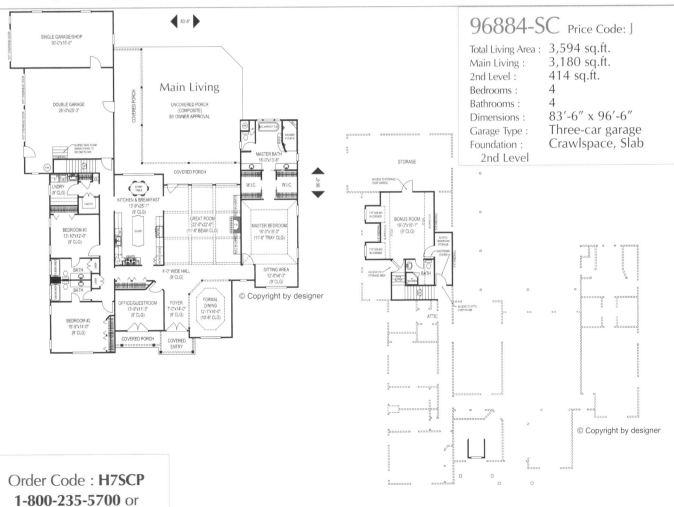

96884-SC Price Code: J

Total Living Area :	3,594 sq.ft.
Main Living :	3,180 sq.ft.
2nd Level :	414 sq.ft.
Bedrooms :	4
Bathrooms :	4
Dimensions :	83'-6" x 96'-6"
Garage Type :	Three-car garage
Foundation :	Crawlspace, Slab

2nd Level

© Copyright by designer

© Copyright by designer

Order Code : **H7SCP**
1-800-235-5700 or
www.familyhomeplans.com

65240-SC Price Code: L

Total Living Area : 4,204 sq.ft.
Main Living : 2,482 sq.ft.
2nd Level : 1,722 sq.ft.
Bedrooms : 5
Bathrooms : 3.5
Dimensions : 95'-0" x 51'-0"
Garage Type : Three-car garage
Foundation : Basement

A computer/study area on the upper level provides a comfortable setting in which to do homework, pay the bills, or just relax with a good book. French doors provide access to the exterior balcony for a enjoying break from studies and getting some fresh air.

Order Code : **H7SCP**
1-800-235-5700 or
www.familyhomeplans.com

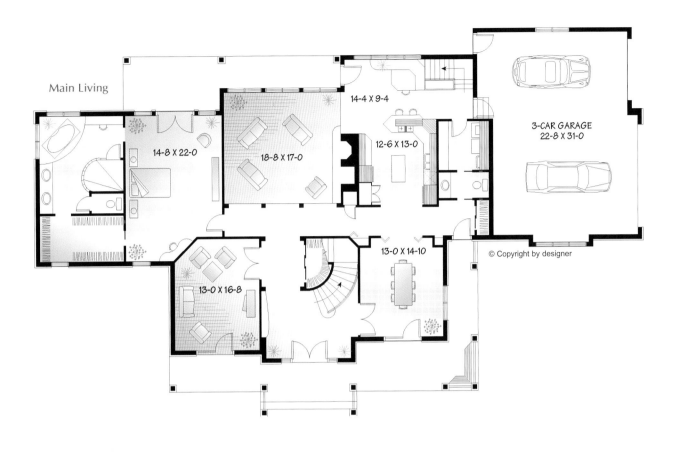

Main Living

14-8 X 22-0

18-8 X 17-0

14-4 X 9-4

12-6 X 13-0

3-CAR GARAGE
22-8 X 31-0

13-0 X 16-8

13-0 X 14-10

© Copyright by designer

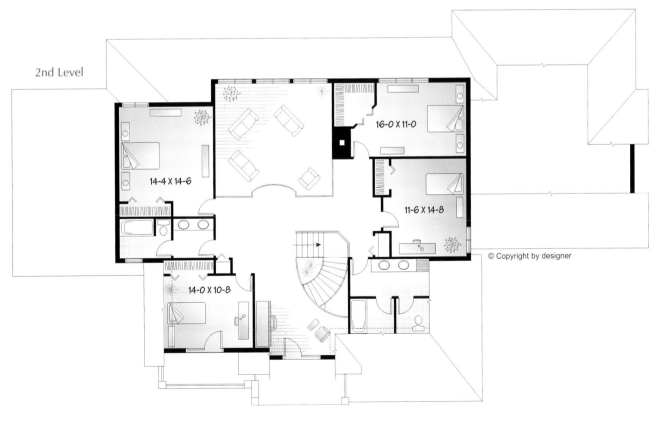

2nd Level

14-4 X 14-6

16-0 X 11-0

11-6 X 14-8

14-0 X 10-8

© Copyright by designer

Cover House

Refined
Living

A striking, 2-story-high entryway greets guests with views of the formal dining room, library and great room.

This home, as shown, may differ from the original design.

Photo Courtesy of The Designer

Tasteful details enhance the character of this stately Southern Colonial design.

A deep front porch ushers guests inside, where a 2-story foyer provides a proper welcome. Views are immediately drawn toward the formal rooms on either side, and to the extraordinary great room beyond. A spacious, well-planned kitchen area opens to the breakfast area and a discreetly located hearth room. On the opposite side of the home, the secluded master suite enjoys a sitting area and private porch. Three spacious secondary bedrooms complete the upper level.

RIGHT: The soaring great room provides an impressive entertaining space, with exquisite trim detailing, a captivating fireplace and built-in display shelves.

ABOVE: The great room's wall of windows brings the outdoors inside with expansive views and an abundance of natural light.

LEFT: The kitchen and adjoining hearth room offer a more private, casual setting for friends and family.

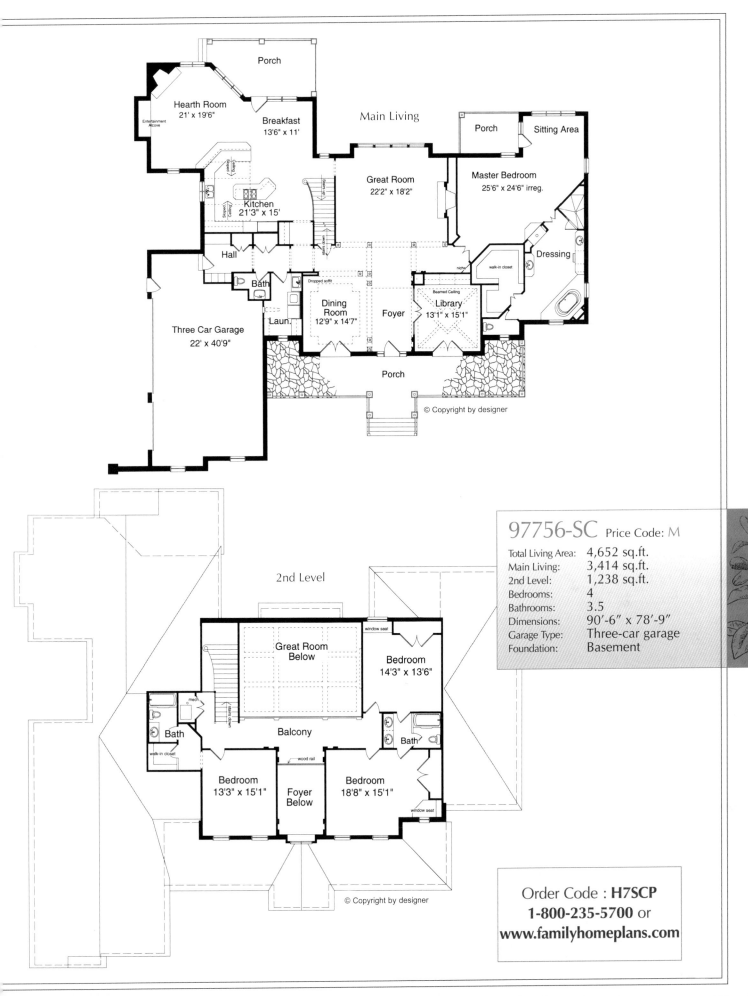

Porch

Hearth Room
21' x 19'6"

Entertainment Alcove

Breakfast
13'6" x 11'

Main Living

Porch

Sitting Area

Great Room
22'2" x 18'2"

Master Bedroom
25'6" x 24'6" irreg.

Kitchen
21'3" x 15'

Hall

Dressing

niche

walk-in closet

Bath

Dropped soffit

Dining Room
12'9" x 14'7"

Foyer

Beamed Ceiling
Library
13'1" x 15'1"

Three Car Garage
22' x 40'9"

Laun.

Porch

© Copyright by designer

2nd Level

Great Room Below

window seat

Bedroom
14'3" x 13'6"

Bath

mech.

Bath

Balcony

walk-in closet

Bedroom
13'3" x 15'1"

Foyer Below

wood rail

Bedroom
18'8" x 15'1"

window seat

© Copyright by designer

97756-SC Price Code: M

Total Living Area:	4,652 sq.ft.
Main Living:	3,414 sq.ft.
2nd Level:	1,238 sq.ft.
Bedrooms:	4
Bathrooms:	3.5
Dimensions:	90'-6" x 78'-9"
Garage Type:	Three-car garage
Foundation:	Basement

Order Code : **H7SCP**
1-800-235-5700 or
www.familyhomeplans.com

Here, an elegant, irresistible covered rear porch becomes the centerpiece of the floor plan. Ceiling details and a fireplace enhance the ambiance of this outdoor living space. Access is gained from the breakfast area, great room and master suite.

50154-SC Price Code: N

Total Living Area :	5,072 sq.ft.
Main Living :	3,648 sq.ft.
2nd Level :	1,424 sq.ft.
Bedrooms :	4
Bathrooms :	4
Dimensions :	88'-4" x 82'-9"
Garage Type :	Three-car garage
Foundation :	Basement

rear view

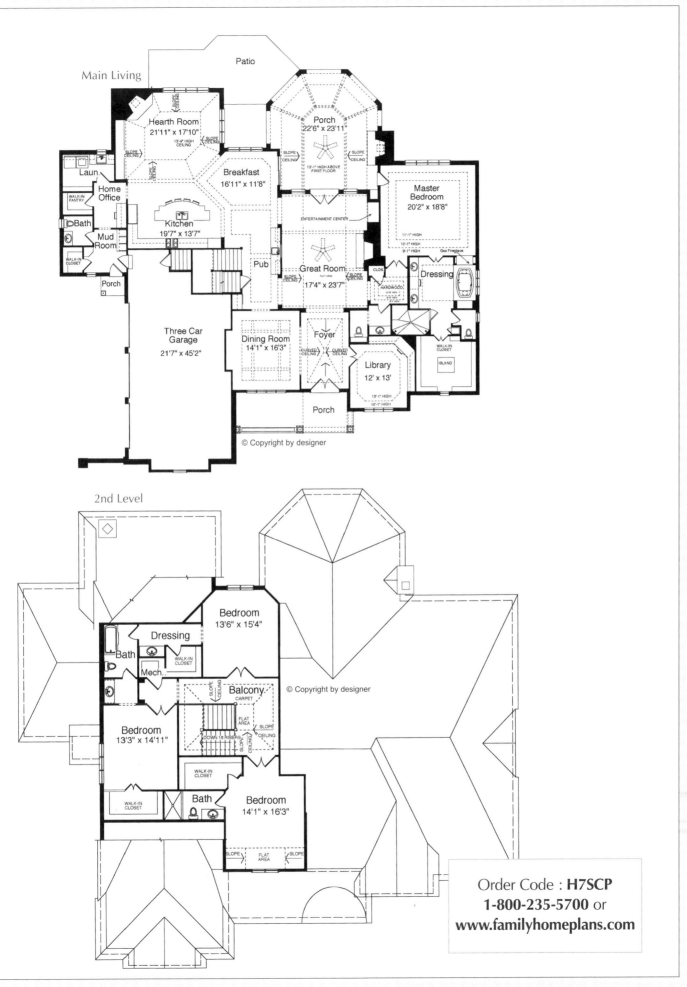

Main Living

Patio

Hearth Room
21'11" x 17'10"

Porch
22'6" x 23'11"

Master Bedroom
20'2" x 18'8"

Breakfast
16'11" x 11'8"

Laun.

Home Office

Kitchen
19'7" x 13'7"

Bath

Mud Room

WALK-IN CLOSET

Porch

Pub

Great Room
17'4" x 23'7"

Dressing

CLOS

Three Car Garage
21'7" x 45'2"

Dining Room
14'1" x 16'3"

Foyer

WALK-IN CLOSET

ISLAND

Library
12' x 13'

Porch

© Copyright by designer

2nd Level

Bedroom
13'6" x 15'4"

Dressing

Bath

WALK-IN CLOSET

Mech.

Balcony
CARPET

© Copyright by designer

Bedroom
13'3" x 14'11"

DOWN 16 RISERS

WALK-IN CLOSET

WALK-IN CLOSET

Bath

Bedroom
14'1" x 16'3"

Order Code : **H7SCP**
1-800-235-5700 or
www.familyhomeplans.com

73068-SC Price Code: J

Total Living Area : 3,697 sq.ft.
Main Living : 2,650 sq.ft.
2nd Level : 1,047 sq.ft.
Bedrooms : 4
Bathrooms : 4
Dimensions : 68'-0" x 84'-4"
Garage Type : Three-car garage
Foundation : Slab*, Crawlspace*,
Walkout Basement

Main Living

SUN. RM.
CATHEDRAL CEILING
17'8"x13'6"

NK.
9'-1 1/8" CEILING
17'8"x12'0"

WOOD DECK
20'0"x18'8"

MBR.
CATHEDRAL CEILING
13'8"x19'8"

KIT.
9'-1 1/8" CEILING
17'8"x16'0"

GRT. RM.
VAULTED-2-STORY
CEILING
21'8"x15'8"

LOCKERS BENCH

3 CAR GARAGE
25'10"x33'6"

DIN.
9'-1 1/8" CEILING
12'8"x13'8"

E.
12'-1 1/8" CEILING

STUDY
TRAY CEILING
12'2"x13'0"

SHELVES

COURTYARD

© Copyright by designer

84'-4"

68'-0"

2nd Level

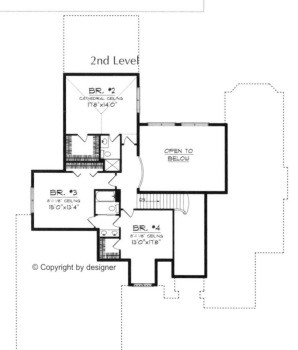

BR. #2
CATHEDRAL CEILING
17'8"x14'0"

OPEN TO
BELOW

BR. #3
8'-1 1/8" CEILING
15'0"x13'4"

BR. #4
8'-1 1/8" CEILING
13'0"x17'8"

© Copyright by designer

99402-SC Price Code: K

Total Living Area :	3,904 sq.ft.
Main Living :	2,813 sq.ft.
2nd Level :	1,091 sq.ft.
Bedrooms :	4
Bathrooms :	4
Dimensions :	85'-5" x 74'-8"
Garage Type :	Three-car garage
Foundation :	Basement, Slab*, Crawlspace*

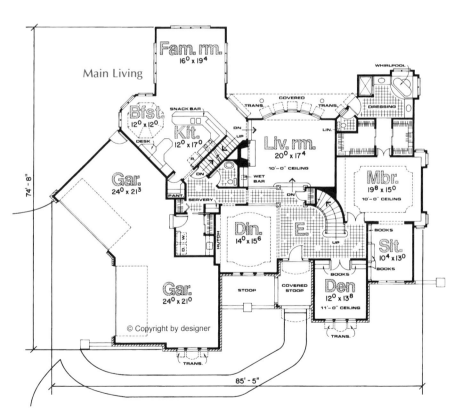

Main Living

Fam. rm.
16⁰ x 19⁴

Bfst.
12⁰ x 12⁰

Kit.
12⁰ x 17⁰

Liv. rm.
20⁰ x 17⁴
10'-0" CEILING

Gar.
24⁰ x 21³

Gar.
24⁰ x 21⁰

Din.
14⁰ x 15⁶

Mbr.
19⁸ x 15⁰
10'-0" CEILING

Sit.
10⁴ x 13⁰

Den
12⁰ x 13⁸
11'-0" CEILING

WHIRLPOOL

DRESSING

© Copyright by designer

74'-8"

85'-5"

2nd Level

Br. 2
13⁰ x 17⁴
10'-0" CLG.

Br. 3
14⁰ x 15⁶

Br. 4
12⁰ x 15⁶
10'-0" CEILING

OPEN TO BELOW

SEAT

© Copyright by designer

73406-SC Price Code: N

Total Living Area :	5,139 sq.ft.
Main Living :	3,989 sq.ft.
2nd Level :	1,150 sq.ft.
Bedrooms :	4
Bathrooms :	4
Dimensions :	102'-4" x 89'-0"
Garage Type :	Three-car garage
Foundation :	Basement

Walls of windows define a stately corner turret that houses a den/library on the main level and a secondary bedroom upstairs. A sensible mudroom, complete with lockers, and a spacious laundry center are much appreciated, practical spaces.

Order Code : **H7SCP**
1-800-235-5700 or
www.familyhomeplans.com

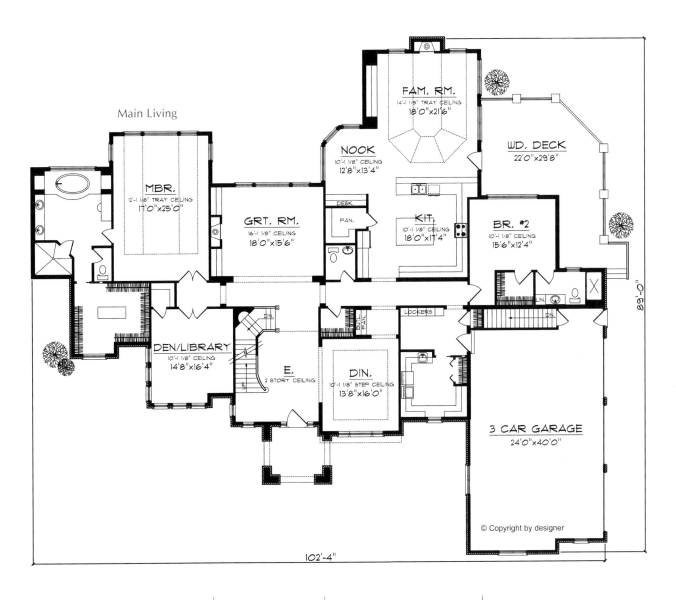

Main Living

MBR.
12'-1 1/8" TRAY CEILING
17'0"x25'0"

GRT. RM.
16'-1 1/8" CEILING
18'0"x15'6"

NOOK
10'-1 1/8" CEILING
12'8"x13'4"

FAM. RM.
14'-1 1/8" TRAY CEILING
18'0"x21'6"

WD. DECK
22'0"x29'8"

KIT.
10'-1 1/8" CEILING
18'0"x17'4"

BR. #2
10'-1 1/8" CEILING
15'6"x12'4"

DESK

PAN.

DEN/LIBRARY
10'-1 1/8" CEILING
14'8"x16'4"

E.
2 STORY CEILING

DIN.
10'-1 1/8" STEP CEILING
13'8"x16'0"

LOCKERS

BUT. PAN.

LIN.

3 CAR GARAGE
24'0"x40'0"

© Copyright by designer

89'-0"

102'-4"

2nd Level

ART NICHE

STOR.

BR. #3
9'-1 1/8" CEILING
14'8"x16'0"

OPEN TO
BELOW

BR. #4
10'-1 1/8" STEP CEILING
13'8"x19'8"

DN.

LIN.

© Copyright by designer

61049-SC Price Code: M

Total Living Area : 4,532 sq.ft.
Main Living : 3,732 sq.ft.
2nd Level : 800 sq.ft.
Bedrooms : 3
Bathrooms : 2
Dimensions : 96'-10" x 75'-10"
Garage Type : Three-car garage
Foundation : Slab, Crawlspace

Appealing outdoor spaces adorn the front and back of this design. On the front, a covered porch is accessed from the bayed study. To the rear, the breakfast room, living room and master suite open to an expansive lanai.

Order Code : **H7SCP**
1-800-235-5700 or
www.familyhomeplans.com

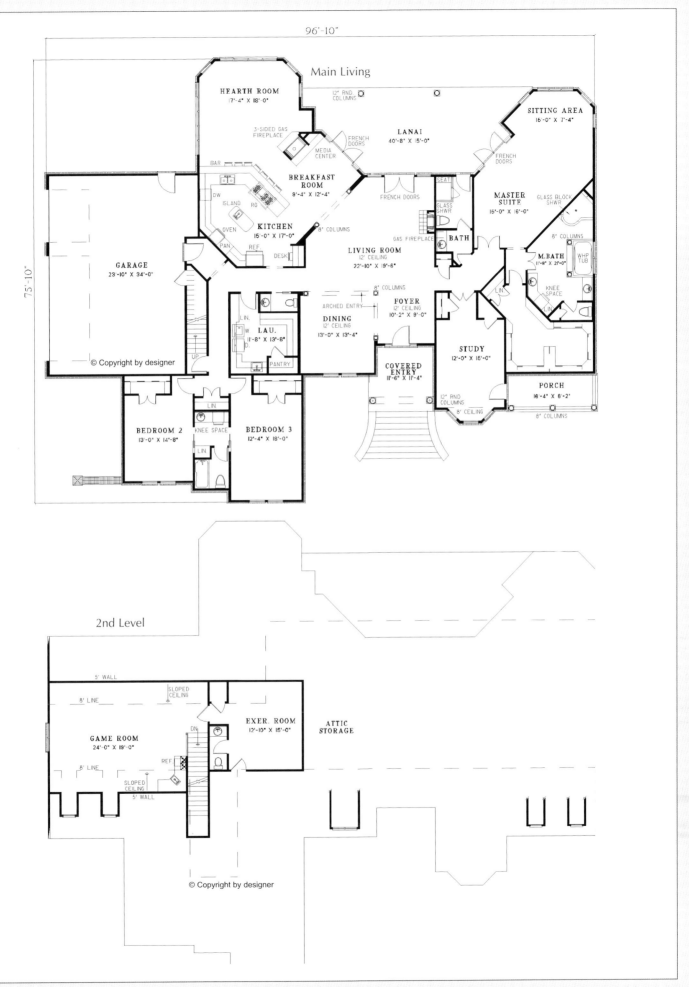

Main Living

HEARTH ROOM
17'-4" X 18'-0"

12" RND.
COLUMNS

SITTING AREA
16'-0" X 7'-4"

3-SIDED GAS
FIREPLACE

LANAI
40'-8" X 15'-0"

MEDIA
CENTER

FRENCH
DOORS

BAR

FRENCH
DOORS

BREAKFAST
ROOM
8'-4" X 12'-4"

DW

MASTER
SUITE
15'-0" X 16'-0"

GLASS BLOCK
SHWR

ISLAND

RG

SEAT

FRENCH DOORS

OVEN

GLASS
SHWR

8' COLUMNS

PAN

KITCHEN
15'-0" X 17'-0"

8" COLUMNS

M.BATH
11'-8" X 21'-0"

WHP
TUB

REF.

DESK

LIVING ROOM
12' CEILING
22'-10" X 19'-6"

GAS FIREPLACE

BATH

KNEE
SPACE

GARAGE
23'-10" X 34'-0"

8" COLUMNS

LIN

ARCHED ENTRY

FOYER
12' CEILING
10'-2" X 9'-0"

LIN

© Copyright by designer

UP

LIN

W

LAU.
11'-8" X 13'-8"

D

DINING
12' CEILING
13'-0" X 13'-4"

STUDY
12'-0" X 15'-0"

PANTRY

COVERED
ENTRY
11'-6" X 11'-4"

PORCH
16'-4" X 8'-2"

BEDROOM 2
13'-0" X 14'-8"

KNEE SPACE

BEDROOM 3
12'-4" X 18'-0"

12" RND
COLUMNS

8' CEILING

8' COLUMNS

LIN

96'-10"

75'-10"

2nd Level

5' WALL

SLOPED
CEILING

8' LINE

GAME ROOM
24'-0" X 19'-0"

DN

EXER. ROOM
12'-10" X 15'-0"

ATTIC
STORAGE

REF.

8' LINE

SLOPED
CEILING

5' WALL

© Copyright by designer

66234-SC Price Code: I

Total Living Area : 3,428 sq.ft.
Main Living : 3,428 sq.ft.
Bedrooms : 4
Bathrooms : 3.5
Dimensions : 112'-0" x 81'-6"
Garage Type : Three-car garage
Foundation : Basement, Slab,
 Crawlspace

2nd Level

Main Living

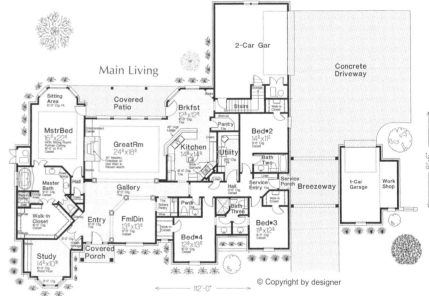

© Copyright by designer

© Copyright by designer

Order Code : **H7SCP**
1-800-235-5700 or
www.familyhomeplans.com

97162-SC Price Code: J

Total Living Area :	3,728 sq.ft.
Main Living :	2,986 sq.ft.
2nd Level :	742 sq.ft.
Bedrooms :	3
Bathrooms :	2.5
Dimensions :	99'-0" x 87'-0"
Garage Type :	Three-car garage
Foundation :	Basement

Main Living

PATIO

SCREEN PORCH
VAULTED CEILING
16'0"X16'0"

FAM. RM.
VAULTED CEILING
18'0"X20'0"

WOOD DECK
32'4"X25'8"

KIT.
15'0"X18'0"

NK
10'8"X11'0"

LIV. RM.
9 STORY CATHEDRAL CEILING
21'4"X17'6"

M.B.R.
16'4"X25'6"

2 CAR GAR.
35'8"X23'0"

DIN. RM.
13'8"X14'8"

E.

2 CAR GAR.
20'0"X24'0"

DEN
14'0"X12'10"

© Copyright by designer

99'-0"

2nd Level

BONUS ROOM
26'6"X22'8"

B.R. #2
15'2"X13'6"

OPEN TO LIV.

B.R. #3
13'8"X11'0"

OPEN TO E.

© Copyright by designer

73030-SC Price Code: O

Total Living Area :	6,223 sq.ft.
Basement :	2,033 sq.ft.
Main Living :	4,190 sq.ft.
Bedrooms :	4
Bathrooms :	5
Dimensions :	113'-4" x 88'-0"
Garage Type :	Three-car garage
Foundation :	Basement

A spacious rear patio, positioned for privacy, has seven points of access from inside the home. Equally inviting is the lower level, which offers space to relax and entertain with a media room, game room and wet bar.

Order Code : **H7SCP**
1-800-235-5700 or
www.familyhomeplans.com

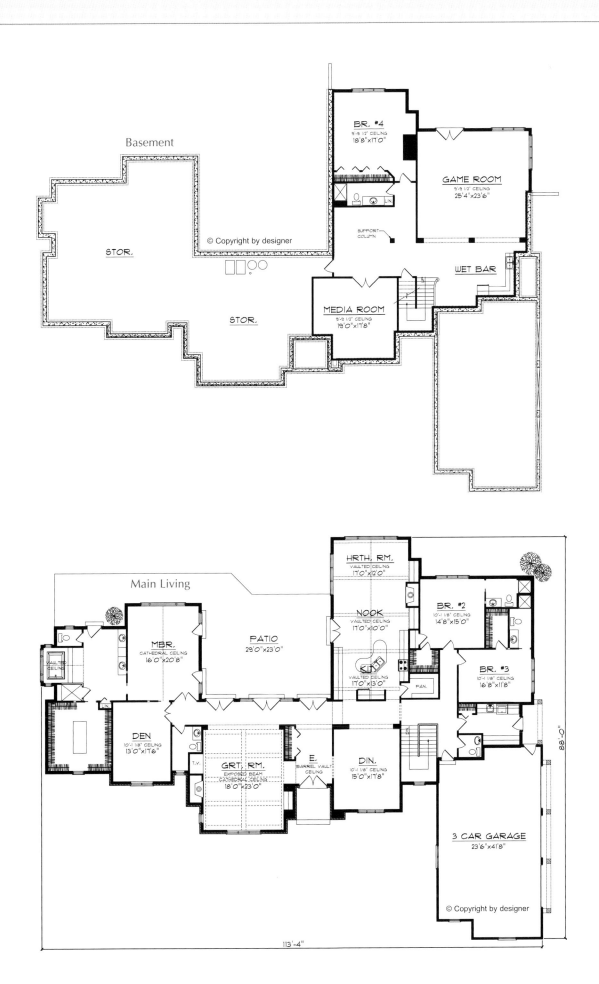

Basement

STOR.

© Copyright by designer

STOR.

BR. #4
9'-9 1/2" ceiling
18'8"x17'0"

GAME ROOM
9'-9 1/2" ceiling
25'4"x23'6"

SUPPORT COLUMN

WET BAR

MEDIA ROOM
9'-9 1/2" ceiling
19'0"x17'8"

Main Living

HRTH. RM.
VAULTED CEILING
17'0"x12'0"

NOOK
VAULTED CEILING
17'0"x10'0"

BR. #2
10'-1 1/8" ceiling
14'8"x15'0"

MBR.
CATHEDRAL CEILING
16'0"x20'8"

PATIO
29'0"x23'0"

KIT.
VAULTED CEILING
17'0"x13'0"

PAN.

BR. #3
10'-1 1/8" ceiling
16'8"x11'8"

VAULTED CEILING

DEN
10'-1 1/8" ceiling
13'0"x17'6"

T.V.

GRT. RM.
EXPOSED BEAM
CATHEDRAL CEILING
18'0"x23'0"

E.
BARREL VAULT
CEILING

DIN.
10'-1 1/8" ceiling
15'0"x17'8"

3 CAR GARAGE
23'6"x41'8"

© Copyright by designer

88'-0"

113'-4"

10670-SC Price Code: K

Total Living Area :	3,935 sq.ft.
Main Living :	2,849 sq.ft.
2nd Level :	1,086 sq.ft.
Bedrooms :	5
Bathrooms :	4.5
Dimensions :	74'-0" x 68'-0"
Garage Type :	Three-car garage
Foundation :	Slab

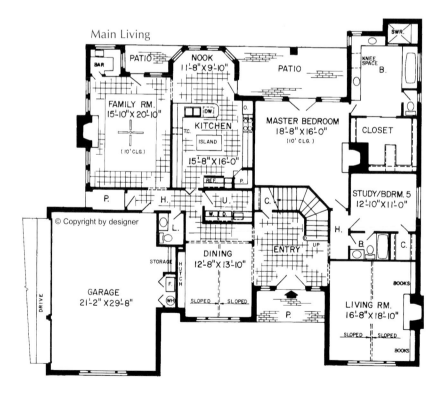

Main Living

PATIO
BAR
NOOK 11'-8" X 9'-10"
PATIO
KNEE SPACE
B.
FAMILY RM. 15'-10" X 20'-10" (10' CLG.)
DW
KITCHEN 15'-8" X 16'-0"
ISLAND
TC.
MASTER BEDROOM 18'-8" X 16'-0" (10' CLG.)
CLOSET
REF.
P.
U.
STUDY/BDRM. 5 12'-10" X 11'-0"
P.
H.
W D
C.
BOOKS
STORAGE
L.
DINING 12'-8" X 13'-10"
ENTRY UP
B.
C.
GARAGE 21'-2" X 29'-8"
HUTCH
F.
WH
SLOPED SLOPED
LIVING RM. 16'-8" X 18'-10"
DRIVE
P.
SLOPED SLOPED
BOOKS

© Copyright by designer

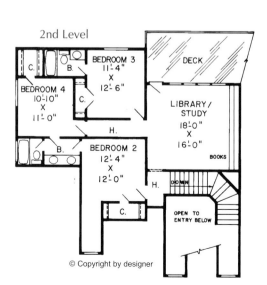

2nd Level

BEDROOM 3 11'-4" X 12'-6"
C.
B.
DECK
BEDROOM 4 10'-10" X 11'-0"
C.
LIBRARY/ STUDY 18'-0" X 16'-0"
H.
B.
BEDROOM 2 12'-4" X 12'-0"
BOOKS
DOWN
H.
C.
OPEN TO ENTRY BELOW

© Copyright by designer

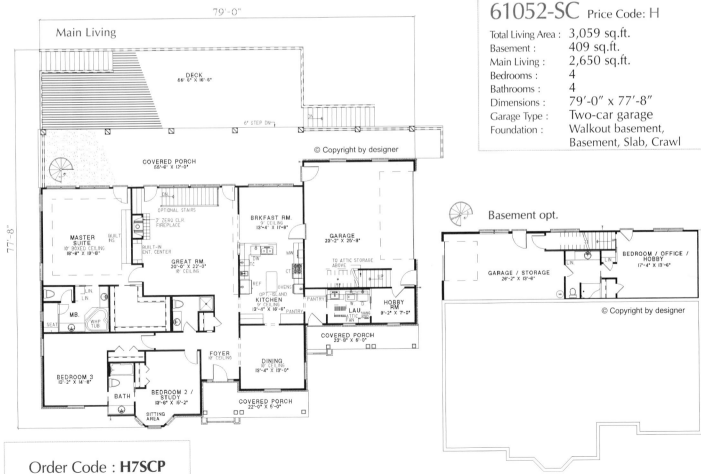

79'-0"

Main Living

77'-8"

DECK
26'-6" X 16'-6"

6' STEP DN.

COVERED PORCH
55'-6" X 12'-0"

© Copyright by designer

OPTIONAL STAIRS

3' ZERO CLR.
FIREPLACE

BRKFAST RM.
13'-4" X 11'-6"
9' CEILING

GARAGE
23'-2" X 25'-8"

BUILT INS

MASTER SUITE
10' BOXED CEILING
18'-6" X 19'-8"

BUILT-IN
ENT. CENTER

GREAT RM.
20'-0" X 22'-0"
10' CEILING

MW
C

TO ATTIC STORAGE
ABOVE

LIN.

DW
C

CT

UP

REF

OVENS

MB.

WHP
TUB

SEAT

OPT. ISLAND

KITCHEN
13'-4" X 16'-6"
9' CEILING

PANTRY

W   D

LAU.
ATTIC FAN

HANG POLE

PANTRY

HOBBY RM.
9'-2" X 7'-0"

BEDROOM 3
13'-2" X 14'-8"

BATH

BEDROOM 2 /
STUDY
13'-8" X 15'-2"

SITTING AREA

FOYER
10' CEILING

DINING
10' CEILING
13'-4" X 13'-0"

COVERED PORCH
22'-0" X 5'-0"

COVERED PORCH
23'-8" X 6'-0"

61052-SC Price Code: H

Total Living Area : 3,059 sq.ft.
Basement : 409 sq.ft.
Main Living : 2,650 sq.ft.
Bedrooms : 4
Bathrooms : 4
Dimensions : 79'-0" x 77'-8"
Garage Type : Two-car garage
Foundation : Walkout basement,
Basement, Slab, Crawl

Basement opt.

GARAGE / STORAGE
26'-2" X 19'-8"

BEDROOM / OFFICE /
HOBBY
17'-4" X 13'-6"

LIN.

LIN.

© Copyright by designer

Order Code : **H7SCP**
1-800-235-5700 or
www.familyhomeplans.com

44084-SC Price Code: K

Total Living Area : 3,823 sq.ft.
Main Living : 3,128 sq.ft.
2nd Level : 695 sq.ft.
Bedrooms : 1
Bathrooms : 1.5
Dimensions : 122'-8" x 85'-1"
Garage Type : Three-car garage
Foundation : Basement, Slab*,
Crawlspace*

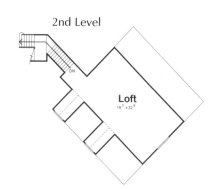

2nd Level

Loft
19⁰ x 32⁸

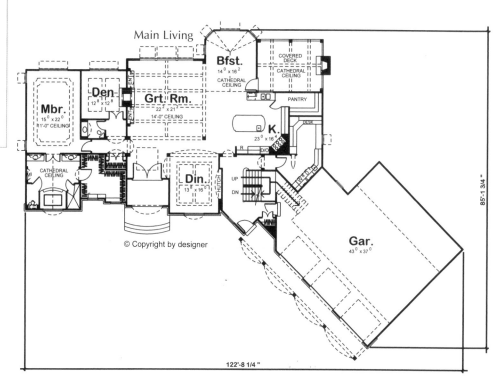

Main Living

Bfst.
14⁰ x 16²
CATHEDRAL CEILING

COVERED DECK
CATHEDRAL CEILING

Den
12⁸ x 12⁸

Grt. Rm.
22⁷ x 21⁷
14'-0" CEILING

PANTRY

Mbr.
15⁰ x 22⁰
11'-0" CEILING

K.
23⁰ x 16⁰

DESK

CATHEDRAL CEILING

Din.
13⁸ x 16⁰

UP
DN

Gar.
43⁰ x 37⁰

© Copyright by designer

85'-1 3/4"

122'-8 1/4"

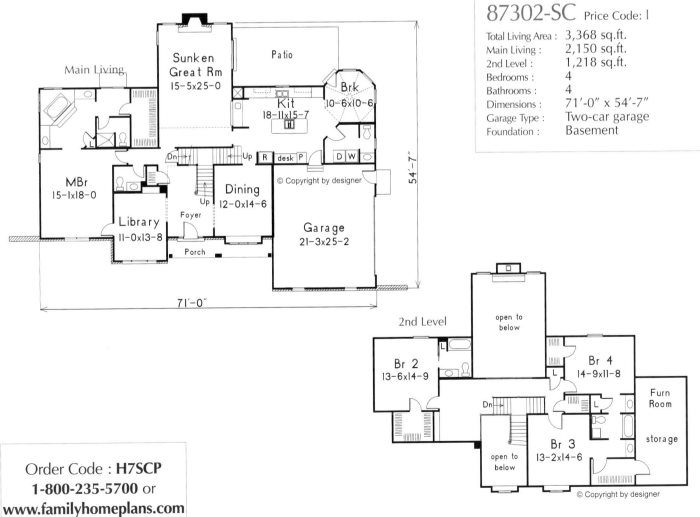

87302-SC Price Code: I

Total Living Area :	3,368 sq.ft.
Main Living :	2,150 sq.ft.
2nd Level :	1,218 sq.ft.
Bedrooms :	4
Bathrooms :	4
Dimensions :	71'-0" x 54'-7"
Garage Type :	Two-car garage
Foundation :	Basement

Main Living

Sunken Great Rm 15-5x25-0

Patio

Brk 10-6x10-6

Kit 18-11x15-7

Dn Up R desk P D W

© Copyright by designer

MBr 15-1x18-0

Dining 12-0x14-6

Up

Library 11-0x13-8

Foyer

Porch

Garage 21-3x25-2

54'-7"

71'-0"

2nd Level

open to below

Br 2 13-6x14-9

Br 4 14-9x11-8

Furn Room

storage

Dn

open to below

Br 3 13-2x14-6

© Copyright by designer

Order Code : **H7SCP**
1-800-235-5700 or
www.familyhomeplans.com

Home Plans Designed with Southern Charm

This home, as shown, may differ from the original design.

The lower level of this home offers nearly as much as the main level – a secondary kitchen, bedroom, office, media room, billiards room and exercise area. This exceptional area would serve well as an inlaw's suite or living space for an older child.

97714-SC Price Code: N

Total Living Area :	5,937 sq.ft.
Basement :	2,367 sq.ft.
Main Living :	3,570 sq.ft.
Bedrooms :	3
Bathrooms :	3.5
Dimensions :	84'-6" x 69'-4"
Garage Type :	Four-car garage
Foundation :	Basement

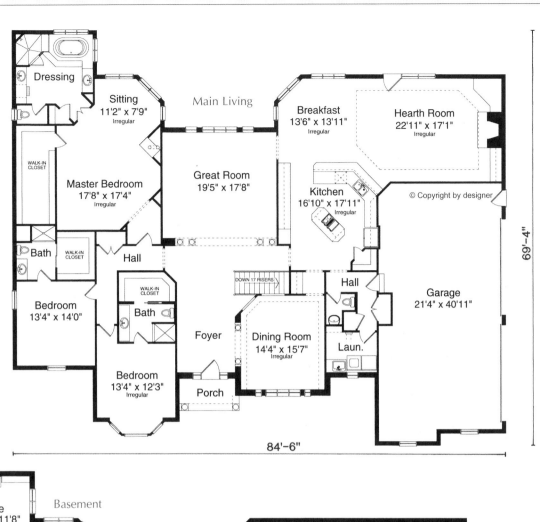

Main Living

Dressing

Sitting
11'2" x 7'9"
Irregular

Breakfast
13'6" x 13'11"
Irregular

Hearth Room
22'11" x 17'1"
Irregular

WALK-IN CLOSET

Master Bedroom
17'8" x 17'4"
Irregular

Great Room
19'5" x 17'8"

Kitchen
16'10" x 17'11"
Irregular

© Copyright by designer

Bath

WALK-IN CLOSET

Hall

Bedroom
13'4" x 14'0"

WALK-IN CLOSET

Bath

DOWN 17 RISERS

Hall

Garage
21'4" x 40'11"

Foyer

Dining Room
14'4" x 15'7"
Irregular

Laun.

Bedroom
13'4" x 12'3"
Irregular

Porch

84'-6"

69'-4"

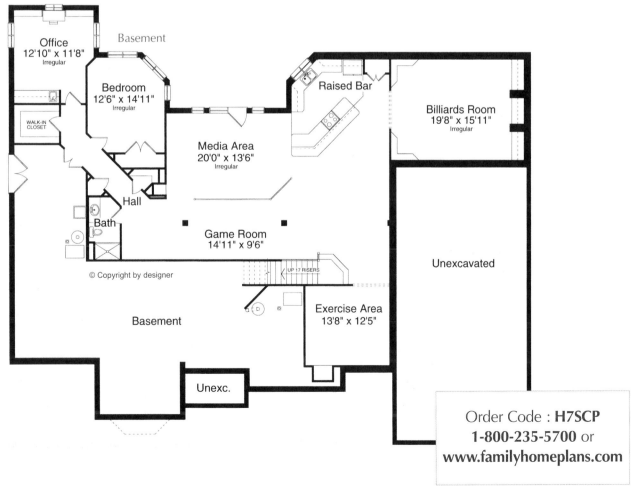

Basement

Office
12'10" x 11'8"
Irregular

Raised Bar

Billiards Room
19'8" x 15'11"
Irregular

Bedroom
12'6" x 14'11"
Irregular

WALK-IN CLOSET

Media Area
20'0" x 13'6"
Irregular

Hall

Bath

© Copyright by designer

Game Room
14'11" x 9'6"

Unexcavated

Basement

UP 17 RISERS

Exercise Area
13'8" x 12'5"

Unexc.

Order Code : **H7SCP**
1-800-235-5700 or
www.familyhomeplans.com

73104-SC Price Code: J

Total Living Area :	3,600 sq.ft.
Main Living :	1,406 sq.ft.
2nd Level :	2,194 sq.ft.
Bedrooms :	4
Bathrooms :	3
Dimensions :	73'-0" x 61'-8"
Garage Type :	Three-car garage
Foundation :	Walkout Basement

A single-car garage, separated from a two-car garage, opens up possibilities as space for a boat, golf carts, workshop – or even, a third car. The lower-level rec room accommodates larger gatherings with a fireplace and wet bar.

Order Code : **H7SCP**
1-800-235-5700 or
www.familyhomeplans.com

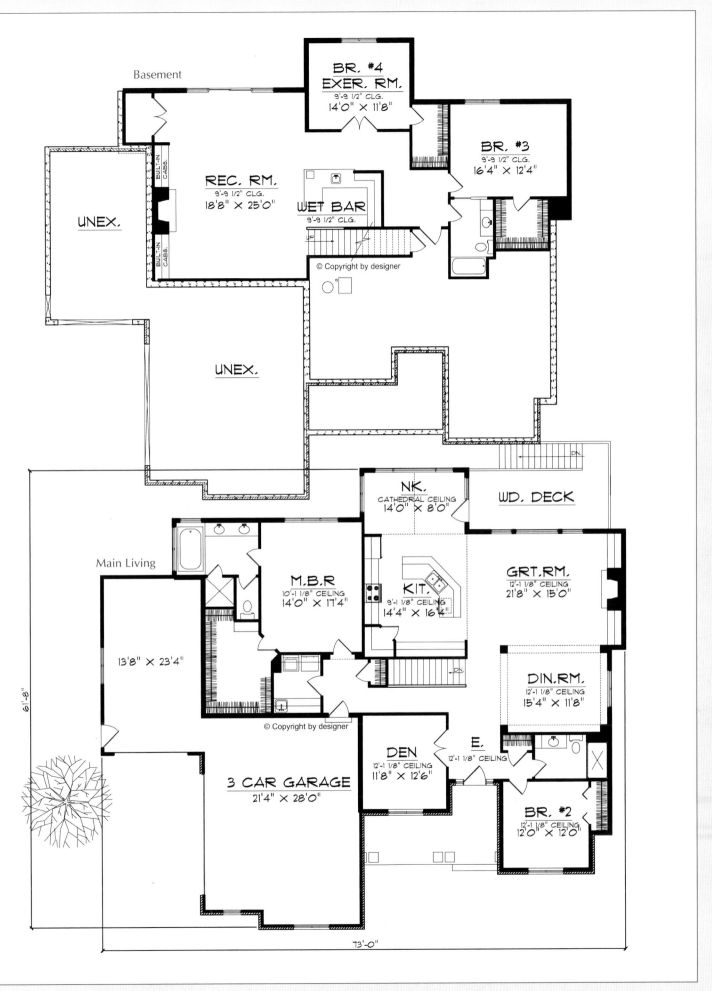

Basement

BR. #4
EXER. RM.
9'-9 1/2" CLG.
14'0" X 11'8"

BR. #3
9'-9 1/2" CLG.
16'4" X 12'4"

UNEX.

REC. RM.
9'-9 1/2" CLG.
18'8" X 25'0"

WET BAR
9'-9 1/2" CLG.

BUILT-IN CABS.

UNEX.

© Copyright by designer

NK.
CATHEDRAL CEILING
14'0" X 8'0"

WD. DECK

Main Living

M.B.R
10'-1 1/8" CEILING
14'0" X 17'4"

KIT.
9'-1 1/8" CEILING
14'4" X 16'4"

GRT.RM.
12'-1 1/8" CEILING
21'8" X 15'0"

13'8" X 23'4"

DIN.RM.
12'-1 1/8" CEILING
15'4" X 11'8"

© Copyright by designer

DEN
12'-1 1/8" CEILING
11'8" X 12'6"

E.
12'-1 1/8" CEILING

3 CAR GARAGE
21'4" X 28'0"

BR. #2
12'-1 1/8" CEILING
12'0" X 12'0"

61'-8"

73'-0"

44064-SC Price Code: I

Total Living Area :	3,365 sq.ft.
Main Living :	3,365 sq.ft.
Bedrooms :	1
Bathrooms :	1.5
Dimensions :	85'-4" x 82'-8"
Garage Type :	Three-car garage
Foundation :	Basement

Order Code : **H7SCP**
1-800-235-5700 or
www.familyhomeplans.com

Main Living

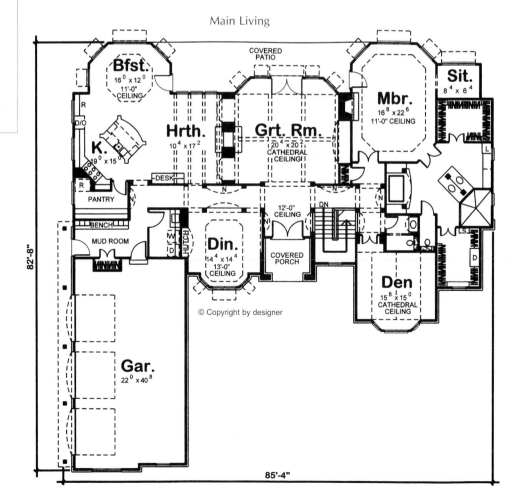

Bfst.
16⁰ x 12⁰
11'-0" CEILING

COVERED PATIO

Sit.
8⁴ x 6⁴

Mbr.
16⁸ x 22⁶
11'-0" CEILING

K.
19⁰ x 15⁰

Hrth.
10⁴ x 17²

Grt. Rm.
20⁴ x 20²
CATHEDRAL CEILING

DESK

PANTRY

BENCH

MUD ROOM

Din.
14⁴ x 14⁴
13'-0" CEILING

COVERED PORCH

12'-0" CEILING

DN

Den
15⁸ x 15⁰
CATHEDRAL CEILING

© Copyright by designer

Gar.
22⁰ x 40⁸

82'-8"

85'-4"

Main Living

125'-0"

65'-0"

Covered Patio

Master Bedroom 17³ x 14⁰

Master Bath

Great Room 20⁵ x 18²

Patio

Util

Three-Car Garage 24⁹ x 32²

Brkfst 13³ x 12⁰

Hall

Kitchen 13³ x 12⁰

Pwdr

Pantry

Gallery

Service Entry

Service Porch

Entry

Formal Dining 13³ x 12⁵

Bed#2 11⁸ x 13³

Bed#3 11⁸ x 13³

Breezeway

Single Garage

Study/ Bed#4 14³ x 15⁵

Cov. Porch

© Copyright by designer

66241-SC Price Code: I

Total Living Area :	3,281 sq.ft.
Main Living :	3,281 sq.ft.
Bedrooms :	4
Bathrooms :	2.5
Dimensions :	125'-0" x 65'-0"
Garage Type :	Three-car garage
Foundation :	Slab

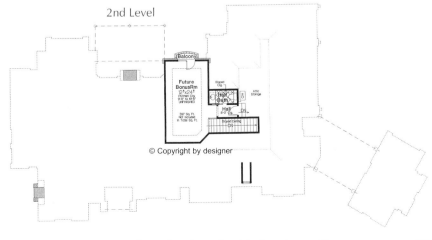

2nd Level

Balcony

Future BonusRm 12⁵ x 24³

Hall

Attic Storage

397 Sq. Ft. Not Included in Total Sq. Ft.

© Copyright by designer

97157-SC Price Code: O

Total Living Area :	6,311 sq.ft.
Basement :	2,537 sq.ft.
Main Living :	3,774 sq.ft.
Bedrooms :	5
Bathrooms :	4.5
Dimensions :	122'-0" x 66'-4"
Garage Type :	Four-car garage
Foundation :	Walkout Basement

An irresistible lower level draws family and friends to gatherings and overnight stays. Directly above, the dining and living rooms mirror this space with two fireplaces and expansive outside views.

Order Code : **H7SCP**
1-800-235-5700 or
www.familyhomeplans.com

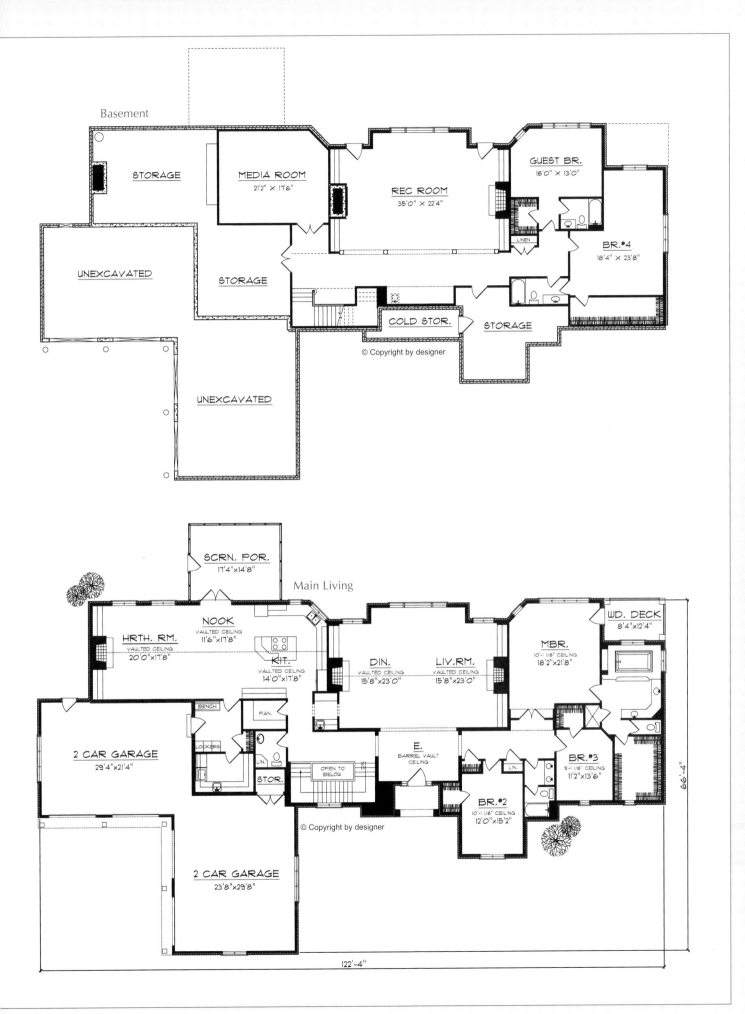

Basement

STORAGE

MEDIA ROOM
21'2" × 17'6"

REC ROOM
35'0" × 22'4"

GUEST BR.
18'0" × 13'0"

UNEXCAVATED

STORAGE

LINEN

BR. #4
18'4" × 23'8"

UNEXCAVATED

COLD STOR.

STORAGE

© Copyright by designer

SCRN. POR.
17'4"×14'8"

Main Living

WD. DECK
8'4"x12'4"

HRTH. RM.
Vaulted Ceiling
20'0"x17'8"

NOOK
Vaulted Ceiling
11'6"x17'8"

KIT.
Vaulted Ceiling
14'0"x17'8"

DIN.
Vaulted Ceiling
15'8"x23'0"

LIV. RM.
Vaulted Ceiling
15'8"x23'0"

MBR.
10'-1 1/8" CEILING
18'2"x21'8"

2 CAR GARAGE
29'4"x21'4"

BENCH

PAN.

LOCKERS

LIN.

STOR.

OPEN TO
BELOW

E.
BARREL VAULT
CEILING

BR. #2
10'-1 1/8" CEILING
12'0"x15'2"

LIN.

BR. #3
9'-11 1/8" CEILING
11'2"x13'6"

2 CAR GARAGE
23'8"x29'8"

© Copyright by designer

122'-4"

66'-4"

44068-SC Price Code: K

Total Living Area :	3,887 sq.ft.
Main Living :	2,872 sq.ft.
2nd Level :	1,015 sq.ft.
Bedrooms :	2
Bathrooms :	2.5
Dimensions :	116'-2" x 87'-8"
Garage Type :	Three-car garage
Foundation :	Basement, Slab*, Crawlspace*

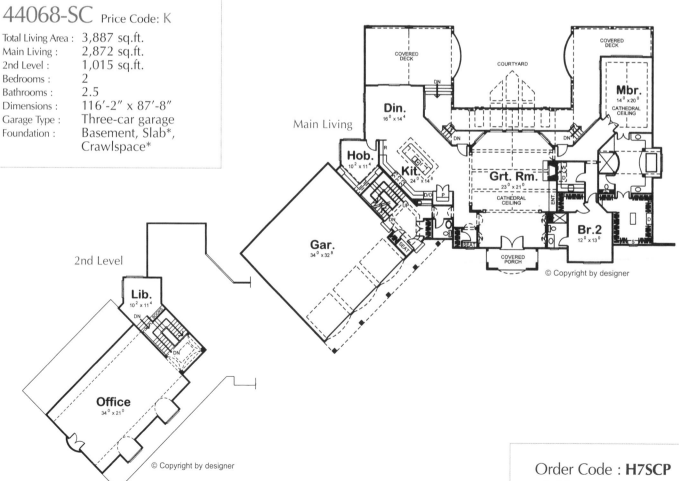

Main Living

COVERED DECK

COVERED DECK

COURTYARD

Din.
16⁰ x 14⁴

Mbr.
14⁰ x 20⁰
CATHEDRAL CEILING

Hob.
10² x 11⁴

Kit.
24⁰ x 14⁸

Grt. Rm.
23⁰ x 21⁰
CATHEDRAL CEILING

Gar.
34⁰ x 32⁸

Br.2
12⁰ x 13⁰

COVERED PORCH

© Copyright by designer

2nd Level

Lib.
10² x 11⁴

Office
34⁰ x 21⁰

© Copyright by designer

82117-SC Price Code: H

Total Living Area :	3,003 sq.ft.
Main Living :	3,003 sq.ft.
Bedrooms :	5
Bathrooms :	4
Dimensions :	84'-10" x 69'-4"
Garage Type :	Three-car garage
Foundation :	Basement*, Slab, Crawlspace

Main Living

84'-10"

REAR ORIENTATION

69'-4"

SITTING ROOM 9'-4" X 9'-4"

GLASS SHWR

WHP TUB

MASTER SUITE 13'-6" X 15'-3"

M.BATH 11'-8" X 22'-0"

LIN.

BEDROOM 4 11'-4" X 10'-8"

MEDIA CENTER

BATH 10'-2" X 5'-0"

COVERED PORCH 21'-0" X 11'-8"

10" COLUMNS

GRILLING PORCH 10'-4" X 7'-8"

GAS BIBB

BREAKFAST ROOM 11'-0" X 10'-8"

IN-LAWS SUITE 15'-2" X 13'-6"

GAS FIREPLACE

GREAT ROOM 13' CEILING 21'-0" X 17'-4"

OVEN

REF.

KITCHEN 10'-4" X 16'-0"

HEARTH ROOM 11'-0" X 16'-0"

OPTIONAL COMPUTER CENTER

LIN.

BATH 10'-8" X 15'-8"

WHP TUB

BEDROOM 3 11'-4" X 10'-11"

LIN.

PANTRY

LAU. 6'-4" X 6'-6"

UP

W D

8" COLUMNS

FOYER 13' CEILING 10'-0" X 12'-6"

DINING ROOM 13' CEILING 11'-0" X 12'-6"

OPT. DOOR

BATH 11'-4" X 5'-4"

BEDROOM 2/ STUDY 14'-0" X 12'-0"

GARAGE 21'-4" X 23'-0"

COURT YARD

© Copyright by designer

GARAGE 21'-4" X 12'-8"

2nd Level

DN

BONUS ROOM 11'-8" X 29'-0"

3' WALLS

6'-8" LINE

© Copyright by designer

Order Code : **H7SCP**
1-800-235-5700 or
www.familyhomeplans.com

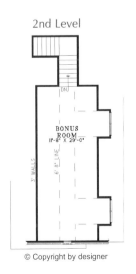

66088-SC Price Code: J

Total Living Area :	3,510 sq.ft.
Main Living :	3,510 sq.ft.
Bedrooms :	4
Bathrooms :	3.5
Dimensions :	91'-0" x 72'-10"
Garage Type :	Two-car garage
Foundation :	Slab

Main Living

© Copyright by designer

Order Code : **H7SCP**
1-800-235-5700 or
www.familyhomeplans.com

Southern Style
Friezes

One of the many decorative flourishes of the Southern Antebellum home was the frieze, an elaborate decorative band on the front exterior of a home, located below the cornice molding and above the architrave (the main beam over the columns). Whether plainly painted or decorated with designs or carvings, the frieze boosted the thickness of the entablature—the area supported by the columns—lending classical dignity to a home.

The frieze traces its roots back to ancient Grecian and Roman architecture, where it was sometimes

used to depict a story using carved scenes in a series of panels. At the Greek temple Parthenon, for example, the famous frieze depicts the "Great Panathenaia," an ancient and important Athenian festival, honoring the deity Athena. Similarly, the United States Capital building contains a frieze depicting scenes of American history. Friezes on the typical Southern home were not carved scenes such as these, but that's not to say they don't tell a story about Southern homes. Their inclusion reveals the Southerners' knowledge of classical architecture and their desire to showcase their sophistication on the exterior of their homes. Purely a decorative element, the frieze on Greek Revival-style homes often was painted white and left plain. If it was carved, natural designs such as a leaf motif were popular.

Today, the frieze is still a common element on many classical architectural styles that incorporate columns or pilasters, including Classical Revival, Greek Revival, and Colonial Revival.

Photography © istockphoto.com

93182-SC Price Code: J

Total Living Area :	3,650 sq.ft.
Main Living :	2,575 sq.ft.
2nd Level :	1,075 sq.ft.
Bedrooms :	4
Bathrooms :	3.5
Dimensions :	85'-0" x 53'-4"
Garage Type :	Three-car garage
Foundation :	Basement

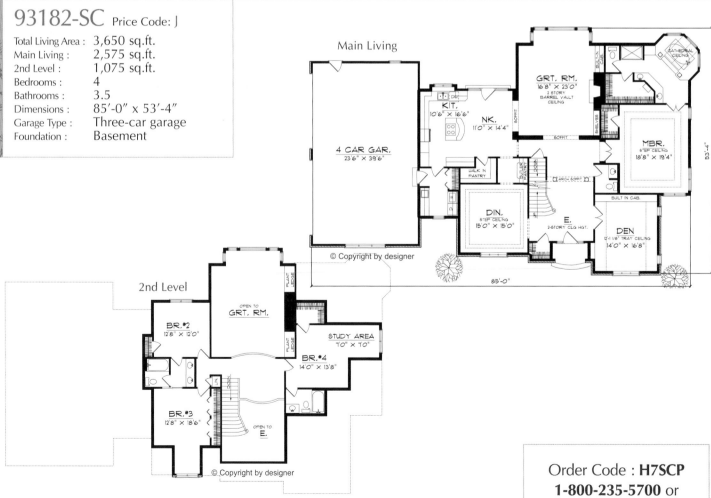

Main Living

GRT. RM.
16'8" X 23'0"
2 STORY
BARREL VAULT
CEILING

KIT.
10'6" X 16'6"

NK.
11'0" X 14'4"

4 CAR GAR.
23'6" X 39'6"

WALK IN
PANTRY

MBR.
18'8" X 19'4"

CATHEDRAL
CEILING

DIN.
15'0" X 15'0"

DEN
14'0" X 16'8"

E.

© Copyright by designer

85'-0"

53'-4"

2nd Level

OPEN TO
GRT. RM.

BR. #2
12'8" X 12'0"

STUDY AREA
7'0" X 7'0"

BR. #4
14'0" X 13'8"

BR. #3
12'8" X 18'6"

OPEN TO
E.

© Copyright by designer

Order Code : **H7SCP**
1-800-235-5700 or
www.familyhomeplans.com

← 96'-0" →

Main Living

Cov'd Patio

MstrBed
18⁶ x 17⁴
Vaulted Clg.
9'-0" to 10'-0"

Brkfst
13' x 11
9'-0" Clg.

Bed#3
12⁸ x 15
9'-0" Clg.

Kitchen
9'-0" Clg.

GreatRm
21⁶ x 17⁴
9'-0" Clg.

Shop
11' x 23²
8'-4" Clg.

Bath 3

Bed#4
10⁴ x 13⁴
9'-0" Clg.

Utility
9'-0" Clg.

Hall

Mstr. Bath
Sloped Clg.

Gallery
9'-0" Clg.

Hall

Bed#2
14⁶ x 12⁵
9'-0" Clg.

Pwdr

Stairs Up

FmlDin
10⁵ x 12⁹
9'-0" Clg.

Entry

Bath 2

Double Garage
8'-4" Clg.

Cov'd Porch

Study
16¹⁰ x 11
9'-0" Clg.

CourtYard

97'-11 1/2'

© Copyright by designer

Breezeway
8'-4" Clg.

Single Garage
8'-4" Clg.

66239-SC Price Code: I

Total Living Area : 3,417 sq.ft.
Main Living : 3,417 sq.ft.
Bedrooms : 4
Bathrooms : 3.5
Dimensions : 96'-0" x 97'-5"
Garage Type : Three-car garage
Foundation : Slab

2nd Level

BonusRm
21' x 19⁹
9'-0" Clg.

Attic Storage

Stairs

Dormer

© Copyright by designer

Order Code : **H7SCP**
1-800-235-5700 or
www.familyhomeplans.com

97166-SC Price Code: L

Total Living Area :	4,247 sq.ft.
Main Living :	3,396 sq.ft.
2nd Level :	851 sq.ft.
Bedrooms :	3
Bathrooms :	2.5
Dimensions :	101'-4" x 88'-0"
Garage Type :	Four-car garage
Foundation :	Basement

A fireplace and a sitting area with a bay of windows make the master suite a welcome place to unwind. Luxury features in this home include three fireplaces, a screen porch, a two-story foyer, and many sets of French doors.

Order Code : **H7SCP**
1-800-235-5700 or
www.familyhomeplans.com

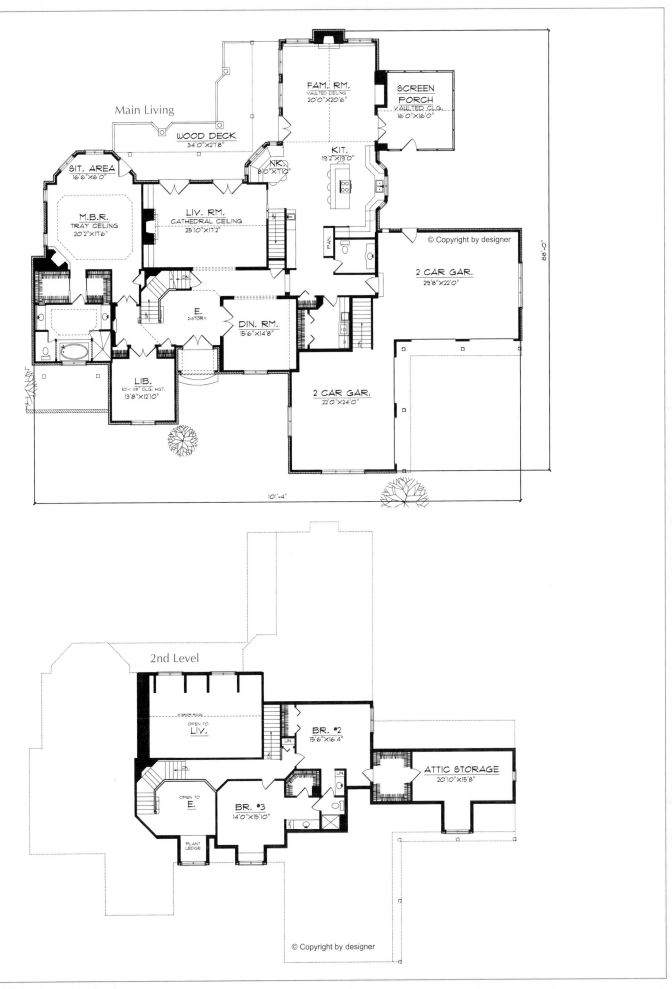

Main Living

WOOD DECK
34'0"X27'8"

FAM. RM.
VAULTED CEILING
20'0"X20'6"

SCREEN
PORCH
VAULTED CLG.
16'0"X16'0"

KIT.
19'2"X19'0"

SIT. AREA
16'6"X6'0"

NK.
8'6"X11'0"

M.B.R.
TRAY CEILING
20'2"X17'6"

LIV. RM.
CATHEDRAL CEILING
25'10"X17'2"

© Copyright by designer

88'-0"

PAN.

2 CAR GAR.
29'8"X22'0"

E.
2-STORY

DIN. RM.
15'6"X14'8"

LIB.
10'-1 1/8" CLG. HGT.
13'8"X12'10"

2 CAR GAR.
22'0"X24'0"

10'-4"

2nd Level

OPEN TO
LIV.

BR. #2
15'6"X16'4"

LIN.

ATTIC STORAGE
20'10"X15'8"

DN.

LIN.

OPEN TO
E.

BR. #3
14'0"X15'10"

LIN.

LIN.

PLANT
LEDGE

© Copyright by designer

99177-SC Price Code: H

Total Living Area : 3,109 sq.ft.
Main Living : 2,224 sq.ft.
2nd Level : 885 sq.ft.
Bedrooms : 4
Bathrooms : 2.5
Dimensions : 91'-8" x 66'-8"
Garage Type : Three-car garage
Foundation : Basement

Main Living

WD. DECK
13'0" X 12'0"

SCREEN PORCH
12'0" X 12'0"

NK.
10'10" X 16'6"

KIT.
12'0" X 14'4"

MBR.
TRAY CEILING
14'0" X 17'0"

GRT. RM.
2-STORY CEILING
18'4" X 20'6"

STUDY
STEP CEILING
12'8" X 13'0"

E.
2-STORY CEILING

DIN.
12'6" X 13'6"

1 1/2 CAR GAR.
22'8" X 20'4"

2 CAR GAR.
23'0" X 22'8"

COURT YARD

© Copyright by designer

91'-8"

66'-8"

2nd Level

OPEN TO
GRT. RM.

BR #2
11'4" X 16'4"

BR #3
11'0" X 16'6"

OPEN TO
E.

BR #4
12'6" X 14'4"

© Copyright by designer

63024-SC Price Code: J

Total Living Area : 3,680 sq.ft.
Main Living : 2,285 sq.ft.
2nd Level : 1,395 sq.ft.
Bedrooms : 3
Bathrooms : 3.5
Dimensions : 73'-8" x 73'-8"
Garage Type : Three-car garage
Foundation : Slab

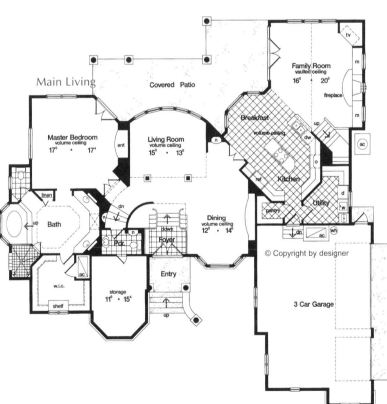

Main Living

Covered Patio

Family Room
vaulted ceiling
16⁰ · 20⁰

tv

m

fireplace

m

Master Bedroom
volume ceiling
17⁰ · 17⁴

Living Room
volume ceiling
15⁰ · 13⁰

Breakfast
volume ceiling

ent

n

dw

ac

linen

Kitchen

d

w

Bath

Dining
volume ceiling
12⁰ · 14⁰

Utility

pantry

dn

ac

wf

w.i.c.

ac

Pdr.

Foyer

dn

© Copyright by designer

storage
11⁰ · 15⁴

Entry

shelf

up

3 Car Garage

2nd Level

Deck

Family Room
Below

Bedroom 3
17⁴ · 11⁴

Living Room
Below

Bath

w.i.c.

Loft

rail

down

down

Bedroom 2
13² · 9⁰

w.i.c.

n

Bonus Room
12⁰ · 24⁰

Den
11⁰ · 15⁴

Balcony

Bath

© Copyright by designer

European
Accents

The library greets guests with a formal welcome, along with the dining room, which also adjoins the foyer.

A chorus of gables, embellished by brick, stone and lap siding, add a decidedly European flavor to this elegant 1 1/2 story home. Sheltering the entry, a wrapping covered front porch maintains the home's Southern balance. Stepping inside, a formal dining room and library open to the foyer. Beyond, a graceful arched opening welcomes guests into the great room, where tall windows bathe the area in natural light. To the side of the great room, the kitchen, breakfast area and hearth room create a comfortable space to interact with family and friends. On the opposite side of the home, the master retreat enjoys its seclusion, along with its direct access to the library. Upstairs, three secondary bedrooms share a conveniently located computer loft, complete with a window seat and built-in shelves.

The great room provides an impressive venue for entertaining, with its soaring ceiling, elaborate fireplace details and built-in displays.

At over 23 feet in length, the hearth room comfortably accommodates larger gatherings, yet is equally at ease with small groups.

The kitchen is well positioned as the hub of the home for lively conversations with family and friends in the breakfast area and hearth room.

Main Living

DECK

STAIRS DOWN

Hearth Room
23'4" x 15'4"

Breakfast

Three Car Garage
22'10" x 38' Irreg.

Laun.

Kitchen
15'9" x 16'6"

Great Room
17'9" x 17'

Gallery

WOOD STAIR RAIL

Mud Room

STAIRS UP

Butler Pantry

WINDOW SEAT

Dining Room
13'2" x 13'6"

Foyer

Library
14'8" x 11'2"

Dressing

Master Bedroom
15' x 19'10"

WALK-IN CLOSET

Bath

Porch

69'10"

90'

© Copyright by designer

2nd Level

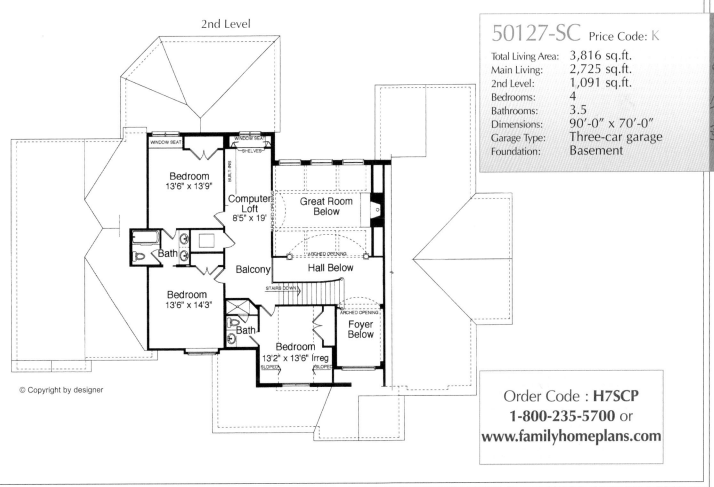

WINDOW SEAT

WINDOW SEAT

SHELVES

Bedroom
13'6" x 13'9"

Computer Loft
8'5" x 19'

Great Room Below

Bath

Balcony

Hall Below

Bedroom
13'6" x 14'3"

STAIRS DOWN

Bath

Bedroom
13'2" x 13'6" Irreg

Foyer Below

© Copyright by designer

50127-SC Price Code: K

Total Living Area:	3,816 sq.ft.
Main Living:	2,725 sq.ft.
2nd Level:	1,091 sq.ft.
Bedrooms:	4
Bathrooms:	3.5
Dimensions:	90'-0" x 70'-0"
Garage Type:	Three-car garage
Foundation:	Basement

Order Code : **H7SCP**
1-800-235-5700 or
www.familyhomeplans.com

97163-SC Price Code: I

Total Living Area : 3,489 sq.ft.
Main Living : 2,514 sq.ft.
2nd Level : 975 sq.ft.
Bedrooms : 4
Bathrooms : 3.5
Dimensions : 74'-8" x 64'-8"
Garage Type : Three-car garage
Foundation : Basement

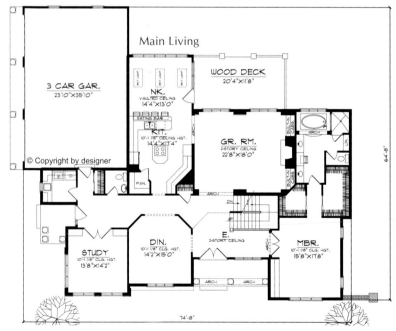

Main Living

3 CAR GAR.
23'10"X35'10"

WOOD DECK
20'4"X11'8"

NK.
VAULTED CEILING
14'4"X13'0"

KIT.
10'-1 1/8" CEILING HGT.
14'4"X17'4"

GR. RM.
2-STORY CEILING
22'8"X18'0"

EATING BAR

PAN.

STUDY
10'-1 1/8" CLG. HGT.
13'8"X14'2"

DIN.
10'-1 1/8" CLG. HGT.
14'2"X15'0"

E.
2-STORY CEILING

MBR.
10'-1 1/8" CLG. HGT.
15'8"X17'8"

64'-8"

74'-8"

© Copyright by designer

2nd Level

BR. #2
14'6"X14'4"

OPEN TO BELOW

BR. #3
17'4"X19'0"

OPEN TO BELOW

BR. #4
14'0"X16'0"

PLANT LEDGE

© Copyright by designer

SUN ROOM
CATHEDRAL CEILING

Main Living

KIT.
VAULTED CEILING
12'4"x15'4"

PAN.

DIN.
10'-1 1/8" CEILING HGT.

GRT. RM.
2-STORY CEILING

MBR.
10'-1 1/8" CEILING HGT.

PAN.

BUILT-IN CABINETS

STUDY
10'-1 1/8" CEILING HGT.

E.
2-STORY
CEILING

© Copyright by designer

2 CAR GAR.

69'-8"

16'-0"

73243-SC Price Code: J

Total Living Area : 3,716 sq.ft.
Main Living : 2,506 sq.ft.
2nd Level : 1,210 sq.ft.
Bedrooms : 4
Bathrooms : 3.5
Dimensions : 69'-8" x 76'-0"
Garage Type : Two-car garage
Foundation : Basement

2nd Level

WINDOW SEAT   WINDOW SEAT

BR. #4   OPEN TO
BELOW   BR. #3

LIN.

BR. #2   OPEN TO
VAULTED CEILING   BELOW
                PLANT
                LEDGE

© Copyright by designer

Order Code : **H7SCP**
1-800-235-5700 or
www.familyhomeplans.com

97169-SC Price Code: I

Total Living Area : 3,259 sq.ft.
Main Living : 2,402 sq.ft.
2nd Level : 857 sq.ft.
Bedrooms : 4
Bathrooms : 3.5
Dimensions : 69'-8" x 74'-8"
Garage Type : Three-car garage
Foundation : Basement

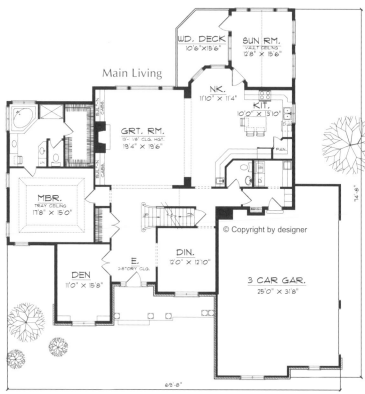

Main Living

WD. DECK
10'6" X 15'6"

SUN RM.
VAULT CEILING
12'8" X 15'6"

NK.
11'10" X 11'4"

KIT.
10'0" X 13'10"

GRT. RM.
13'-1/8" CLG. HGT.
19'4" X 19'6"

MBR.
TRAY CEILING
17'8" X 15'0"

© Copyright by designer

DIN.
12'0" X 12'10"

DEN
11'0" X 15'8"

E.
2-STORY CLG.

3 CAR GAR.
25'0" X 31'8"

74'-8"

69'-8"

2nd Level

BR. #4
TRAY CEILING
11'0" X 13'10"

BR. #2
TRAY CEILING
11'10" X 13'4"

BR. #3
TRAY CEILING
12'0" X 13'0"

© Copyright by designer

Southern Style
Central Entryways

The front hall was the public face of the typical Southern home in the Antebellum era. Reflecting the social standing of the family, the entryway was designed to make an instant impression. Typically located in the center of the home just behind the front door, it followed the symmetrical design of typical Southern homes of the pre-war period. In larger homes, the center hall would have spanned the length of the house, with doors at the front and the rear, and may have even been used as a parlor. Other public rooms such as the library, dining room, and parlor were typically located next to the entryway. For families with smaller means, such an expansive layout would not have been possible. A more common layout would have been a front hall that extended half the length of the floor plan with work rooms, such as the kitchen, scullery, and laundry behind it. Other typical features—depending on the size and proportion of the home—might include fireplaces, grand staircases, and the best furnishings in the home.

As the main reception area, the central hall served a broad swath of functions, from important to mundane including the place from which to greet guests and from which to accept the mail and deliveries. The layout isolated the cold and would have helped corral outside dirt and mud so that it could be easily cleaned. Social visits, or "calling," were required by proper society, and the central hall would have served as a place to greet friends and acquaintances. In addition, business transactions were almost always handled in person and the main entryway provided a place to conduct such dealings.

66240-SC Price Code: M

Total Living Area:	4,599 sq.ft.
Main Living:	4,599 sq.ft.
Bedrooms:	4
Bathrooms:	3.5
Dimensions:	108'-6" x 76'-6"
Garage Type:	Three-car garage
Foundation:	Slab

This home's master suite goes above and beyond what one might expect in the way of amenities, with separate his and her bathrooms. Additionally, her walk-in closet opens to a heavily reinforced safe room.

Order Code : **H7SCP**
1-800-235-5700 or
www.familyhomeplans.com

108'-6"

Main Living

Safe Room
8'-0" Clg.

Her Walk-In Closet
Chest
10'-0" Clg.

36" x 72" Whirlpool

Linen

Her Bath
10'-0" Clg.

Cov'd Patio
10'-0" Clg.

Brkfst
15⁷ x 16
10'-0" Clg.

Storage
8 x 8⁴
Sloped Clg.
7'-6" to 10'-0"

Three-Car Garage
9'-4" Clg.

Attic Pull Dn. Ladder

Shower Seat

Shl'vs

42" High Brkfst Bar

Rear Hall
10'-0" Clg.

Wash/Dryer

C/H

HW

Walk-In Closet

Storage Area

Drying Area

His Bath
10'-0" Clg.

Linen

MstrBed
24⁴ x 16⁴
10'-0" Clg.

GreatRm
24³ x 19
Vaulted Clg.
12'-0" to 14'-0"

48" Masonary Fireplace w/ Gas Starter & Raised Hearth

Dbl. Sink w/ Disp.

Kitchen
10'-0" Clg.

Dn. Draft Cook-Top

Ref.

DW

Dbl. Oven

MW

Freezer

Utility
10'-0" Clg.

Brooms

Recreation/ MediaRm
23² x 14⁶
Pullman Clg.
9'-0" to 10'-6"

His Walk-In Closet
10'-0" Clg.

C/H

HW

Chest

5'-0" Tub w/ Shower

Walk-In Closet

Coats

Hall
10'-0" Clg.

Butlers Pantry

Pantry

Hall
10'-0" Clg.

Hutch

Pwdr.

Linen

Hall
10'-0" Clg.

Storage

Walk-In Closet

Wet Bar

Ref. Ice

Bath 2

Chest

Books

Gallery
12'-0" Clg.

Chest

Walk-In Closet

Linen

5'-0" Tub w/ Shower

Bed#2
14³ x 14⁸
10'-0" Clg.

Study
11² x 13⁴
12'-0" Clg.

Foyer
12'-0" Clg.

FmlDin
12² x 13⁹
Pullman Clg.
12'-0" to 13'-0"

Bed#3
14³ x 11⁴
9'-0" Clg.

Bath 3

Bed#4
10¹⁰ x 14⁸
9'-0" Clg.

Sitting Area

Cov'd Porch

© Copyright by designer

76'-6"

72049-SC Price Code: I

Total Living Area : 3,270 sq.ft.
Main Living : 1,660 sq.ft.
2nd Level : 1,610 sq.ft.
Bedrooms : 4
Bathrooms : 3
Dimensions : 74'-0" x 74'-0"
Garage Type : Four-car garage
Foundation : Slab,
Walkout Basement

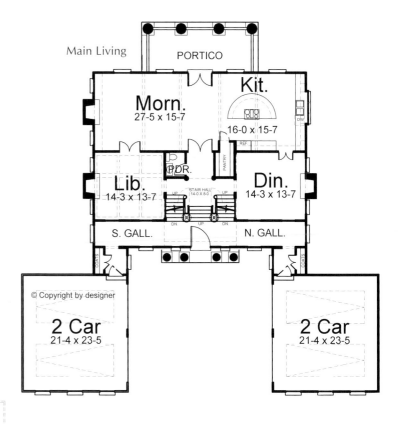

Main Living

PORTICO

Morn.
27-5 x 15-7

Kit.
16-0 x 15-7

PDR.

Lib.
14-3 x 13-7

STAIR HALL
14-0 x 8-0

Din.
14-3 x 13-7

S. GALL.

N. GALL.

© Copyright by designer

2 Car
21-4 x 23-5

2 Car
21-4 x 23-5

2nd Level

PORTICO

Bdr.
12-5 X 14-0

Mstr.
18 DIA.
DOME CLG

M. BATH

BATH

BATH

Bdr.
14-6 X 12-5

Bdr.
14-6 x 12-5

© Copyright by designer

66238-SC Price Code: I

Total Living Area :	3,428 sq.ft.
Main Living :	2,713 sq.ft.
2nd Level :	715 sq.ft.
Bedrooms :	4
Bathrooms :	4.5
Dimensions :	70'-0" x 71'-10"
Garage Type :	Three-car garage
Foundation :	Basement, Slab

Main Living

Stoop

Stor.

Potting Shed

3 Car Garage

Bath 2

Driveway

Sitting Area

Stor.

Serv Porch

Util
9'-0" Clg.

Bed#2
12'²x14'⁴
10'-0" Clg.

Brkfst
12'⁰x12'⁵
10'-0" Clg.
Wood Plank Flooring

Covered Patio

Kitchen
13'x12'⁵
10'-0" Clg.
Wood Plank Flooring

Family Room
18'⁸x18'⁴
10'-0" Clg.
Wood Plank Flooring

Hall
Wood Plank Flooring

Closet

Closet

Whirl-pool Tub

Shower

Her Walk-in Closet

Pwdr

Linen

Pantry

Linen

Mstr. Bath

Hall
10'-0" Clg.

Gallery
10'-0" Clg.

His Walk-In Closet

MstrBed
14'⁸x17'⁰
Vaulted Clg.
10'-0" to 12'-0"

Study
10'⁸x10'¹⁰

Formal Dining
12'⁸x12'⁴
Wood Plank Flooring

Entry

Formal Living
14'⁵x12'⁴
Pullman Clg.
10'-0" to 9'-0"

Pvt. Lanai
9'⁸x9'⁸

Covered Porch

70'-0"

71'-10"

© Copyright by designer

2nd Level

Future Playroom

Bed#3
11'⁴x11'⁴

Bath2

Optional Bedroom

Walk-In Closet

Laundry Chute

Balcony

Stairway

Bath4

Bed#4
12'⁸x12'⁴

Walk-In Closet

Open To Entry Below

© Copyright by designer

Order Code : H7SCP
1-800-235-5700 or
www.familyhomeplans.com

This home, as shown, may differ from the original design.

Elegance and symmetry define the character of this home, both outside and in. Soaring above it all, a widow's walk surrounds an observation cupola for breathtaking views.

68186-SC Price Code: I

Total Living Area : 3,335 sq.ft.
Basement : 2,054 sq.ft.
Main Living : 1,281 sq.ft.
Bedrooms : 4
Bathrooms : 2 Fulls, One 3/4 bath, One Half
Dimensions : 82'-0" x 60'-8"
Garage Type : Four-car garage
Foundation : Slab, Basement

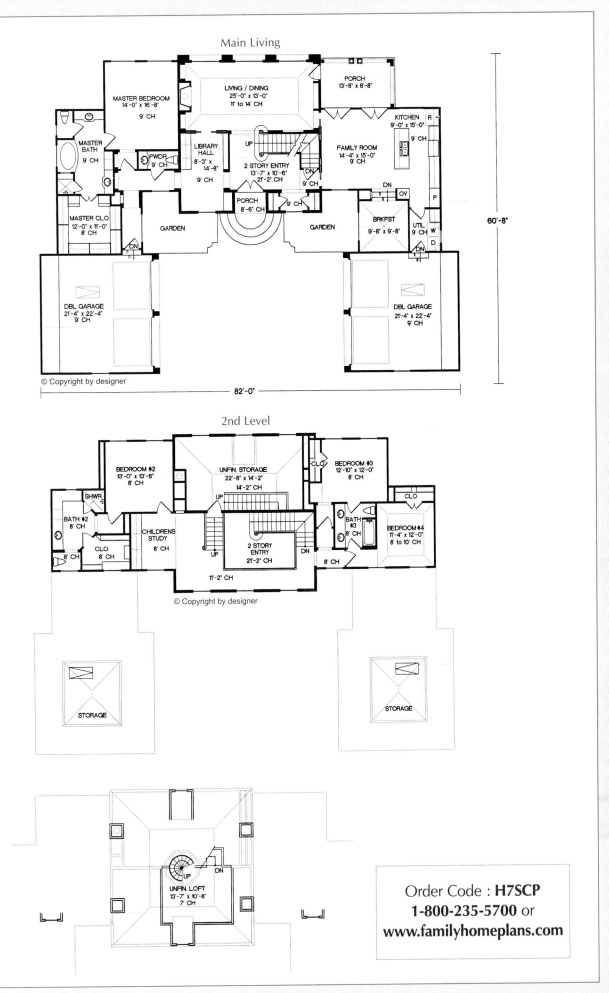

Main Living

MASTER BEDROOM
14'-0" x 16'-8"
9' CH

LIVING / DINING
25'-0" x 13'-0"
11' to 14' CH

PORCH
13'-8" x 8'-8"

MASTER BATH
9' CH

PWDR
9' CH

LIBRARY HALL
8'-3" x 14'-8"
9' CH

UP

KITCHEN
9'-0" x 15'-0"
9' CH

FAMILY ROOM
14'-4" x 15'-0"
9' CH

2 STORY ENTRY
13'-7" x 10'-6"
21'-2" CH

DN
9' CH

MASTER CLO
12'-0" x 11'-0"
8' CH

DN

GARDEN

PORCH
8'-6" CH

9' CH

GARDEN

DN
OV

BRKFST
9'-8" x 9'-8"

UTIL
9' CH
W D

P

DN

DBL GARAGE
21'-4" x 22'-4"
9' CH

DBL GARAGE
21'-4" x 22'-4"
9' CH

© Copyright by designer

82'-0"

60'-8"

2nd Level

BEDROOM #2
13'-0" x 13'-6"
8' CH

UNFIN. STORAGE
22'-8" x 14'-2"
14'-2" CH

CLO

BEDROOM #3
12'-10" x 12'-0"
8' CH

SHWR

BATH #2
8' CH

CHILDRENS STUDY
8' CH

UP

CLO

BATH #3
8' CH

CLO

BEDROOM #4
11'-4" x 12'-0"
8' to 10' CH

CLO
8' CH

8' CH

CLO
8' CH

UP

2 STORY ENTRY
21'-2" CH

DN

8' CH

11'-2" CH

© Copyright by designer

STORAGE

STORAGE

UP
DN

UNFIN. LOFT
13'-7" x 10'-8"
7' CH

Order Code : **H7SCP**
1-800-235-5700 or
www.familyhomeplans.com

66243-SC Price Code: I

Total Living Area : 3,355 sq.ft.
Main Living : 2,397 sq.ft.
2nd Level : 958 sq.ft.
Bedrooms : 3
Bathrooms : 2.5
Dimensions : 80'-4" x 83'-4"
Garage Type : Three-car garage
Foundation : Slab, Crawlspace

Main Living

© Copyright by designer

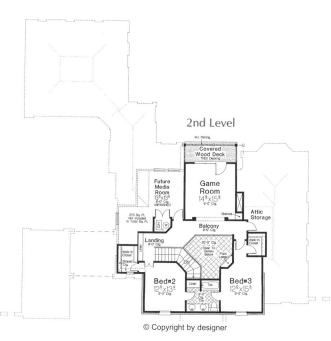

2nd Level

© Copyright by designer

Order Code : **H7SCP**
1-800-235-5700 or
www.familyhomeplans.com

124   ❧ Home Plans Designed with Southern Charm ❧

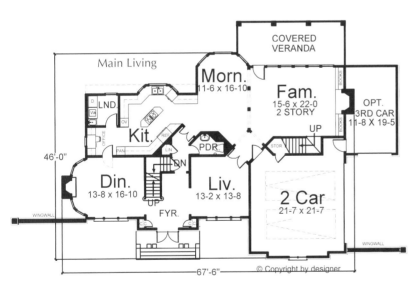

72031-SC Price Code: I

Total Living Area :	3,385 sq.ft.
Main Living :	1,692 sq.ft.
2nd Level :	1,693 sq.ft.
Bedrooms :	4
Bathrooms :	3
Dimensions :	68'-0" x 46'-0"
Garage Type :	Two-car garage
Foundation :	Walkout Basement

Main Living

COVERED VERANDA

Morn.
11-6 x 16-10

Fam.
15-6 x 22-0
2 STORY

OPT.
3RD CAR
11-8 X 19-5

UP

Kit.

LND.

D
W

OV

OFFICE

REF

PAN

LIN

PDR.

STOR

BOOKS

BOOKS

BOOKS

46'-0"

Din.
13-8 x 16-10

DN

UP

Liv.
13-2 x 13-8

FYR.

2 Car
21-7 x 21-7

WINGWALL

WINGWALL

67'-6"

© Copyright by designer

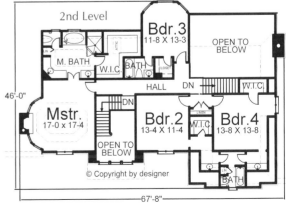

2nd Level

Bdr. 3
11-8 x 13-3

OPEN TO BELOW

M. BATH

W.I.C.

BATH

CLOSET

HALL

DN

W.T.C.

46'-0"

Mstr.
17-0 x 17-4

DN

Bdr. 2
13-4 X 11-4

W.I.C.

LINEN

Bdr. 4
13-8 X 13-8

OPEN TO BELOW

BATH

© Copyright by designer

67'-8"

53734-SC Price Code: L

Total Living Area :	4,170 sq.ft.
Main Living :	2,583 sq.ft.
2nd Level :	1,587 sq.ft.
Bedrooms :	5
Bathrooms :	5.5
Dimensions :	108'-1" x 112'-1"
Garage Type :	Four-car garage
Foundation :	Basement, Crawlspace, Walkout Basement

Terraces grace the rear of the home, providing space to entertain or spend private moments in outdoor elegance.

A tasteful porte-cochere provides aesthetic access to the home's four-car garage.

Order Code : **H7SCP**
1-800-235-5700 or
www.familyhomeplans.com

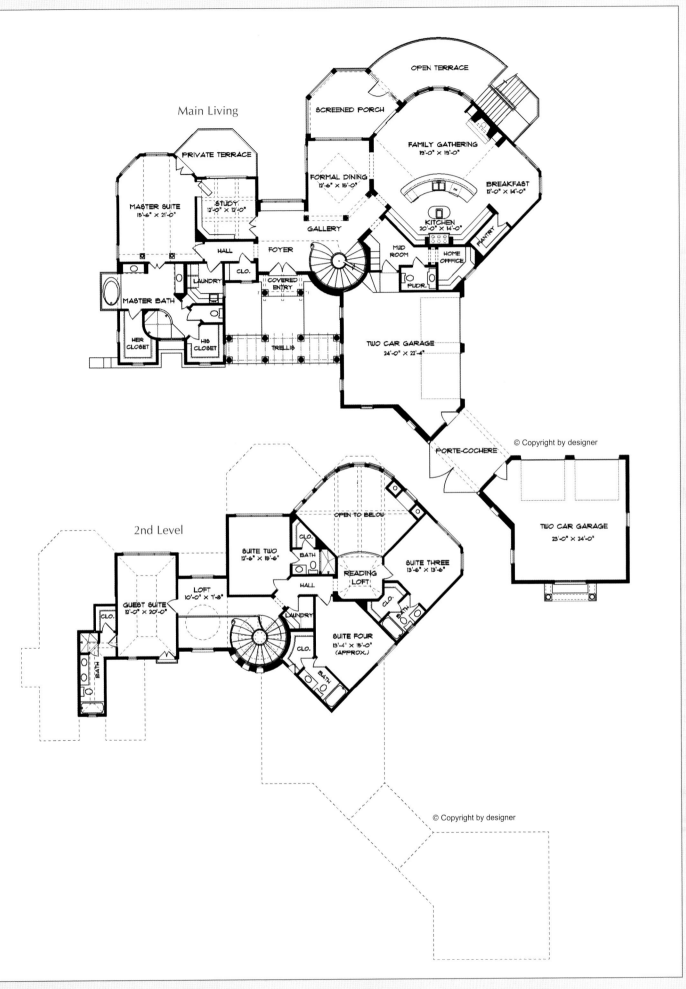

Main Living

PRIVATE TERRACE

OPEN TERRACE

SCREENED PORCH

FAMILY GATHERING
19'-0" × 19'-0"

MASTER SUITE
15'-6" × 21'-0"

STUDY
12'-0" × 12'-0"

FORMAL DINING
12'-6" × 15'-0"

BREAKFAST
12'-0" × 14'-0"

GALLERY

KITCHEN
20'-0" × 14'-0"

PANTRY

HALL

FOYER

MUD ROOM

HOME OFFICE

LAUNDRY

CLO.

COVERED ENTRY

PWDR.

MASTER BATH

HER CLOSET

HIS CLOSET

TRELLIS

TWO CAR GARAGE
24'-0" × 22'-4"

© Copyright by designer

PORTE-COCHERE

2nd Level

OPEN TO BELOW

SUITE TWO
12'-6" × 15'-6"

CLO.

BATH

SUITE THREE
13'-6" × 13'-6"

TWO CAR GARAGE
23'-0" × 24'-0"

GUEST SUITE
12'-0" × 20'-0"

LOFT
10'-0" × 7'-8"

HALL

READING LOFT

CLO.

BATH

CLO.

BATH

LAUNDRY

CLO.

SUITE FOUR
13'-4" × 15'-0"
(APPROX.)

BATH

© Copyright by designer

98281-SC Price Code: J

Total Living Area :	3,698 sq.ft.
Main Living :	1,893 sq.ft.
2nd Level :	1,805 sq.ft.
Bedrooms :	5
Bathrooms :	4
Dimensions :	75'-0" x 65'-0"
Garage Type :	Three-car garage
Foundation :	Walkout Basement

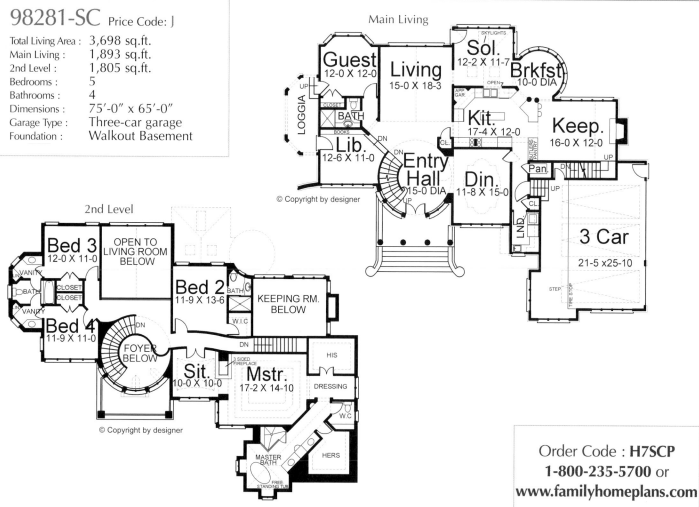

Main Living

Guest
12-0 X 12-0

Living
15-0 X 18-3

Sol.
12-2 X 11-7

Brkfst
10-0 DIA

LOGGIA

UP

CLOSET

BATH

BOOKS

Lib.
12-6 X 11-0

DN

DN

Entry Hall
15-0 DIA

UP

APP.
GAR.

OPEN

Kit.
17-4 X 12-0

CL

Din.
11-8 X 15-0

Pan.

CL

LND

BUTLERS PANTRY

Keep.
16-0 X 12-0

UP

UP

DN

UP

3 Car
21-5 x25-10

STEP

TIRE STOP

© Copyright by designer

2nd Level

Bed 3
12-0 X 11-0

OPEN TO LIVING ROOM BELOW

Bed 2
11-9 X 13-6

KEEPING RM. BELOW

VANITY

LIN

BATH

CLOSET

CLOSET

BATH

W.I.C

VANITY

Bed 4
11-9 X 11-0

DN

FOYER BELOW

DN

Sit.
10-0 X 10-0

3 SIDED FIREPLACE

Mstr.
17-2 X 14-10

HIS

DRESSING

W.C

MASTER BATH

FREE STANDING TUB

HERS

© Copyright by designer

Order Code : **H7SCP**
1-800-235-5700 or
www.familyhomeplans.com

Home Plans Designed with Southern Charm

Southern Style
Ballrooms

Ballroom dancing as a social event was popular in the South at the turn of the 19th Century through the Antebellum period to the turn of the next century. Formal events, such "subscription" dances were a form of entertainment for the middle and upper-crust classes. (Folk dancing was reserved for the lower classes.) Traditionally, most ballroom dances were held in private residences, and this fact would have been true for the mostly rural orientation of the pre-war South. To some aristocrats, public balls would have been considered in poor taste, even though in some areas of the country, public balls were quite common.

Even though many have survived in historic homes, most formal ballrooms actually were found in only the largest and most elaborate Southern mansions. Ballrooms typically were generous, highly decorative, and featured tall ceilings—perhaps even taller than most of the other rooms in the house. Ideally, ballrooms were fashioned in a large square or rectangle, avoiding a long and narrow layout, which would have been confining for dancers. The floor typically consisted of polished wood. Spaciousness was important; it helped ensure that the dancers would have sufficient room to move about and that the orchestra's sound would fill the entire room. If a home didn't have a ballroom, then a large room in the house, such as a grand front hall, could suffice, as long as it was spacious enough to accommodate a large group.

As other forms of private and social entertainment became popular, ballrooms fell out of fashion as entertaining rooms in private homes. Ballroom dancing gradually shifted to public venues where most ballroom dances are still held today. The desire for social entertaining in private residences, however, has never fallen out of fashion. In the larger homes of today, the entertaining space that once may have been reserved for a ballroom is now reserved for a media room or a home theater—areas where friends can gather for entertainment of a more relaxed nature.

This home, as shown, may differ from the original design.

Every aspect of luxury living is addressed throughout both levels of this richly appointed, palatial design. Perhaps the most appreciated areas will be found adjoining the garage and porte cochere – the home office/workshop with a private retreat above.

63082-SC Price Code: O

Total Living Area :	6,462 sq.ft.
Main Living :	3,874 sq.ft.
2nd Level :	2,588 sq.ft.
Bedrooms :	5
Bathrooms :	8
Dimensions :	137'-8" x 91'-7"
Garage Type :	Three-car garage
Foundation :	Slab

rear view

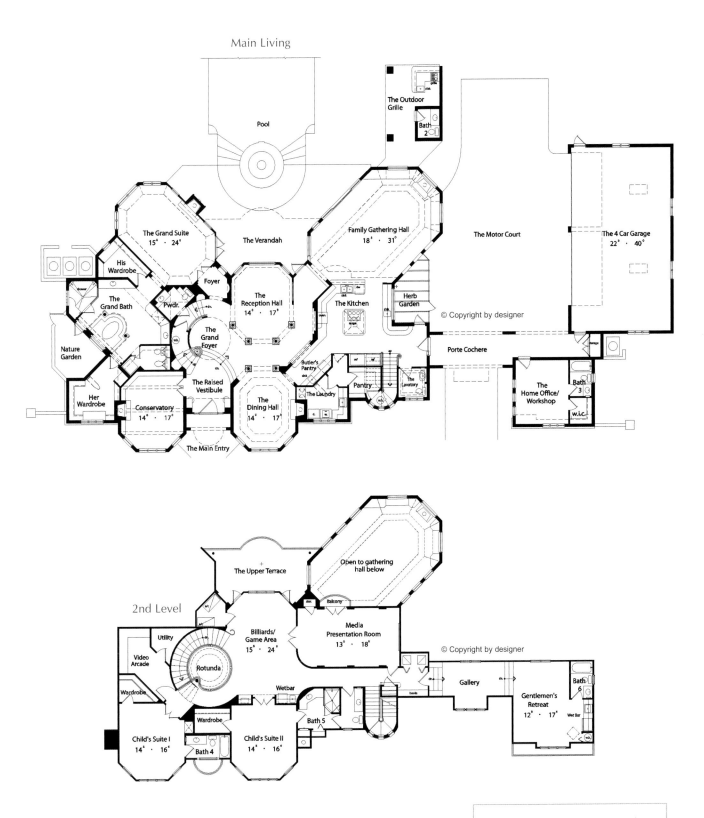

Main Living

Pool

The Outdoor Grille

Bath 2

The Grand Suite
15⁸ · 24⁰

The Verandah

Family Gathering Hall
18⁸ · 31⁰

The Motor Court

The 4 Car Garage
22⁸ · 40⁰

His Wardrobe

Foyer

The Grand Bath

Pwdr.

The Reception Hall
14⁰ · 17⁰

The Kitchen

Herb Garden

© Copyright by designer

Nature Garden

The Grand Foyer

Porte Cochere

Her Wardrobe

The Raised Vestibule

Conservatory
14⁰ · 17⁰

The Dining Hall
14⁰ · 17⁰

Butler's Pantry

The Laundry

Pantry

The Lavatory

The Home Office/ Workshop

Bath 3

w.l.c.

The Main Entry

2nd Level

The Upper Terrace

Open to gathering hall below

Balcony

Utility

Billiards/ Game Area
15⁸ · 24⁰

Media Presentation Room
13⁰ · 18⁰

© Copyright by designer

Video Arcade

Rotunda

Gallery

Bath 6

Wardrobe

Wetbar

Gentlemen's Retreat
12⁰ · 17⁰

Wet Bar

Wardrobe

Bath 5

Child's Suite I
14⁴ · 16⁰

Bath 4

Child's Suite II
14⁴ · 16⁰

Order Code : **H7SCP**
1-800-235-5700 or
www.familyhomeplans.com

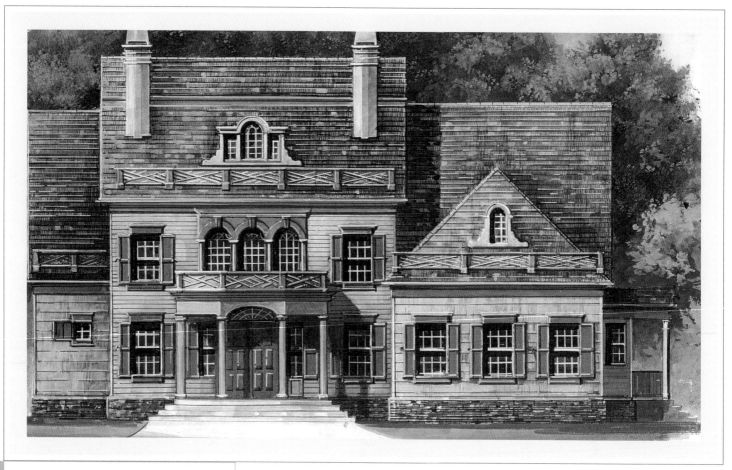

72029-SC Price Code: H

Total Living Area :	3,159 sq.ft.
Main Living :	2,173 sq.ft.
2nd Level :	986 sq.ft.
Bedrooms :	4
Bathrooms :	3.5
Dimensions :	63'-0" x 58'-0"
Garage Type :	Three-car garage
Foundation :	Walkout Basement

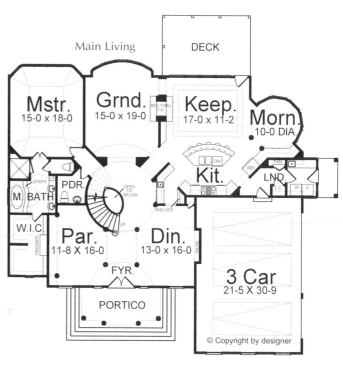

Main Living

DECK

Mstr. 15-0 x 18-0

Grnd. 15-0 x 19-0

Keep. 17-0 x 11-2

Morn. 10-0 DIA.

Kit.

LND.

BATH

PDR.

W.I.C.

Par. 11-8 X 16-0

Din. 13-0 x 16-0

3 Car 21-5 X 30-9

FYR.

PORTICO

© Copyright by designer

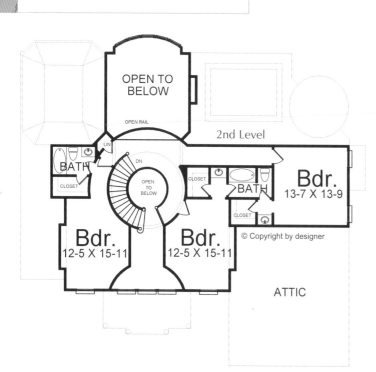

OPEN TO BELOW

OPEN RAIL

2nd Level

BATH

CLOSET

DN

OPEN TO BELOW

Bdr. 13-7 X 13-9

BATH

CLOSET

Bdr. 12-5 X 15-11

Bdr. 12-5 X 15-11

© Copyright by designer

ATTIC

72030-SC Price Code: I

Total Living Area :	3,265 sq.ft.
Main Living :	1,657 sq.ft.
2nd Level :	1,608 sq.ft.
Bedrooms :	5
Bathrooms :	5
Dimensions :	53'-0" x 56'-0"
Garage Type :	Two-car garage
Foundation :	Walkout basement

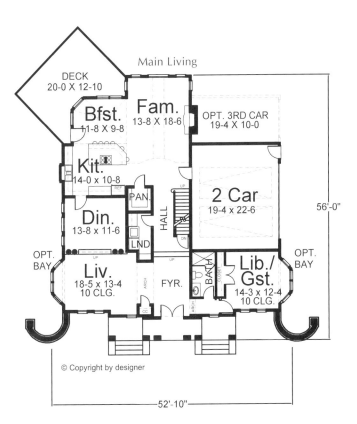

Main Living

DECK
20-0 X 12-10

Bfst.
11-8 X 9-8

Fam.
13-8 X 18-6

OPT. 3RD CAR
19-4 X 10-0

Kit.
14-0 x 10-8

PAN.

REF

HALL

2 Car
19-4 x 22-6

56'-0"

Din.
13-8 x 11-6

LND

OPT.
BAY

Liv.
18-5 x 13-4
10 CLG.

UP

FYR.

BATH

CLOSET

Lib./
Gst.
14-3 x 12-4
10 CLG.

OPT.
BAY

ARCH

ARCH

CC

© Copyright by designer

52'-10"

UPPER
FAM.

2nd Level

CLOSET

Bdr.
13-7 x 10-8

BATH

HALL

UP
TO ATTIC

Mstr.
19-4 X 15-6

54'-0"

Bdr
11-4 x 11-3

CLOSET

LINEN

DN

LIN

HER BATH

ATTIC

BATH

Bdr.
13-4 x 13-4

CLOSET

OPEN
RAIL

UPPER
FYR.

HIS
BATH

HIS
CLO.

DRESSER

LIN

HER
CLO.

DRESSER

© Copyright by designer

48'-0"

66236-SC Price Code: O

Total Living Area :	6,274 sq.ft.
Main Living :	4,336 sq.ft.
2nd Level :	1,938 sq.ft.
Bedrooms :	5
Bathrooms :	6
Dimensions :	112'-0" x 81'-10"
Garage Type :	Four-car garage
Foundation :	Basement, Slab

Privacy is well preserved in the master suite and nearby study, where both areas are discretely tucked away from the main level's living spaces. With the same spirit of discretion, a secondary stairway just off the service entry ascends to the upper level.

Order Code : **H7SCP**
1-800-235-5700 or
www.familyhomeplans.com

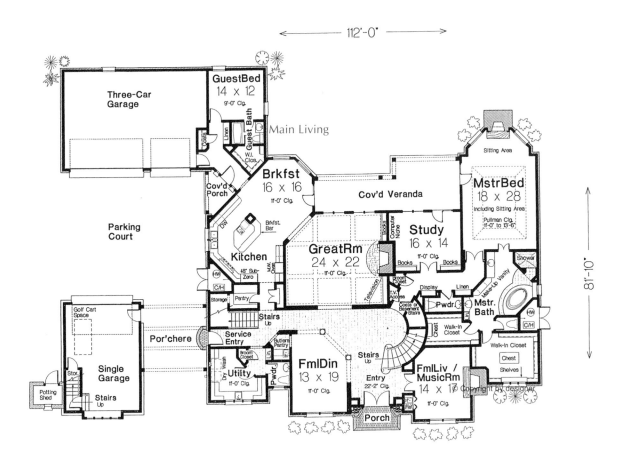

112'-0"

81'-10"

Three-Car Garage

GuestBed
14 x 12
9'-0" Clg.

Guest Bath

Linen

W.I. Clos.

Main Living

Cov'd Porch

Brkfst
16 x 16
11'-0" Clg.

Cov'd Veranda

Sitting Area

MstrBed
18 x 28
Including Sitting Area
Pullman Clg.
11'-0" to 13'-6"

Parking Court

Brkfst. Bar

DW

Kitchen

48" Sub-Zero

M.W. Oven

GreatRm
24 x 22
11'-0" Clg.

Computer Niche

Study
16 x 14
11'-0" Clg.

Books

Books

Shower

HW

C/H

Storage

Pantry

Television

Broom Closet

T.V. Access

Display

Linen

Make-Up Vanity

Mstr. Bath

Golf Cart Space

Service Entry

Broom Closet

Butler's Pantry

Coats or Basement Stairs

Pwdr.

Walk-In Closet

HW

C/H

Por'chere

Stairs Up

Dy Wash

Utility
11'-0" Clg.

Pwdr.

FmlDin
13 x 19
11'-0" Clg.

Stairs Up

Entry
22'-2" Clg.

FmlLiv / MusicRm
14 x 17
11'-0" Clg.

Walk-In Closet

Chest

Shelves

Single Garage

Stor.

Potting Shed

Stairs Up

Porch

© Copyright by designer

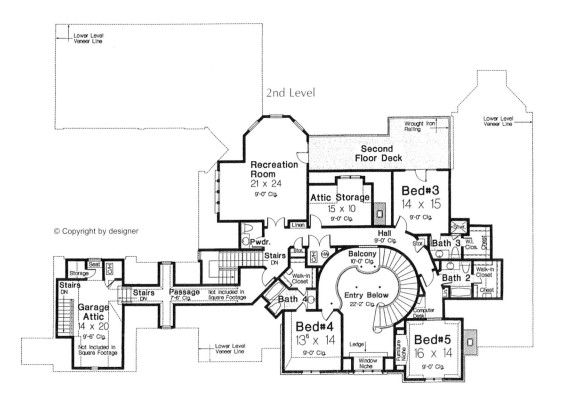

Lower Level Veneer Line

2nd Level

Lower Level Veneer Line

Wrought Iron Railing

Second Floor Deck

Recreation Room
21 x 24
9'-0" Clg.

Attic Storage
15 x 10
9'-0" Clg.

Bed#3
14 x 15
9'-0" Clg.

© Copyright by designer

Linen

Pwdr.

Stairs DN

Stor.

C/H

HW

Hall
9'-0" Clg.

Shwr.

Bath 3

W.I. Clos.

Seat

HW

Storage

Stairs DN

Stairs DN

Passage
7'-6" Clg.

Not included in Square Footage

Walk-In Closet

Balcony
10'-0" Clg.

Entry Below
22'-2" Clg.

Bath 4

Bath 2

Walk-In Closet

Chest

Garage Attic
14 x 20
9'-6" Clg.
Not Included in Square Footage

Lower Level Veneer Line

Bed#4
13'6 x 14
9'-0" Clg.

Ledge

Window Niche

Furniture Niche

Computer Desk

Bed#5
16 x 14
9'-0" Clg.

72059-SC Price Code: J

Total Living Area :	3,691 sq.ft.
Main Living :	2,531 sq.ft.
2nd Level :	1,160 sq.ft.
Bedrooms :	5
Bathrooms :	5.5
Dimensions :	72'-0" x 74'-0"
Garage Type :	Three-car garage
Foundation :	Walkout Basement

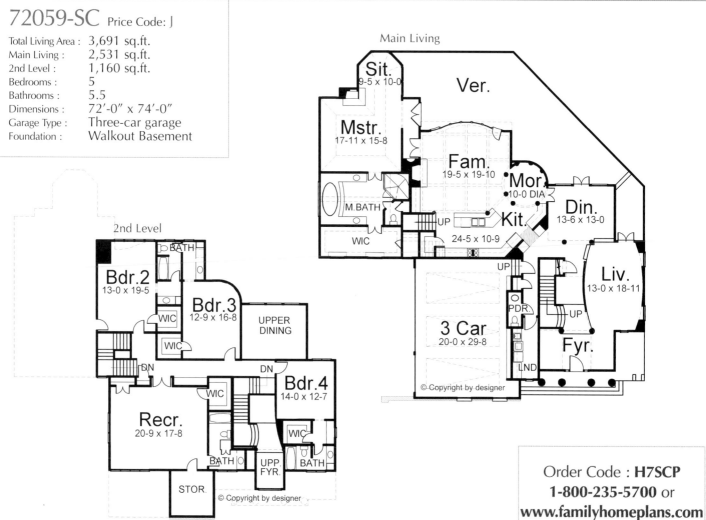

Main Living

Sit.
9-5 x 10-0

Ver.

Mstr.
17-11 x 15-8

Fam.
19-5 x 19-10

Mor
10-0 DIA

Din.
13-6 x 13-0

M.BATH

WIC

Kit.
24-5 x 10-9

UP

Liv.
13-0 x 18-11

UP

PDR

3 Car
20-0 x 29-8

UP

Fyr.

LND

© Copyright by designer

2nd Level

BATH

Bdr.2
13-0 x 19-5

WIC

Bdr.3
12-9 x 16-8

UPPER DINING

WIC

DN

DN

Bdr.4
14-0 x 12-7

WIC

Recr.
20-9 x 17-8

WIC

BATH

UPP. FYR.

BATH

WIC

STOR.

© Copyright by designer

65650-SC Price Code: H

Total Living Area :	3,096 sq.ft.
Main Living :	2,111 sq.ft.
2nd Level :	985 sq.ft.
Bedrooms :	4
Bathrooms :	4.5
Dimensions :	70'-0" x 78'-0"
Garage Type :	Two-car garage
Foundation :	Basement, Slab, Crawlspace

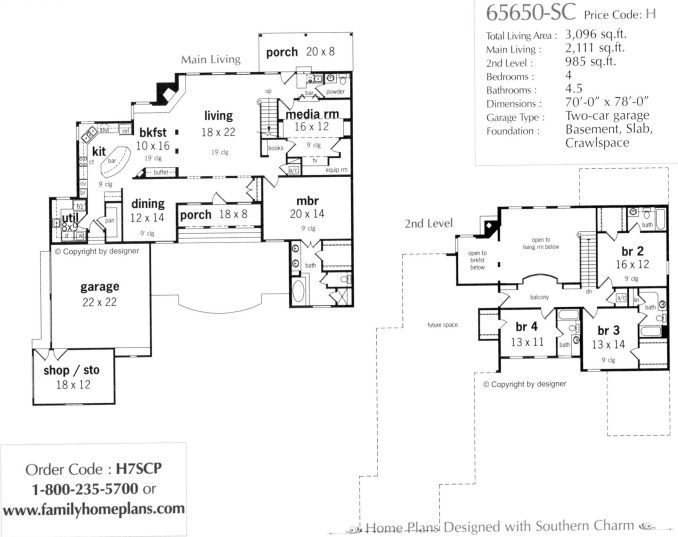

Main Living

porch 20 x 8

up

bar   powder

living
18 x 22
19' clg

bkfst
10 x 16
19' clg

kit
bar

ct

media rm
16 x 12

books

9' clg

tv

buffet

a/c   equip rm

ov
br
frz

util
8x9

pan

dining
12 x 14
9' clg

porch 18 x 8

mbr
20 x 14
9' clg

d   w

© Copyright by designer

bath

garage
22 x 22

shop / sto
18 x 12

2nd Level

open to
living rm below

open to
brkfst
below

bath

br 2
16 x 12
9' clg

dn

a/c   lin

bath

balcony

future space

br 4
13 x 11

bath

br 3
13 x 14
9' clg

© Copyright by designer

Home Plans Designed with Southern Charm

Visiting guests or live-in relatives have easy access to their quarters just inside the service entry. On the opposite side of the home, the master suite enjoys seclusion from secondary bedrooms as well as the main level's living areas.

66237-SC Price Code: L

Total Living Area : 4,182 sq.ft.
Main Living : 3,142 sq.ft.
2nd Level : 1,040 sq.ft.
Bedrooms : 3
Bathrooms : 3.5
Dimensions : 86'-0" x 85'-4"
Garage Type : Three-car garage
Foundation : Basement, Slab, Crawlspace

rear view

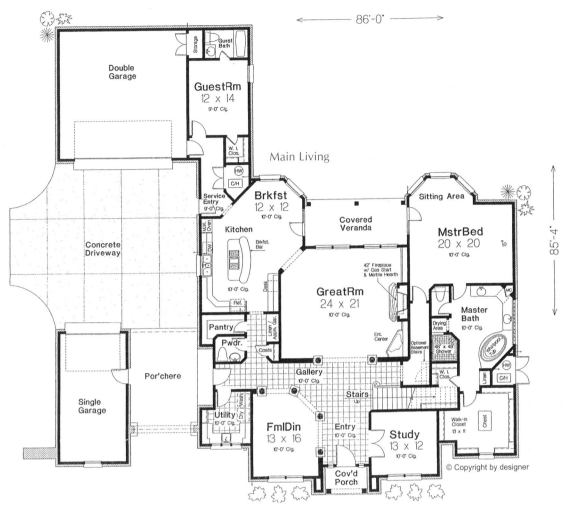

86'-0"

Double Garage

Guest Bath

Storage

GuestRm
12 x 14
9'-0" Clg.

W. I. Clos.

Main Living

HW

C/H

Service Entry
9'-0" Clg.

Brkfst
12 x 12
10'-0" Clg.

Covered Veranda

Sitting Area

MstrBed
20 x 20
10'-0" Clg.

85'-4"

M.W. Oven

Kitchen

Brkfst. Bar

10'-0" Clg.

Desk

Concrete Driveway

DW

Ref.

GreatRm
24 x 21
10'-0" Clg.

42" Fireplace w/ Gas Start & Marble Hearth

Drying Area

Master Bath
10'-0" Clg.

MC

Whirlpool Tub

Pantry

Linen / Appln. Gar.

Ent. Center

48" x 48" Shower

HW

PWdr.

Costs

Optional Basement Stairs

W. I. Clos.

Linen

C/H

Gallery
10'-0" Clg.

Por'chere

Single Garage

Utility
10'-0" Clg.

Dry / Wash

FmlDin
13 x 16
10'-0" Clg.

Stairs
Up

Entry
10'-0" Clg.

Study
13 x 12
10'-0" Clg.

Walk-In Closet
13 x 11

Chest

© Copyright by designer

Cov'd Porch

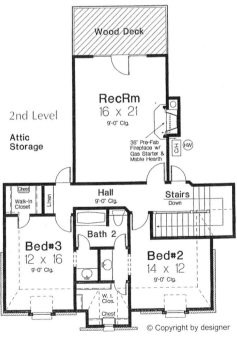

Wood Deck

2nd Level

Attic Storage

RecRm
16 x 21
9'-0" Clg.

36" Pre-Fab Fireplace w/ Gas Starter & Mable Hearth

C/H

HW

Chest

Walk-In Closet

Linen

Hall
9'-0" Clg.

Stairs
Down

Bed#3
12 x 16
9'-0" Clg.

Bath 2

Bed#2
14 x 12
9'-0" Clg.

W. I. Clos.

Chest

© Copyright by designer

Order Code : **H7SCP**
1-800-235-5700 or
www.familyhomeplans.com

72016-SC Price Code: J

Total Living Area : 3,620 sq.ft.
Main Living : 2,610 sq.ft.
2nd Level : 1,010 sq.ft.
Bedrooms : 4
Bathrooms : 4
Dimensions : 60'-0" x 68'-0"
Garage Type : Three-car garage
Foundation : Walkout Basement

Main Living

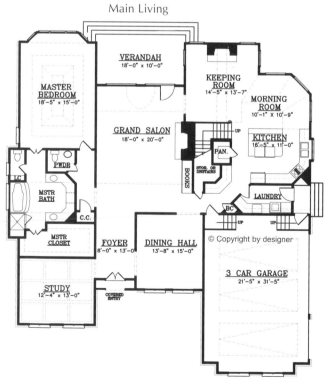

VERANDAH
18'-0" x 10'-0"

MASTER
BEDROOM
18'-5" x 15'-0"

KEEPING
ROOM
14'-5" X 13'-7"

MORNING
ROOM
10'-1" X 10'-9"

GRAND SALON
18'-0" x 20'-0"

KITCHEN
16'-5" x 11'-0"

PWDR

MSTR
BATH

PAN.

BOOKS

STOR. OR
DNSTAIRS

LC

C.C.

LAUNDRY

MSTR
CLOSET

FOYER
8'-0" x 13'-0"

DINING HALL
13'-8" x 15'-0"

BC

© Copyright by designer

STUDY
12'-4" x 13'-0"

COVERED
ENTRY

3 CAR GARAGE
21'-5" x 31'-5"

2nd Level

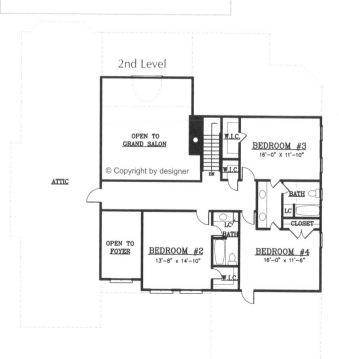

OPEN TO
GRAND SALON

© Copyright by designer

W.I.C.

BEDROOM #3
16'-0" X 11'-10"

W.I.C.

DN

ATTIC

BATH

LC

CLOSET

OPEN TO
FOYER

BEDROOM #2
13'-8" x 14'-10"

LC
BATH

BEDROOM #4
16'-0" x 11'-6"

W.I.C.

Southern Style
Pediments

The white-pillared Southern home had many facets. Among the most recognizable features of these homes was the pediment, a projecting low-pitch triangular gable that typically rested atop the portico, or porch and was sometimes supported by a colonnade. If the pediment recessed into the structure, it was occasionally anchored by pilasters, or flat columns set against the facade. The classical pediment features clean lines and little ornamentation.

Pediments trace their roots to the architecture of ancient Greece, where they were commonly used on ancient temples. The famous 16th Century Italian architect Andrea Palladio, who was heavily influenced by Grecian architecture, widely used pediments and porticos in his buildings. As the Greek Revival style helped the budding republic of the United States gain a national identity, numerous pattern books were published that helped popularize the style. These books made it easy for the Southern builder to recreate the look using locally available materials. (The ancient classical orders were all intended for stone to be used. But many Southerners—depending upon which region they lived—turned to stucco, brick, and wood as alternatives.)

Photography © istockphoto.com

Photo Courtesy of The Pella Corporation

Not exclusive to the Greek Revival style, pediments of many kinds decorated other Southern architectural styles, including Colonial and Classical Revival styles. Broken pediments are common in Colonial styles of architecture. Open-bed pediments feature a gap in the base molding and triangular-shape returns at the corners. The sloping sides of broken-apex pediments are returned before reaching the apex. Another popular broken-style pediment is the swan's neck; a pediment featuring scroll-like S curves that flank a central finial.

The popularity of the pediment may stem from its unique ability to draw attention to the façade of a home, facilitate a sense of exterior balance, and showcase the front entrance. Pediments even can be found on the Southern homes being built today, a testament to its enduring qualities.

Photo Courtesy of The Designer

This home, as shown, may differ from the original design.

Exceptional spaces for outdoor entertaining are found at the front and rear of this design.

To the front, guests are greeted by an inviting courtyard, complete with fireplace. To the rear, a double-stacked covered porch is accessed by the main-level breakfast room and upper-level game room.

68359-SC Price Code: M

Total Living Area:	4,629 sq.ft.
Main Living:	3,337 sq.ft.
2nd Level:	1,292 sq.ft.
Bedrooms:	4
Bathrooms:	4.5
Dimensions:	84'-10" x 102'-3"
Garage Type:	Four-car garage
Foundation:	Basement, Slab

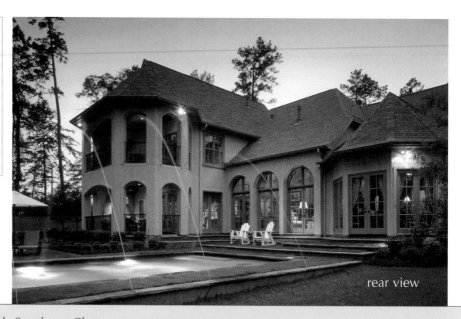

rear view

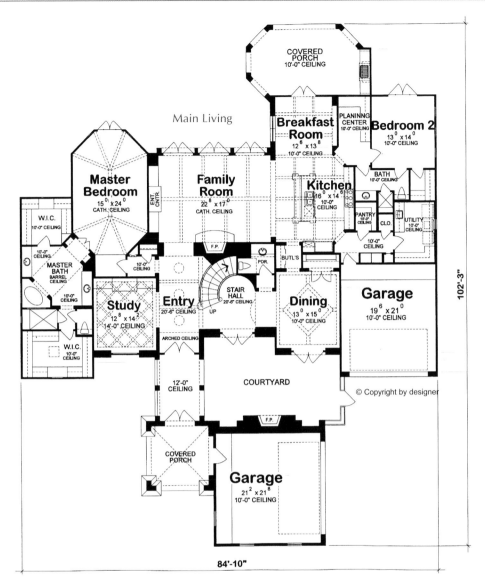

Main Living

COVERED
PORCH
10'-0" CEILING

Breakfast
Room
12⁶ x 13⁸
10'-0" CEILING

PLANNING
CENTER
10'-0" CEILING

Bedroom 2
13⁰ x 14⁰
10'-0" CEILING

Master
Bedroom
15⁰ x 24⁰
CATH. CEILING

Family
Room
22⁸ x 17⁰
CATH. CEILING

Kitchen
16⁰ x 14⁰
10'-0" CEILING

BATH
10'-0" CEILING

W.I.C.
10'-0" CEILING

ENT
CNTR

F.P.

PDR.

BUTL'S

PANTRY
10'-0"
CEILING

CLO.

UTILITY
10'-0"
CEILING

10'-0"
CEILING

MASTER
BATH
BARREL
CEILING

10'-0"
CEILING

10'-0"
CEILING

Study
12⁸ x 14²
14'-0" CEILING

Entry
20'-6" CEILING

STAIR
HALL
20'-6" CEILING

UP

Dining
13⁰ x 15⁰
10'-0" CEILING

Garage
19⁶ x 21⁰
10'-0" CEILING

W.I.C.
10'-0"
CEILING

ARCHED CEILING

© Copyright by designer

12'-0"
CEILING

COURTYARD

COVERED
PORCH

F.P.

Garage
21² x 21⁸
10'-0" CEILING

102'-3"

84'-10"

2nd Level

COVERED
PORCH
9'-11' CEILING

Game
Room
13⁸ x 27⁶
BARREL CEILING

ENT
CNTR

Bedroom 4
13⁰ x 14⁰
11'-0" CEILING

SLP

9'-0"
CEILING

9'-0"
CEILING

W.I.C.

2-STORY
FAMILY ROOM

9'-0"
CEILING

9'-0"
CEILING

LIN.

9'-0"
CEILING

2-STORY
ENTRY

DN

W.I.C.

9'-0"
CEILING

9'-0"
CEILING

Bedroom 3
13⁴ x 15⁰
CATH. CEILING

UNFINISHED
STORAGE

© Copyright by designer

Order Code : **H7SCP**
1-800-235-5700 or
www.familyhomeplans.com

66242-SC Price Code: I

Total Living Area : 3,273 sq.ft.
Main Living : 2,307 sq.ft.
2nd Level : 966 sq.ft.
Bedrooms : 4
Bathrooms : 3.5
Dimensions : 68'-10" x 62'-1"
Garage Type : Three-car garage

Main Living

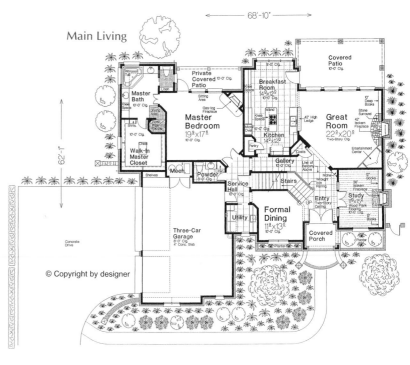

© Copyright by designer

2nd Level

Bedroom Four 13⁸x15⁰ 9'-0" Clg.

Bath Three

Bedroom Three 12⁶x13⁰ 9'-0" Clg.

Open to Below

Walk-In Closet

Walk-In Linen

Mech.

Walk-In Closet

Balcony
Wrought-Iron Railing

Stairs

Romeo & Juliet Wrought Iron Balcony

Open to Below

Future BonusRm 13⁸x27³ 9'-0" Clg. 412 Sq. ft. NOT included in Total

Bath Two

Bedroom Two 11⁴x13⁰ 9'-0" Clg.

Open to Below

5'-8" High Wall

© Copyright by designer

53710-SC Price Code: J

Total Living Area :	3,687 sq.ft.
Main Living :	3,151 sq.ft.
2nd Level :	536 sq.ft.
Bedrooms :	4
Bathrooms :	4
Dimensions :	86'-4" x 70'-6"
Garage Type :	Three-car garage
Foundation :	Basement, Crawlspace, Walkout Basement

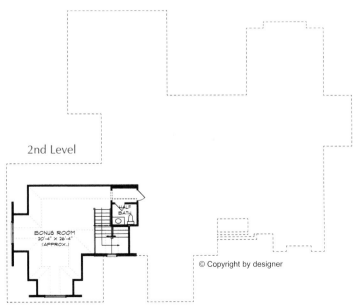

Main Living

SUITE TWO
12'-0" × 14'-8"

SUITE THREE
12'-0" × 16'-0"

OPEN VERANDA

MASTER SUITE
18'-4" × 16'-0"

BATH

CLOSET

CLOSET

HALL

TRELLIS

MASTER BATH

HER CLOSET

HIS CLOSET

DINING ROOM
15'-8" × 12'-0"

GREAT ROOM
20'-0" × 20'-0"

BATH

MUD HALL

PWD.

FOYER

STUDY/
GUEST SUITE
12'-0" × 15'-0"

THREE CAR GARAGE
23'-0" × 33'-0"

LAUNDRY

KITCHEN
14'-0" × 18'-0"

COVERED ENTRY

CLOSET

PANTRY

STOOP

BREAKFAST
10'-8" × 10'-8"

© Copyright by designer

2nd Level

HALF BATH

BONUS ROOM
20'-4" × 26'-4"
(APPROX.)

© Copyright by designer

Order Code : H7SCP
1-800-235-5700 or
www.familyhomeplans.com

Home Plans Designed with Southern Charm   145

An entire wing of the upper level of this design

is set apart for fun, with a home theater, game room and wet bar. More sedate entertaining options are offered on the main level, where a fireplaced screened porch and a covered veranda sweep the rear of the home.

53744-SC Price Code: N

Total Living Area :	5,087 sq.ft.
Main Living :	2,872 sq.ft.
2nd Level :	2,215 sq.ft.
Bedrooms :	4
Bathrooms :	4
Dimensions :	131'-0" x 84'-6"
Garage Type :	Three-car garage
Foundation :	Basement, Crawlspace, Walkout Basement

Photo Courtesy of The Designer

This home, as shown, may differ from the original design.

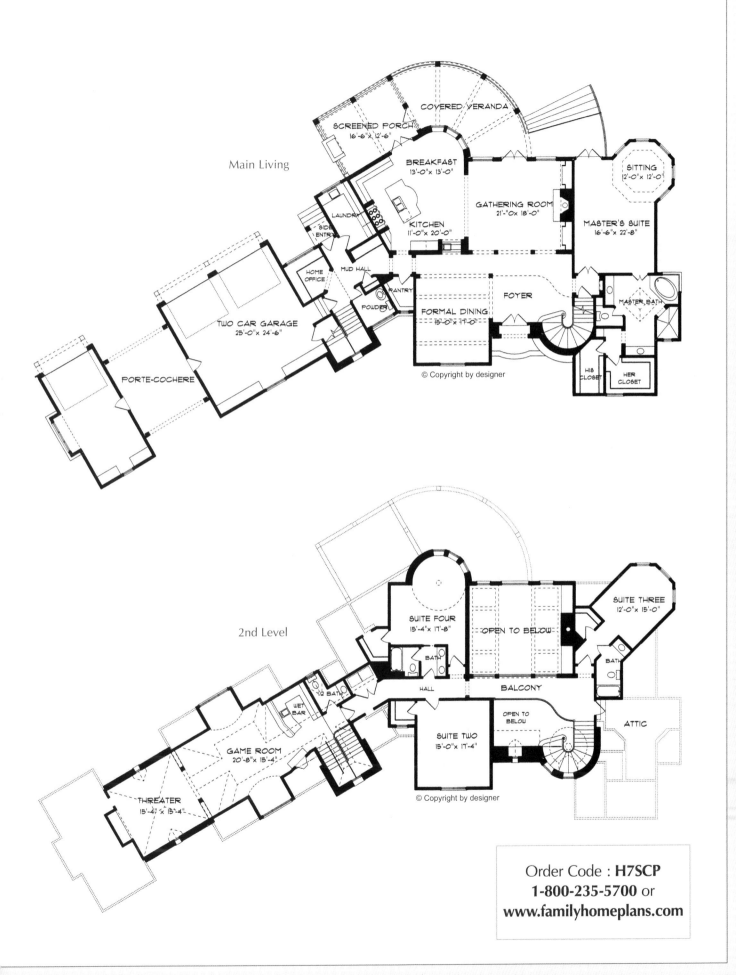

Main Living

SCREENED PORCH
16'-6"x 12'-6"

COVERED VERANDA

BREAKFAST
13'-0"x 13'-0"

GATHERING ROOM
21'-"0x 18'-0"

SITTING
12'-0"x 12'-0"

MASTER'S SUITE
16'-6"x 22'-8"

LAUNDRY

SIDE ENTRY

KITCHEN
11'-0"x 20'-0"

HOME OFFICE

MUD HALL

PANTRY

POWDER

FOYER

MASTER BATH

TWO CAR GARAGE
25'-0"x 24'-6"

FORMAL DINING
15'-0"x 17'-0"

PORTE-COCHERE

HIS CLOSET

HER CLOSET

© Copyright by designer

2nd Level

SUITE FOUR
15'-4"x 17'-8"

OPEN TO BELOW

SUITE THREE
12'-0"x 15'-0"

BATH

BATH

WET BAR

1/2 BATH

HALL

BALCONY

OPEN TO BELOW

ATTIC

GAME ROOM
20'-8"x 15'-4"

SUITE TWO
15'-0"x 17'-4"

THEATER
15'-4"x 15'-4"

© Copyright by designer

Order Code : **H7SCP**
1-800-235-5700 or
www.familyhomeplans.com

94937-SC Price Code: K

Total Living Area : 3,806 sq.ft.
Main Living : 2,126 sq.ft.
2nd Level : 1,680 sq.ft.
Bedrooms : 4
Bathrooms : 4
Dimensions : 67'-4" x 66'-0"
Garage Type : Three-car garage
Foundation : Basement

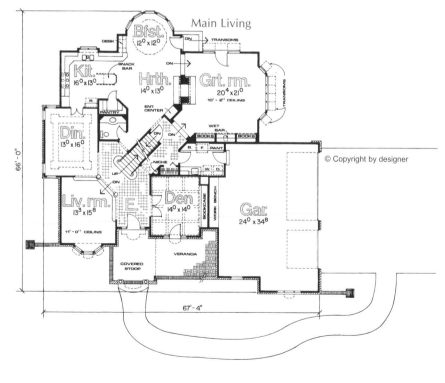

Main Living

Bfst.
12⁰ x 12⁰

Kit.
16⁰ x 13⁰

Hrth.
14⁰ x 13⁰

Grt. rm.
20⁴ x 21⁰
10' - 2" CEILING

Din.
13⁰ x 16⁰

Liv. rm.
13³ x 15⁸
11' - 0" CEILING

Den
14⁰ x 14⁰

Gar.
24⁰ x 34⁸

66' - 0"

67' - 4"

© Copyright by designer

2nd Level

Br. 3
14⁰ x 15⁰
9' - 0" CEILING

Mbr.
16³ x 18⁷
9' - 6" CLG.

Br. 2
14⁰ x 12⁰
9' - 0" CEILING

Br. 4
12⁰ x 12⁴
10' - 0" CLG.

© Copyright by designer

53798-SC Price Code: J

Total Living Area : 3,609 sq.ft.
Main Living : 2,249 sq.ft.
2nd Level : 1,360 sq.ft.
Bedrooms : 4
Bathrooms : 3.5
Dimensions : 88'-4" x 49'-6"
Garage Type : Three-car garage
Foundation : Basement,
Crawlspace, Walkout Basement

Main Living

© Copyright by designer

THREE CAR GARAGE 22'-0" x 32'-2"

COATS

STOR.

POWDER

LAUNDRY

PANTRY

OPEN

DINING 14'-0" x 13'-0"

KITCHEN 14'-0" x 15'-8"

OPT. OUTDOOR LIVING

GREAT ROOM 20'-4" x 26'-0"

FORMAL SPACE 14'-0" x 13'-0"

MASTER SUITE 19'-0" x 14'-4"

COATS

MASTER BATH

W.I.C.

VESTIBULE

COV. PORCH

2nd Level

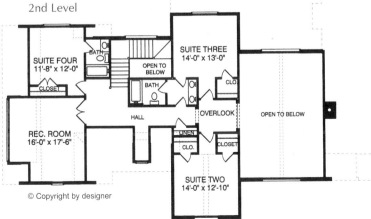

© Copyright by designer

SUITE FOUR 11'-8" x 12'-0"

CLOSET

REC. ROOM 16'-0" x 17'-6"

BATH

OPEN TO BELOW

BATH

HALL

SUITE THREE 14'-0" x 13'-0"

CLO.

OVERLOOK

LINEN

CLO.

CLOSET

OPEN TO BELOW

SUITE TWO 14'-0" x 12'-10"

Order Code : **H7SCP**
1-800-235-5700 or
www.familyhomeplans.com

This home, as shown, may differ from the original design.

Plenty of "fun space" is found in the upper level family room and home theater. The main level is conducive to more formal gatherings, with its dining room and spacious great room that opens to the rear covered porch.

96885-SC Price Code: M

Total Living Area :	4,626 sq.ft.
Main Living :	3,800 sq.ft.
2nd Level :	826 sq.ft.
Bedrooms :	4
Bathrooms :	3.5
Dimensions :	103'-0" x 75'-6"
Garage Type :	Three-car garage
Foundation :	Basement, Slab, Crawlspace

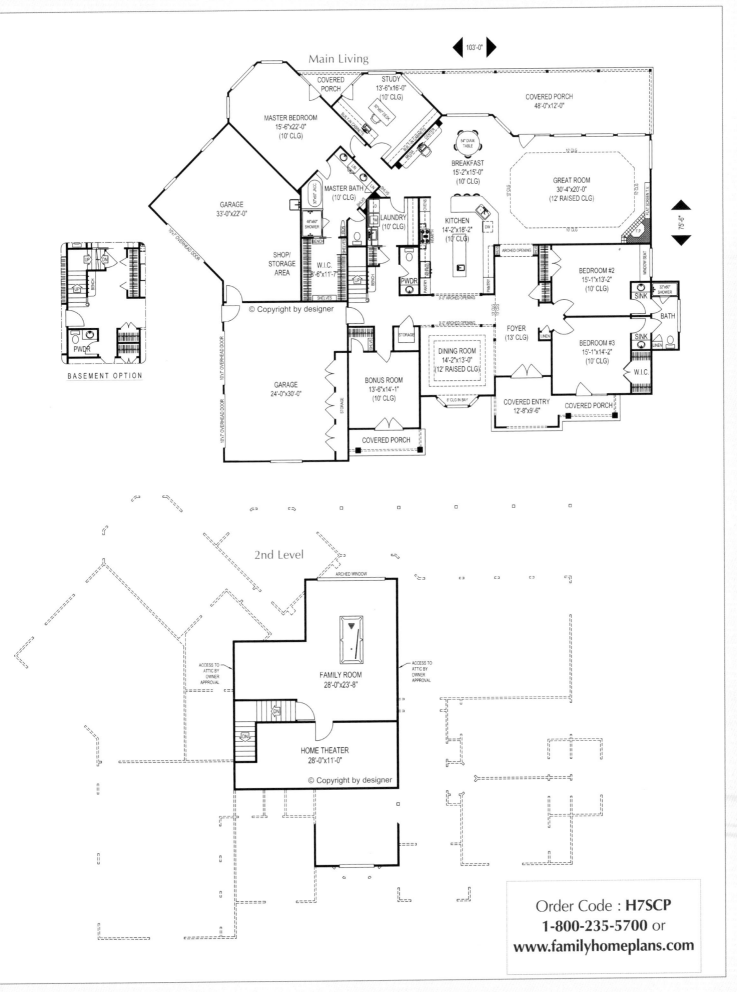

Main Living

103'-0"

COVERED PORCH

STUDY
13'-6"x16'-0"
(10' CLG)

MASTER BEDROOM
15'-6"x22'-0"
(10' CLG)

COVERED PORCH
48'-0"x12'-0"

BREAKFAST
15'-2"x15'-0"
(10' CLG)

54" DIAM
TABLE

GREAT ROOM
30'-4"x20'-0"
(12' RAISED CLG)

GARAGE
33'-0"x22'-0"

MASTER BATH
(10' CLG)

LAUNDRY
(10' CLG)

KITCHEN
14'-2"x18'-2"
(10' CLG)

BEDROOM #2
15'-1"x13'-2"
(10' CLG)

SHOP/
STORAGE
AREA

W.I.C.
8'-6"x11'-7"

PWDR

SINK

BATH

SINK

LINEN

FOYER
(13' CLG)

BEDROOM #3
15'-1"x14'-2"
(10' CLG)

LINEN

© Copyright by designer

STORAGE

DINING ROOM
14'-2"x13'-0"
(12' RAISED CLG)

W.I.C.

GARAGE
24'-0"x30'-0"

BONUS ROOM
13'-6"x14'-1"
(10' CLG)

COVERED ENTRY
12'-8"x9'-6"

COVERED PORCH

COVERED PORCH

BASEMENT OPTION

UP

DN

BENCH

UP

PWDR

75'-6"

2nd Level

ARCHED WINDOW

ACCESS TO
ATTIC BY
OWNER
APPROVAL

FAMILY ROOM
28'-0"x23'-8"

ACCESS TO
ATTIC BY
OWNER
APPROVAL

DN

DN

HOME THEATER
28'-0"x11'-0"

© Copyright by designer

Order Code : **H7SCP**
1-800-235-5700 or
www.familyhomeplans.com

Home Plans Designed with Southern Charm   151

This exceptional design offers an abundance of space in which to entertain – both casually and formally. For outdoor entertaining, an especially impressive loggia facilitates larger groups with its fireplace and outdoor kitchen area.

68361-SC Price Code: P

Total Living Area :	7,004 sq.ft.
Main Living :	4,323 sq.ft.
2nd Level :	2,681 sq.ft.
Bedrooms :	5
Bathrooms :	5.5
Dimensions :	77'-0" x 128'-4"
Garage Type :	Three-car garage
Foundation :	Basement*, Slab

This home, as shown, may differ from the original design.

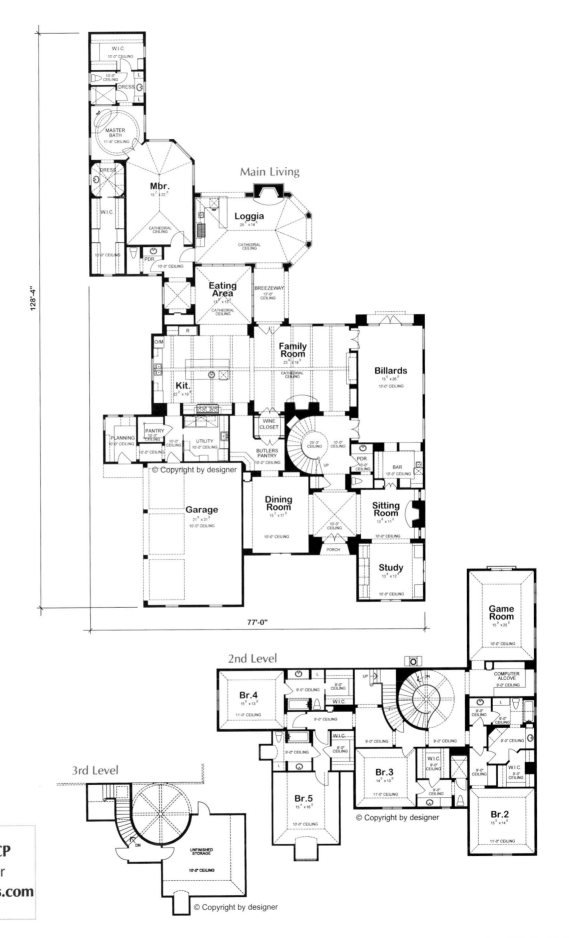

Main Living

Mbr.
15² x 22⁰

Loggia
25⁶ x 14⁶

Eating Area
13⁸ x 13⁰

BREEZEWAY
12'-0" CEILING

Family Room
23⁴ x 19⁰

Billards
15⁵ x 26⁰

Kit.
22⁶ x 19⁴

Garage
21⁵ x 31⁸

Dining Room
15² x 17⁰

Sitting Room
13⁸ x 11⁰

Study
13⁸ x 12⁶

© Copyright by designer

128'-4"

77'-0"

Game Room
15⁰ x 20⁰

2nd Level

Br.4
15⁰ x 13⁰

COMPUTER ALCOVE

Br.3
14⁰ x 13⁰

Br.5
15⁴ x 16⁰

Br.2
15⁰ x 14⁶

© Copyright by designer

3rd Level

UNFINISHED STORAGE
10'-0" CEILING

© Copyright by designer

53708-SC Price Code: J

Total Living Area :	3,669 sq.ft.
Main Living :	2,063 sq.ft.
2nd Level :	1,606 sq.ft.
Bedrooms :	4
Bathrooms :	4.5
Dimensions :	82'-4" x 79'-9"
Garage Type :	Three-car garage
Foundation :	Basement*, Crawlspace
	Walkout Basement*

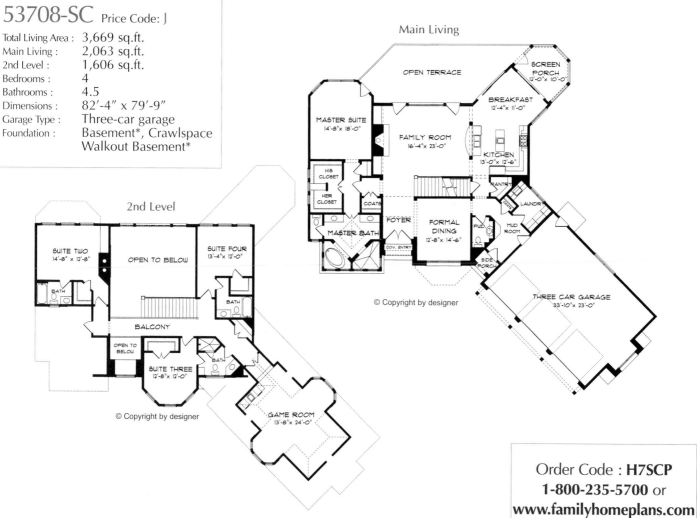

Main Living

OPEN TERRACE

SCREEN PORCH
12'-0"x 10'-0"

MASTER SUITE
14'-8"x 18'-0"

BREAKFAST
12'-4"x 11'-0"

FAMILY ROOM
16'-4"x 23'-0"

KITCHEN
13'-0"x 12'-6"

HIS CLOSET

HER CLOSET

COATS

PANTRY

LAUNDRY

FOYER

FORMAL DINING
12'-8"x 14'-6"

PWD

MUD ROOM

MASTER BATH

COV. ENTRY

SIDE PORCH

© Copyright by designer

THREE CAR GARAGE
33'-10"x 23'-0"

2nd Level

SUITE TWO
14'-8"x 12'-8"

OPEN TO BELOW

SUITE FOUR
13'-4"x 12'-0"

BATH

BATH

BALCONY

OPEN TO BELOW

SUITE THREE
12'-8"x 12'-0"

BATH

GAME ROOM
13'-8"x 24'-0"

© Copyright by designer

Main Living

SUN RM.
CATHEDRAL CEILING
11'6"x11'6"

NOOK
9'-1 1/8" CEILING
10'8"x16'4"

KIT.
9'-1 1/8" CEILING
12'0"x14'4"

PAN.

LIN.

9'6"x23'6"

GRT. RM.
2-STORY CEILING
16'6"x20'6"

MBR.
9'-1 1/8" TRAY CEILING
14'0"x17'0"

E.
2-STORY
CEILING

DIN.
9'-1 1/8" CEILING
12'4"x13'6"

STUDY
9'-1 1/8" STEP CEILING
12'8"x13'0"

3 CAR GARAGE
26'0"x34'8"

© Copyright by designer

95'-7¼"

78'-3¼"

73176-SC Price Code: I

Total Living Area :	3,332 sq.ft.
Main Living :	2,374 sq.ft.
2nd Level :	958 sq.ft.
Bedrooms :	3
Bathrooms :	3
Dimensions :	95'-7" x 78'-3"
Garage Type :	Three-car garage
Foundation :	Basement

2nd Level

BR. #2
8'-1 1/8" CEILING
11'0"x16'4"

LOFT
9'-1 1/8" CEILING
9'0"x16'4"

OPEN TO
BELOW

© Copyright by designer

BR. #3
8'-1 1/8" CEILING
12'4"x12'0"

OPEN TO
BELOW

97358-SC Price Code: N

Total Living Area :	5,752 sq.ft.
Main Living :	4,017 sq.ft.
2nd Level :	1,735 sq.ft.
Bedrooms :	4
Bathrooms :	4.5
Dimensions :	121'-0" x 84'-8"
Garage Type :	Three-car garage
Foundation :	Crawlspace, Slab, Walkout Basement

A sprawling rear deck and spacious screened porch are perfect spots for greeting the sun with morning coffee, or winding-down at the end of the day. A well-appointed master suite provides a pampering retreat on the inside of the home.

Order Code : **H7SCP**
1-800-235-5700 or
www.familyhomeplans.com

Main Living

FAMILY ROOM
CATHEDRAL CEILING
19'0"X21'0"

WOOD
DECK

SCREEN
PORCH
CATHEDRAL CEILING
17'6"X19'6"

NOOK
13'10"X17'8"

EATING BAR

KITCHEN
10'-1 1/8" CLG. HGT.
26'0"X19'4"

LIVING RM.
15'-1 1/8" CEILING HGT.
21'4"X18'4"

BARREL
VAULT

19'0"X15'8"

OFFICE
10'-1 1/8" CLG. HGT.
14'8"X6'0"

RAISED COUNTER

© Copyright by designer

10'8"X8'2"

ISLAND

PAN.
8'0"X6'8"

ARCH SOFFIT

7'2"X12'0"

7'2"X12'0"

BARREL
VAULT

BARREL
VAULT

SHELVES

SHELVES

2 CAR GARAGE
29'4" X 27'8"

STORAGE SHELVES

BENCH

LOCKERS

7'4"X5'8"

MUD RM.
12'0"X13'4"

LOCKERS

DN

DINING RM.
10'-1 1/8" CLG. HGT.
15'0"X14'0"

UP

ART
NICHE

DN

ART
NICHE

BUILT-INS

ART
NICHE

MBR.
14'-1 1/8" TRAY CLG.
23'6"X20'0"

10'-1 1/8" CLG. HGT.

FOYER
2-STORY CLG.

STUDY
10'-1 1/8" CEILING HGT.
15'0"X18'0"

1 CAR GARAGE
28'4"X24'0"

84'-8"

121'-0"

2nd Level

BR. #4
9'-1 1/8" CEILING HGT.
15'4"X14'8"

SEAT

BR. #3
9'-1 1/8" CEILING HGT.
19'0"X16'8"

SEAT

LIN

DESK

UNFINISHED
ATTIC STORAGE
15'8"X17'8"

LIN

DESK

SHELVES

ART NICHE

5'4"X18'0"

DN

STUDY LOFT
9'-1 1/8" CEILING HGT.
15'4"X14'0"

© Copyright by designer

BR. #2
9'-1 1/8" CEILING HGT.
15'0"X12'0"

DESK

SHELVES

SEAT

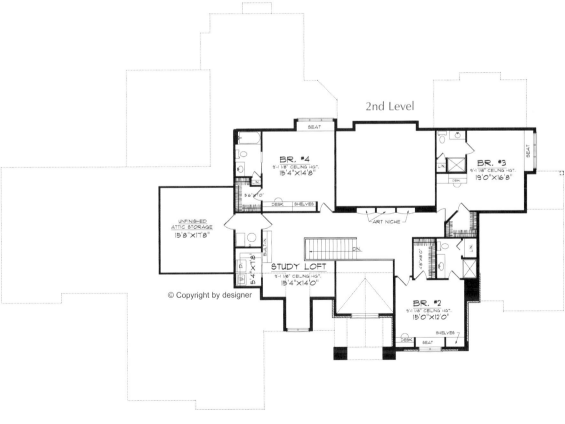

53719-SC Price Code: H

Total Living Area : 3,091 sq.ft.
Main Living : 1,833 sq.ft.
2nd Level : 1,258 sq.ft.
Bedrooms : 4
Bathrooms : 3.5
Dimensions : 87'-9" x 73'-2"
Garage Type : Three-car garage
Foundation : Basement*, Crawlspace,
 Walkout Basement*

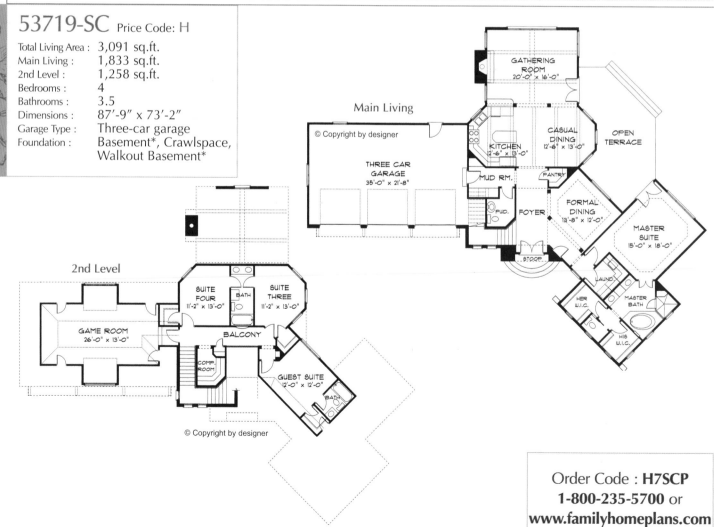

Main Living

© Copyright by designer

GATHERING ROOM
20'-0" x 16'-0"

THREE CAR GARAGE
35'-0" x 21'-8"

KITCHEN
12'-6" x 13'-0"

CASUAL DINING
12'-6" x 13'-0"

OPEN TERRACE

MUD RM.

PANTRY

PWD.

FOYER

FORMAL DINING
13'-8" x 12'-0"

MASTER SUITE
15'-0" x 18'-0"

STOOP

LAUND.

HER W.I.C.

MASTER BATH

HIS W.I.C.

2nd Level

GAME ROOM
26'-0" x 13'-0"

SUITE FOUR
11'-2" x 13'-0"

BATH

SUITE THREE
11'-2" x 13'-0"

BALCONY

COMP. ROOM

GUEST SUITE
12'-0" x 12'-0"

BATH

© Copyright by designer

Order Code : **H7SCP**
1-800-235-5700 or
www.family home plans.com

Southern Style
Grand Staircases

Staircases were the crown jewel of the center hall in the majority of Southern Antebellum homes. Curving elliptical and spiral staircases provided instant aesthetic appeal to anyone entering the home. Next to white pillars, a circular staircase was the most coveted feature of a plantation owner's home. Evidence of this fact is the many pattern books of the day devoted exclusively to stair design and construction.

The prestige and majesty of the grand staircase, though, did not originate in the Southern states. Its fate, having moved through the centuries of architecture from simple transport vestige to status symbol was sealed during the Baroque period in Europe. During this era, many reception rooms were located on the second level, so the staircase in the center hall provided a functional connection between the spaces. Yet, as staircases tend to overshadow a space, attention to their aesthetic side was inevitable. Staircase design gradually became more ornate and it soon became part of the trappings of social status. The stature of the staircase would have been well-known to European settlers who emigrated to America.

It's fair to say that the status of a Southern family was expressed as much by his staircase as by the façade of his home. It was thought that the sweeping shape of the stairwell allowed the home's inhabitants to ascend and descend with the ease and grace befitting their importance. But as aesthetic appeal often trumped functionality in the Southern home, grand staircases became art objects themselves—the main showpiece of the central hall or entryway.

Photography © istockphoto.com

This home, as shown, may differ from the original design.

A single-car garage, separated from the two-car garage, offers the perfect space for hobby enthusiasts to pursue their passions without disturbing the household or making messes that might be tracked inside the home. Golfers will appreciate a space for their cart.

96886-SC Price Code: N

Total Living Area :	5,183 sq.ft.
Main Living :	3,404 sq.ft.
2nd Level :	1,780 sq.ft.
Bedrooms :	5
Bathrooms :	5.5
Dimensions :	70'-0" x 73'-6"
Garage Type :	Three-car garage
Foundation :	Basement, Slab, Crawlspace

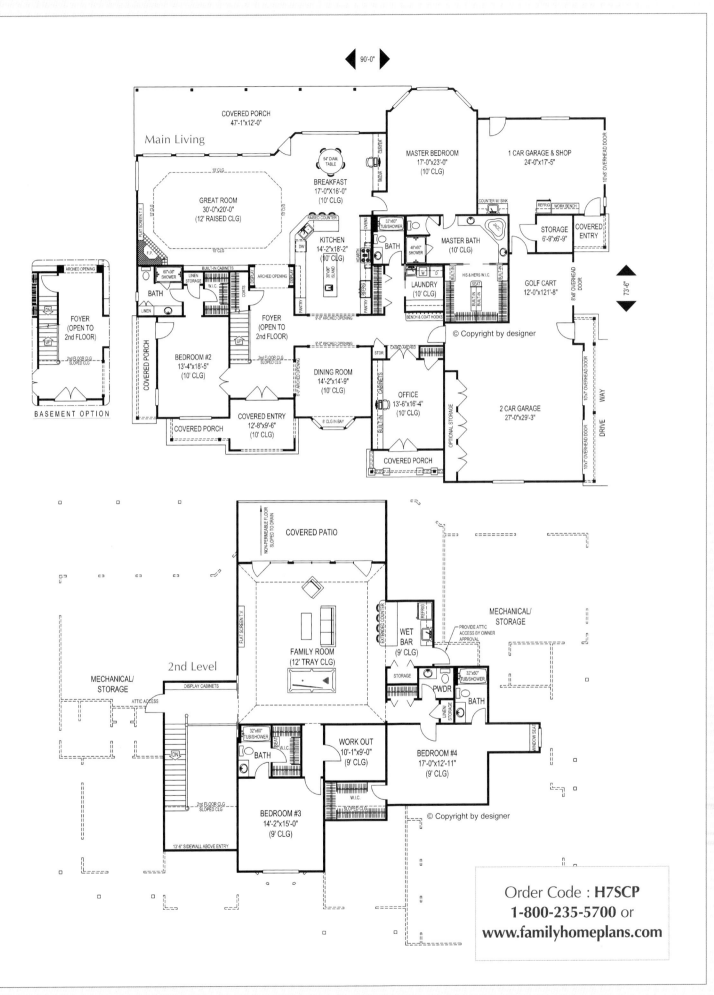

90'-0"

COVERED PORCH
47'-1"x12'-0"

Main Living

MASTER BEDROOM
17'-0"x23'-0"
(10' CLG)

1 CAR GARAGE & SHOP
24'-0"x17'-5"

10'x8' OVERHEAD DOOR

54" DIAM. TABLE

BREAKFAST
17'-0"X16'-0"
(10' CLG)

10' CLG

GREAT ROOM
30'-0"x20'-0"
(12' RAISED CLG)

RAISED COUNTER

KITCHEN
14'-2"x18'-2"
(10' CLG)

COUNTER W/ SINK

REFRIG WORK BENCH

STORAGE
6'-9"x6'-9"

COVERED
ENTRY

32"x60"
TUB/SHOWER

BATH

MASTER BATH
(10' CLG)

ARCHED OPENING

FOYER
(OPEN TO
2nd FLOOR)

48"x60"
SHOWER

BATH

60"x38"
SHOWER

LINEN STORAGE

BUILT-IN CABINETS

W.I.C.

COATS

LAUNDRY
(10' CLG)

HIS & HERS W.I.C.

73'-6"

8'x8' OVERHEAD DOOR

LINEN

FOYER
(OPEN TO
2nd FLOOR)

PANTRY

ARCHED OPENING

BENCH & COAT HOOKS

GOLF CART
12'-0"x121'-8"

DN

UP

2nd FLOOR CLG
SLOPED CLG

BASEMENT OPTION

BEDROOM #2
13'-4"x18'-5"
(10' CLG)

UP

2nd FLOOR CLG
SLOPED CLG

DINING ROOM
14'-2"x14'-9"
(10' CLG)

STOR

OFFICE
13'-6"x16'-4"
(10' CLG)

RAISED COUNTER

© Copyright by designer

10'x7' OVERHEAD DOOR

DRIVE WAY

COVERED PORCH

COVERED ENTRY
12'-8"x9'-6"
(10' CLG)

COVERED PORCH

8' CLG IN BAY

BUILT-IN CABINETS

OPTIONAL STORAGE

2 CAR GARAGE
27'-0"x29'-3"

10'x7' OVERHEAD DOOR

COVERED PORCH

COVERED PATIO

NON-PERMEABLE FLOOR SLOPED TO DRAIN

MECHANICAL/
STORAGE

FLAT SCREEN T.V.

2nd Level

FAMILY ROOM
(12' TRAY CLG)

EXTENDED COUNTER

WET BAR
(9' CLG)

REFRIG

PROVIDE ATTIC ACCESS BY OWNER APPROVAL

MECHANICAL/
STORAGE

MECHANICAL/
STORAGE

DISPLAY CABINETS

STORAGE

PWDR

LINEN STORAGE

32"x60"
TUB/SHOWER

BATH

ATTIC ACCESS

DN

2nd FLOOR CLG
SLOPED CLG

32"x60"
TUB/SHOWER

BATH

W.I.C.

WORK OUT
10'-1"x9'-0"
(9' CLG)

W.I.C.

BEDROOM #4
17'-0"x12'-11"
(9' CLG)

WINDOW SEAT

SLOPED CLG

BEDROOM #3
14'-2"x15'-0"
(9' CLG)

13'-6" SIDEWALL ABOVE ENTRY

© Copyright by designer

Order Code : H7SCP
1-800-235-5700 or
www.familyhomeplans.com

53802-SC Price Code: L

Total Living Area :	4,004 sq.ft.
Main Living :	2,292 sq.ft.
2nd Level :	1,712 sq.ft.
Bedrooms :	4
Bathrooms :	3.5
Dimensions :	64'-8" x 86'-6"
Garage Type :	Three-car garage
Foundation :	Basement, Crawlspace, Walkout Basement

The most appreciated space in this design may not be inside the home itself. An outdoor living area to the rear of the home invites family and friends to take in the fresh air and views of an enticing fireplace.

Order Code : **H7SCP**
1-800-235-5700 or
www.familyhomeplans.com

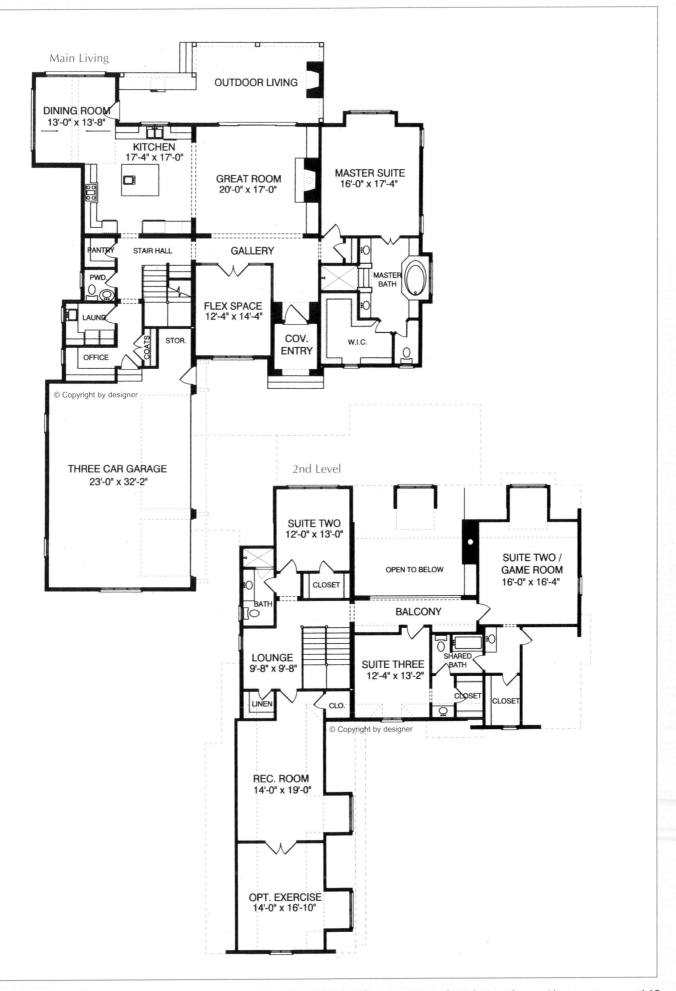

Main Living

OUTDOOR LIVING

DINING ROOM
13'-0" x 13'-8"

KITCHEN
17'-4" x 17'-0"

GREAT ROOM
20'-0" x 17'-0"

MASTER SUITE
16'-0" x 17'-4"

PANTRY

STAIR HALL

GALLERY

PWD.

MASTER BATH

LAUND

FLEX SPACE
12'-4" x 14'-4"

OFFICE

COATS

STOR.

COV. ENTRY

W.I.C.

© Copyright by designer

THREE CAR GARAGE
23'-0" x 32'-2"

2nd Level

SUITE TWO
12'-0" x 13'-0"

CLOSET

OPEN TO BELOW

SUITE TWO /
GAME ROOM
16'-0" x 16'-4"

BATH

BALCONY

LOUNGE
9'-8" x 9'-8"

SUITE THREE
12'-4" x 13'-2"

SHARED BATH

CLOSET

CLOSET

LINEN

CLO.

© Copyright by designer

REC. ROOM
14'-0" x 19'-0"

OPT. EXERCISE
14'-0" x 16'-10"

53705-SC Price Code: I

Total Living Area :	3,467 sq.ft.
Main Living :	2,222 sq.ft.
2nd Level :	1,245 sq.ft.
Bedrooms :	4
Bathrooms :	3.5
Dimensions :	67'-0" x 69'-4"
Garage Type :	Three-car garage
Foundation :	Basement*, Crawlspace, Walkout Basement*

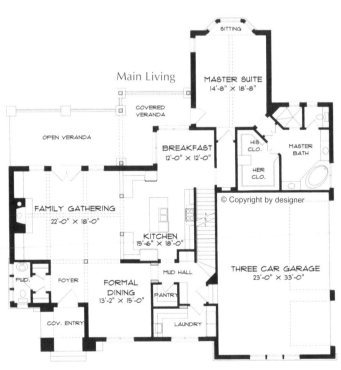

Main Living

SITTING

MASTER SUITE
14'-8" X 18'-8"

COVERED VERANDA

OPEN VERANDA

BREAKFAST
12'-0" X 12'-0"

HIS. CLO.

HER. CLO.

MASTER BATH

FAMILY GATHERING
22'-0" X 18'-0"

© Copyright by designer

KITCHEN
15'-6" X 18'-0"

PWD.

FOYER

FORMAL DINING
13'-2" X 15'-0"

MUD HALL

PANTRY

THREE CAR GARAGE
23'-0" X 33'-0"

COV. ENTRY

LAUNDRY

2nd Level

OPEN TO BELOW

SUITE THREE
15'-0" X 12'-0"

BATH

LOFT
15'-0" X 10'-4"

SUITE FOUR / GAME ROOM
18'-4" X 15'-4"

BATH

SUITE TWO
16'-0" X 12'-0"

© Copyright by designer

ATTIC

Main Living

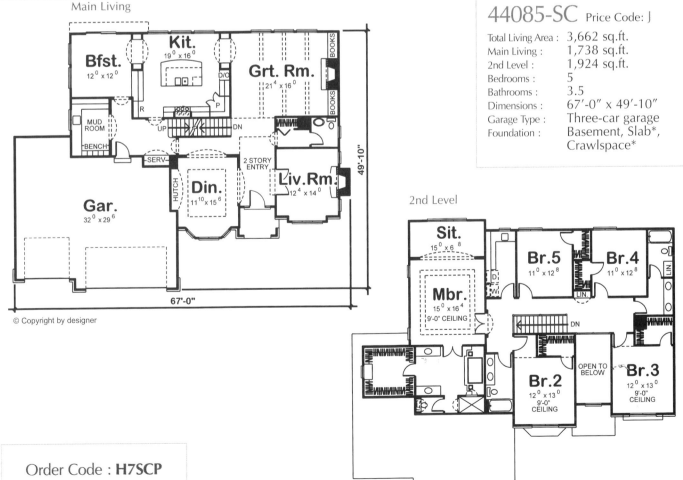

Kit.
19⁰ x 16⁰

Bfst.
12⁰ x 12⁰

MUD ROOM

BENCH

Grt. Rm.
21⁴ x 16⁰

BOOKS

BOOKS

BOOKS

UP

DN

P

R

D/O

SERV.

2 STORY ENTRY

HUTCH

Din.
11¹⁰ x 15⁶

Liv. Rm.
12⁴ x 14⁰

Gar.
32⁰ x 29⁶

49'-10"

67'-0"

© Copyright by designer

44085-SC Price Code: J

Total Living Area : 3,662 sq.ft.
Main Living : 1,738 sq.ft.
2nd Level : 1,924 sq.ft.
Bedrooms : 5
Bathrooms : 3.5
Dimensions : 67'-0" x 49'-10"
Garage Type : Three-car garage
Foundation : Basement, Slab*, Crawlspace*

2nd Level

Sit.
15⁰ x 6⁸

Mbr.
15⁰ x 16⁴
9'-0" CEILING

Br.5
11⁰ x 12⁸

Br.4
11⁰ x 12⁸

Br.2
12⁰ x 13⁰
9'-0" CEILING

OPEN TO BELOW

Br.3
12⁰ x 13⁰
9'-0" CEILING

DN

D

W

LIN.

LIN.

LIN.

© Copyright by designer

An irresistible detail of this design is the charming potting shed, which adds a stylish European touch. Inside the home, both luxurious and practical amenities abound – from the master suite's decadent Roman bath, to the sensible mudroom.

53743-SC   Price Code : M

Total Living Area :	4,934 sq.ft.
Main Living :	2,948 sq.ft.
2nd Level :	1,986 sq.ft.
Bedrooms :	4
Bathrooms :	4.5
Dimensions :	89'-7" x 69'-3"
Garage Type :	Three-car garage
Foundation :	Basement, Crawlspace, Walkout Basement

Photo Courtesy of The Designer

This home, as shown, may differ from the original design.

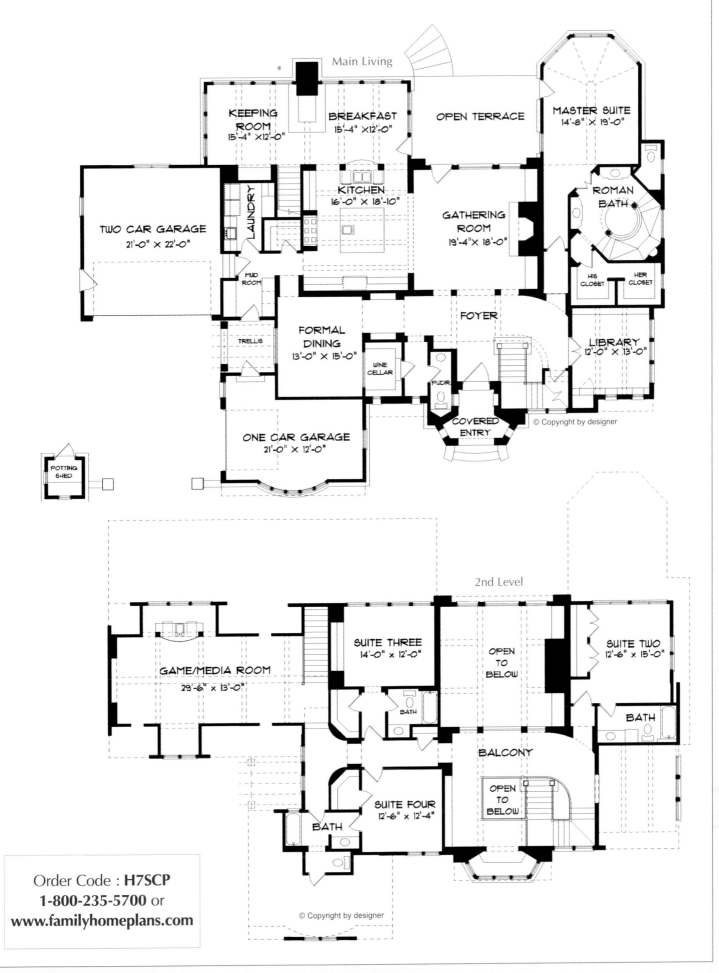

Main Living

KEEPING ROOM
15'-4" × 12'-0"

BREAKFAST
15'-4" × 12'-0"

OPEN TERRACE

MASTER SUITE
14'-8" × 19'-0"

LAUNDRY

KITCHEN
16'-0" × 18'-10"

ROMAN BATH

TWO CAR GARAGE
21'-0" × 22'-0"

GATHERING ROOM
19'-4" × 18'-0"

MUD ROOM

HIS CLOSET   HER CLOSET

TRELLIS

FORMAL DINING
13'-0" × 15'-0"

WINE CELLAR

FOYER

LIBRARY
12'-0" × 13'-0"

PWDR

ONE CAR GARAGE
21'-0" × 12'-0"

COVERED ENTRY

© Copyright by designer

POTTING SHED

2nd Level

GAME/MEDIA ROOM
29'-6" × 13'-0"

SUITE THREE
14'-0" × 12'-0"

OPEN TO BELOW

SUITE TWO
12'-6" × 15'-0"

BATH

BATH

BALCONY

SUITE FOUR
12'-6" × 12'-4"

OPEN TO BELOW

BATH

© Copyright by designer

Order Code : **H7SCP**
1-800-235-5700 or
www.familyhomeplans.com

53702-SC Price Code: I

Total Living Area : 3,430 sq. ft.
Main Living : 1,981 sq. ft.
2nd Level : 1,449 sq. ft.
Bedrooms : 4
Bathrooms : 3.5
Dimensions : 53'-2" x 63'-8"
Garage Type : Two-car garage
Foundation : Basement*, Crawlspace,
Walkout Basement*

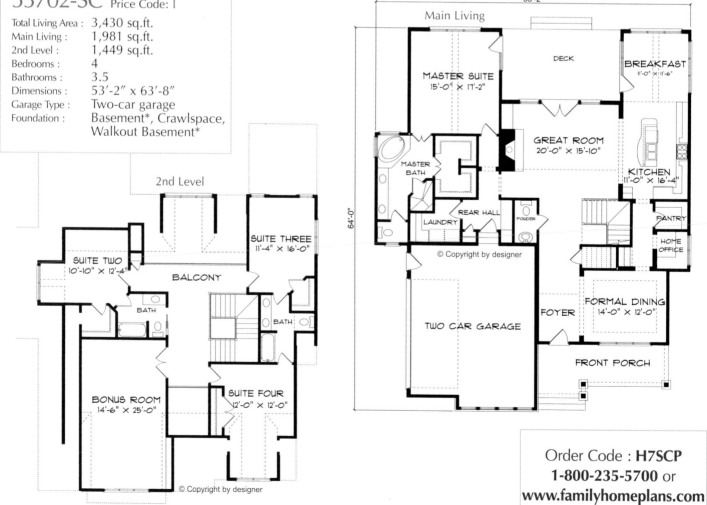

2nd Level

SUITE TWO
10'-10" x 12'-4"

BALCONY

SUITE THREE
11'-4" x 16'-0"

BATH

BATH

BONUS ROOM
14'-6" x 25'-0"

SUITE FOUR
12'-0" x 12'-0"

© Copyright by designer

Main Living

53'-2"

64'-0"

MASTER SUITE
15'-0" x 17'-2"

DECK

BREAKFAST
11'-0" x 11'-6"

MASTER BATH

GREAT ROOM
20'-0" x 15'-10"

KITCHEN
11'-0" x 16'-4"

LAUNDRY

REAR HALL

POWDER

PANTRY

HOME OFFICE

© Copyright by designer

TWO CAR GARAGE

FORMAL DINING
14'-0" x 12'-0"

FOYER

FRONT PORCH

Order Code : **H7SCP**
1-800-235-5700 or
www.familyhomeplans.com

Photo Courtesy of The Designer

This home, as shown, may differ from the original design.

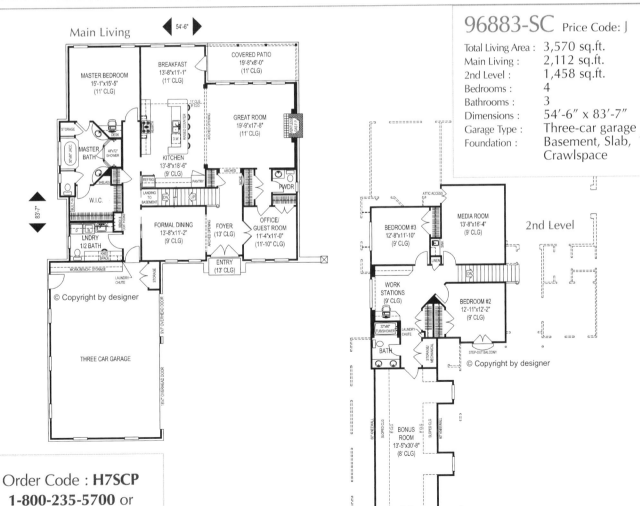

Main Living

54'-6"

83'-7"

MASTER BEDROOM
15'-1"x15'-5"
(11' CLG)

STORAGE

MASTER BATH
48"x72" SHOWER

W.I.C.

LNDRY
1/2 BATH

KNEE SPACE

WORK BENCH- STORAGE

LAUNDRY CHUTE

STORAGE

THREE CAR GARAGE

© Copyright by designer

18'x7' OVERHEAD DOOR

DESK

BREAKFAST
13'-8"x11'-1"
(11' CLG)

KITCHEN
13'-8"x18'-6"
(9' CLG)

RAISED COUNTER

D.W.

REFRIG

PANTRY

LANDING TO BASEMENT

DN

UP

FORMAL DINING
13'-8"x11'-2"
(9' CLG)

COVERED PATIO
19'-8"x8'-0"
(11' CLG)

GREAT ROOM
19'-9"x17'-8"
(11' CLG)

ARCHED

ARCHED OPENING

PWDR

FOYER
(13' CLG)

OFFICE/
GUEST ROOM
11'-4"x11'-0"
(11'-10" CLG)

ENTRY
(13' CLG)

96883-SC Price Code: J

Total Living Area :	3,570 sq.ft.
Main Living :	2,112 sq.ft.
2nd Level :	1,458 sq.ft.
Bedrooms :	4
Bathrooms :	3
Dimensions :	54'-6" x 83'-7"
Garage Type :	Three-car garage
Foundation :	Basement, Slab, Crawlspace

2nd Level

ATTIC ACCESS

BEDROOM #3
12'-8"x11'-10"
(9' CLG)

MEDIA ROOM
13'-8"x16'-4"
(9' CLG)

LINEN

DN

WORK STATIONS
(9' CLG)

BEDROOM #2
12'-11"x12'-2"
(9' CLG)

32"x60" TUB/SHOWER

LAUNDRY CHUTE

BATH

STORAGE/ MECHANICAL

STEP-OUT BALCONY

© Copyright by designer

SLOPED CLG

SLOPED CLG

BONUS ROOM
13'-5"x30'-8"
(8' CLG)

STEP-OUT BALCONY

73027-SC Price Code: I

Total Living Area :	3,256 sq.ft.
Main Living :	2,284 sq.ft.
2nd Level :	972 sq.ft.
Bedrooms :	4
Bathrooms :	3.5
Dimensions :	66'-0" x 89'-10"
Garage Type :	Three-car garage
Foundation :	Basement

Main Living

WD. DECK
17'0"x12'0"

NOOK
10'-1 1/8" CEILING
16'0"x12'6"

GRT. RM.
2 STORY CEILING
16'0"x18'8"

MBR.
CATHEDRAL CEILING
14'0"x16'4"

KIT.
10'-1 1/8" CEILING
16'0"x15'0"

BENCH

DIN.
10'-1 1/8" CEILING
12'0"x13'0"

E.
2 STORY
CEILING

DEN
10'-1 1/8" CEILING
14'0"x12'8"

© Copyright by designer

3 CAR GARAGE
23'6"x42'8"

66'-0"

89'-10"

2nd Level

BR. #3
8'-1 1/8" CEILING
11'0"x13'0"

OPEN TO
BELOW

BR. #4
8'-1 1/8" CEILING
12'8"x12'4"

OPEN TO
BELOW

BR. #2
8'-1 1/8" CEILING
16'0"x11'8"

© Copyright by designer

53768-SC Price Code: K

Total Living Area : 3,798 sq.ft.
Main Living : 2,390 sq.ft.
2nd Level : 1,408 sq.ft.
Bedrooms : 4
Bathrooms : 3.5
Dimensions : 89'-8" x 71'-0"
Garage Type : Two-car garage
Foundation : Crawlspace

Main Living

MASTER SUITE
15'-0" x 20'-0"

GREAT ROOM
22'-4" x 17'-8"

COVERED LOGGIA
24'-4" x 13'-0"

MASTER BATH

DINING ROOM
12'-0" x 13'-6"

KITCHEN
14'-8" x 15'-0"

OFFICE

HIS CLO.

HER CLO.

FORMAL SPACE
12'-4" x 13'-0"

FOYER

MUD ROOM

PWD.

COV. ENTRY

PANTRY

LAUND.

FUT. ELEV.

STORAGE

SIDE ENTRY

TWO CAR GARAGE
23'-0" x 22'-4"

GOLF-CART GARAGE
10'-0" x 8'-0"

© Copyright by designer

2nd Level

SUITE FOUR
15'-0" x 12'-8"

GAME ROOM
22'-4" x 15'-0"

BATH

BALCONY

BATH

SUITE FOUR
12'-4" x 13'-6"

OPEN TO BELOW

HALL

CLO.

© Copyright by designer

SUITE THREE
14'-8" x 12'-0"

FUT. ELEV.

OPT. BONUS ROOM
13'-4" x 22'-4"

Order Code : **H7SCP**
1-800-235-5700 or
www.familyhomeplans.com

53775-SC Price Code: M

Total Living Area :	4,547 sq.ft.
Main Living :	2,573 sq.ft.
2nd Level :	1,974 sq.ft.
Bedrooms :	4
Bathrooms :	3.5
Dimensions :	65'-9" x 87'-1"
Garage Type :	Three-car garage
Foundation :	Crawlspace

Luxury meets practicality with this home's side porch, mudroom, home office and laundry, located just off the garage. Upstairs, an enormous bonus room offers endless possibilities.

Order Code : **H7SCP**
1-800-235-5700 or
www.familyhomeplans.com

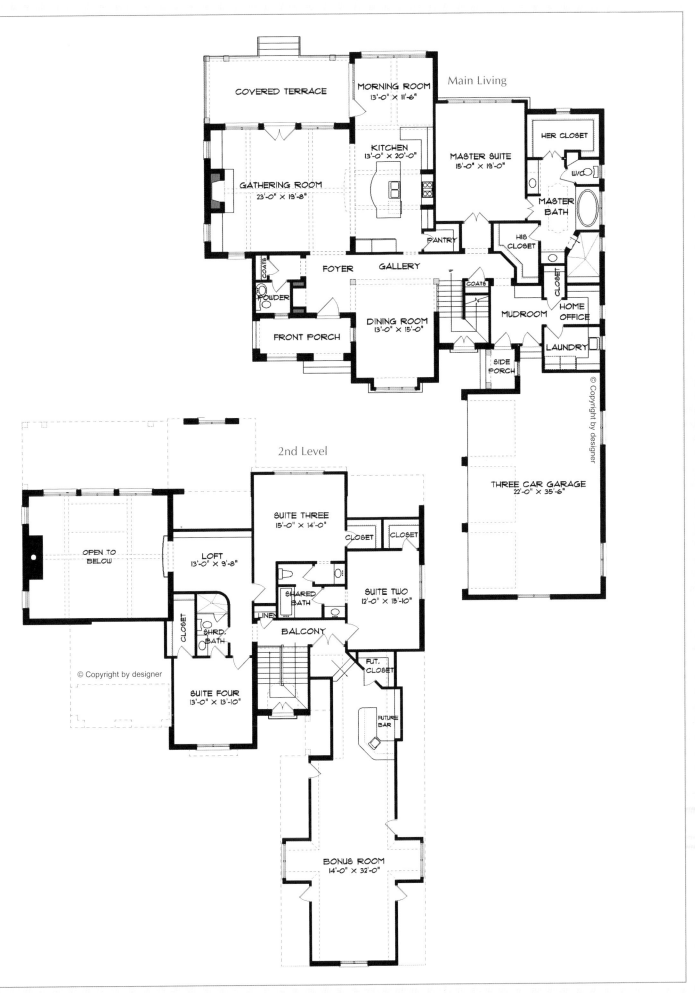

Main Living

COVERED TERRACE

MORNING ROOM
13'-0" x 11'-6"

KITCHEN
13'-0" x 20'-0"

MASTER SUITE
15'-0" x 19'-0"

HER CLOSET

W/C

GATHERING ROOM
23'-0" x 19'-8"

MASTER BATH

PANTRY

HIS CLOSET

CLOSET

COAT

COATS

FOYER

GALLERY

POWDER

MUDROOM

HOME OFFICE

DINING ROOM
13'-0" x 15'-0"

FRONT PORCH

SIDE PORCH

LAUNDRY

© Copyright by designer

THREE CAR GARAGE
22'-0" x 35'-6"

2nd Level

OPEN TO BELOW

SUITE THREE
15'-0" x 14'-0"

CLOSET

CLOSET

LOFT
13'-0" x 9'-8"

SHARED BATH

SUITE TWO
12'-0" x 15'-10"

CLOSET

SHRD. BATH

LINEN

BALCONY

© Copyright by designer

FUT. CLOSET

SUITE FOUR
13'-0" x 13'-10"

FUTURE BAR

BONUS ROOM
14'-0" x 32'-0"

63023-SC Price Code: J

Total Living Area : 3,557 sq.ft.
Main Living : 2,761 sq.ft.
2nd Level : 796 sq.ft.
Bedrooms : 4
Bathrooms : 4.5
Dimensions : 72'-0" x 85'-0"
Garage Type : Three-car garage
Foundation : Slab

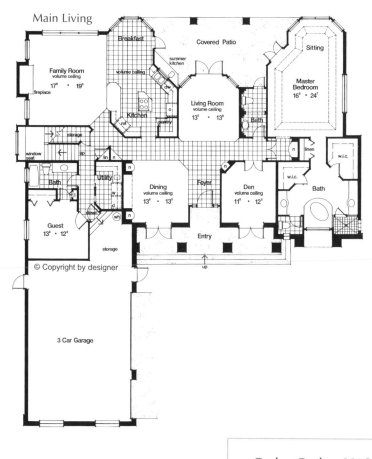

Main Living

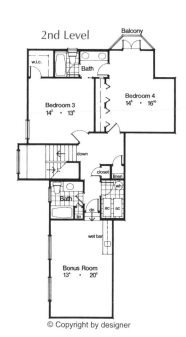

2nd Level

Order Code : **H7SCP**
1-800-235-5700 or
www.familyhomeplans.com

❧ Home Plans Designed with Southern Charm ❧

This home, as shown, may differ from the original design.

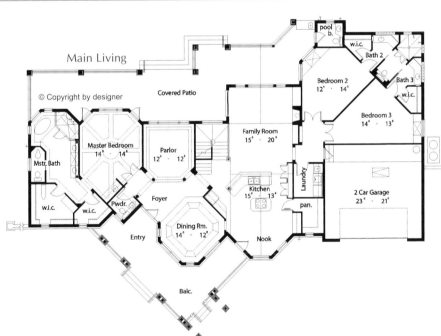

Main Living

© Copyright by designer

Covered Patio

Master Bedroom
14⁴ · 14⁴

Mstr. Bath

w.i.c.   w.i.c.

Pwdr.

Foyer

Parlor
12⁰ · 12⁴

Kitchen
15¹ · 13⁴

Entry

Dining Rm.
14⁴ · 12⁰

Nook

Balc.

Family Room
15¹ · 20⁰

Laundry

pan.

pool b.

w.i.c.

Bath 2

Bedroom 2
12⁴ · 14⁰

Bath 3

w.i.c.

Bedroom 3
14⁴ · 13⁴

2 Car Garage
23⁸ · 21⁴

63162-SC Price Code: I

Total Living Area :	3,436 sq.ft.
Main Living :	3,146 sq.ft.
2nd Level :	290 sq.ft.
Bedrooms :	4
Bathrooms :	4
Dimensions :	94'-0" x 113'-5"
Garage Type :	Three-car garage
Foundation :	Slab

Sun Deck

Bonus Rm.
12² · 16⁵

Guest Quarters
14⁰ · 13⁴

w.i.c.

Bath

1 Car Garage
14⁰ · 23⁴

Order Code : **H7SCP**
1-800-235-5700 or
www.familyhomeplans.com

Jewel
BOX

An abundance of natural light floods the main living areas of the home. Here, the living room's generous windows provide expansive views to the outside.

BELOW: The home's rear deck expands entertaining options to the outside and is directly accessed from the sunroom and screened porch.

This home, as shown, may differ from the original design.

With design amenities usually found in homes twice its size, this elegant one story accommodates more discriminating lifestyles at just over 2,500 square feet. A gabled front porch opens to the foyer, revealing immediate views of the living room with its breathtaking wall of windows. Joining this airy, open space is the kitchen, breakfast area and sunroom, which flow together seamlessly. On the opposite side of the home, sleeping quarters reside. The master suite lives large with an abundance of amenities and access to a spacious rear screened porch. Practicality rules the garage area, with golf cart storage, a workshop and entrance to the home through a mudroom area. An unfinished bonus room above the garage adds more than 400 square feet of space for future use.

A fireplace and built-in display cabinet enhance the living room's sophisticated yet relaxed atmosphere.

ABOVE: Walls of windows in the sunroom bring the outdoors inside.

Order Code : **H7SCP**
1-800-235-5700 or
www.familyhomeplans.com

Main Living

45667-SC Price Code: F

Total Living Area:	2,525 sq.ft.
Main Living:	2,525 sq.ft.
Bedrooms:	3
Bathrooms:	2.5
Dimensions:	82'-2" x 98'-8"
Garage Type:	Two-car garage
Foundation:	Crawlspace

© Copyright by designer

This home, as shown, may differ from the original design.

63260-SC Price Code: I

Total Living Area :	3,430 sq.ft.
Main Living :	3,064 sq.ft.
2nd Level :	366 sq.ft.
Bedrooms :	4
Bathrooms :	4
Dimensions :	80'-0" x 91'-0"
Garage Type :	Three-car garage
Foundation :	Basement, Slab

Main Living

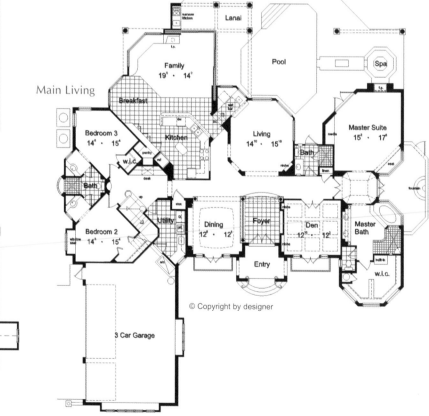

© Copyright by designer

76131-SC   Price Code: I

Total Living Area :	3,448 sq.ft.
Main Living :	2,085 sq.ft.
2nd Level :	1,363 sq.ft.
Bedrooms :	6
Bathrooms :	4.5
Dimensions :	64'-8" x 58'-8"
Garage Type :	Three-car garage
Foundation :	Slab

Main Living

16-0 X 16-0

15-0 X 15-0

10-0 X 10-0

13-0 X 14-8

12-8 X 14-6

13-0 X 14-8

14-0 X 14-4

10-4 X 12-8

3-CAR GARAGE
22-0 X 32-0

© Copyright by designer

2nd Level

12-8 X 15-0

11-4 X 10-4

11-4 X 11-4

11-4 X 11-4

12-8 X 12-4

© Copyright by designer

55836-SC Price Code: I

Total Living Area :	3,276 sq.ft.
Main Living :	3,276 sq.ft.
Bedrooms :	4
Bathrooms :	3.5
Dimensions :	76'-2" x 73'-10"
Foundation :	Slab

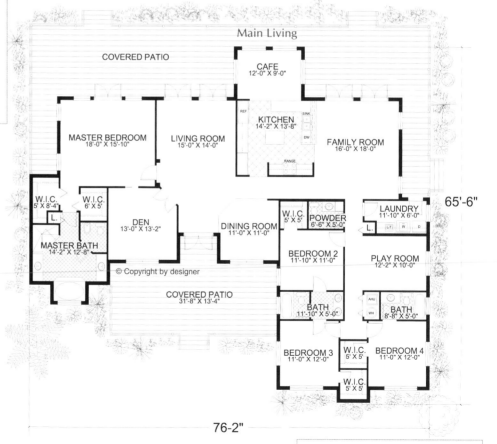

Main Living

COVERED PATIO

CAFE
12'-0" X 9'-0"

KITCHEN
14'-2" X 13'-8"

REF SINK

DW

RANGE

MASTER BEDROOM
18'-0" X 15'-10"

LIVING ROOM
15'-0" X 14'-0"

FAMILY ROOM
16'-0" X 18'-0"

65'-6"

W.I.C.
5' X 8'-4"

W.I.C.
6' X 5'

L.

DEN
13'-0" X 13'-2"

DINING ROOM
11'-0" X 11'-0"

W.I.C.
5' X 5'

POWDER
6'-6" X 5'-0"

LAUNDRY
11'-10" X 6'-0"

L. W D

MASTER BATH
14'-2" X 12'-8"

BEDROOM 2
11'-10" X 11'-0"

PLAY ROOM
12'-2" X 10'-0"

© Copyright by designer

COVERED PATIO
31'-8" X 13'-4"

BATH
11'-10" X 5'-0"

AHU
WH

BATH
8'-8" X 5'-0"

BEDROOM 3
11'-0" X 12'-0"

W.I.C.
5' X 5'

BEDROOM 4
11'-0" X 12'-0"

W.I.C.
5' X 5'

76-2"

97511-SC Price Code: H

Total Living Area : 3,032 sq.ft.
Main Living : 3,032 sq.ft.
Bedrooms : 3
Bathrooms : 3
Dimensions : 73'-0" x 87'-8"
Garage Type : Three-car garage
Foundation : Slab

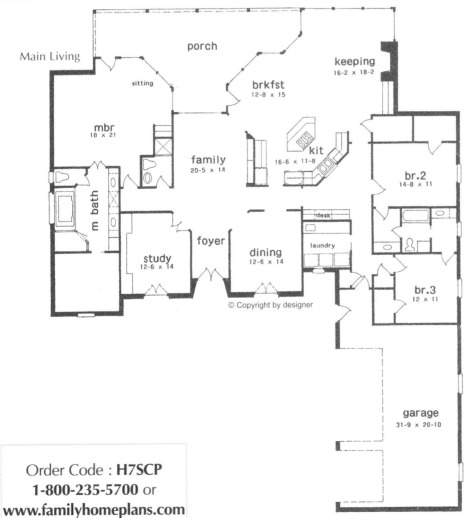

Main Living

porch

sitting

keeping
16-2 x 18-2

brkfst
12-8 x 15

mbr
18 x 21

family
20-5 x 14

kit
16-6 x 11-8

m bath

br.2
14-8 x 11

study
12-6 x 14

foyer

dining
12-6 x 14

desk

laundry

© Copyright by designer

br.3
12 x 11

garage
31-9 x 20-10

Order Code : **H7SCP**
1-800-235-5700 or
www.familyhomeplans.com

55730-SC Price Code: I

Total Living Area :	3,323 sq.ft.
Main Living :	2,020 sq.ft.
2nd Level :	1,303 sq.ft.
Bedrooms :	3
Bathrooms :	3
Dimensions :	48'-0" x 80'-0"
Garage Type :	Two-car garage
Foundation :	Slab

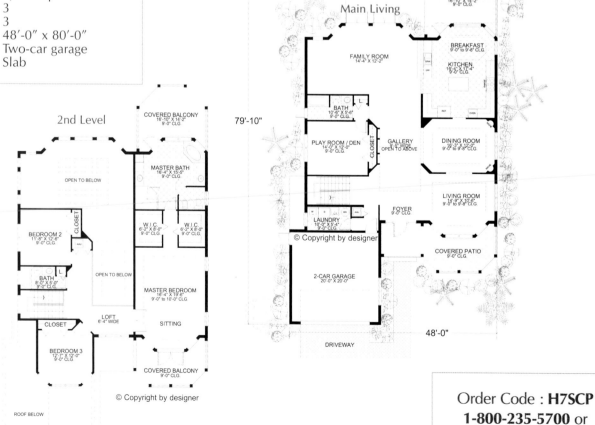

2nd Level

COVERED BALCONY
16'-10" X 14'-2"
9'-0" CLG.

MASTER BATH
16'-4" X 15'-6"
9'-0" CLG.

OPEN TO BELOW

BEDROOM 2
11'-8" X 12'-6"
9'-0" CLG.

CLOSET

W.I.C.
6'-2" X 8'-0"
9'-0" CLG.

W.I.C.
6'-2" X 8'-0"
9'-0" CLG.

BATH
8'-0" X 5'-0"
9'-0" CLG.

OPEN TO BELOW

MASTER BEDROOM
16'-4" X 19'-6"
9'-0" to 10'-0" CLG.

CLOSET

LOFT
6'-4" WIDE

SITTING

BEDROOM 3
12'-7" X 12'-0"
9'-0" CLG.

COVERED BALCONY
9'-0" CLG.

© Copyright by designer

ROOF BELOW

Main Living

COVERED PATIO
16'-10" X 14'-2"
9'-0" CLG.

FAMILY ROOM
14'-4" X 12'-2"

BREAKFAST
9'-0" to 9'-8" CLG.

KITCHEN
16'-0" X 17'-4"
9'-0" CLG.

BATH
10'-6" X 5'-6"
9'-0" CLG.

79'-10"

PLAY ROOM / DEN
14'-0" X 12'-0"
9'-0" CLG.

GALLERY
3'-6" WIDE
OPEN TO ABOVE

CLOSET

DINING ROOM
16'-3" X 12'-0"
9'-0" to 9'-8" CLG.

LIVING ROOM
14'-9" X 10'-6"
9'-0" to 9'-8" CLG.

LAUNDRY
10'-0" X 5'-4"
9'-0" CLG.

FOYER
9'-0" CLG.

COVERED PATIO
9'-0" CLG.

© Copyright by designer

2-CAR GARAGE
20'-0" X 20'-0"

DRIVEWAY

48'-0"

❧ Home Plans Designed with Southern Charm ❧

Order Code : **H7SCP**
1-800-235-5700 or
www.familyhomeplans.com

97515-SC Price Code: J

Total Living Area : 3,658 sq.ft.
Main Living : 2,780 sq.ft.
2nd Level : 878 sq.ft.
Bedrooms : 4
Bathrooms : 4
Dimensions : 68'-3" x 89'-1"
Garage Type : Two-car garage
Foundation : Slab

Main Living

sitting
8-8 X 12-10

mbr
15 X 17-8

hers

his

hers

his

family
23-9 X 19

keeping
13-4 X 12-10

brkfst
13 X 13

kit.
14 X 17-6

study
14-3 X 13

foyer

dining
14-3 X 13-2

laundry

br.2
11 X 12-10

© Copyright by designer

garage
21 X 24-5

2nd Level

gameroom
18 X 17

open to below

© Copyright by designer

br.3
14-2 X 11

br.4
14-3 X 11

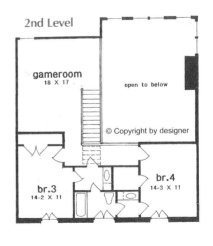

Order Code : **H7SCP**
1-800-235-5700 or
www.familyhomeplans.com

97525-SC Price Code: H

Total Living Area : 3,029 sq.ft.
Main Living : 2,298 sq.ft.
2nd Level : 731 sq.ft.
Bedrooms : 4
Bathrooms : 3
Dimensions : 71'-10" x 78'-0"
Garage Type : Three-car garage
Foundation : Slab

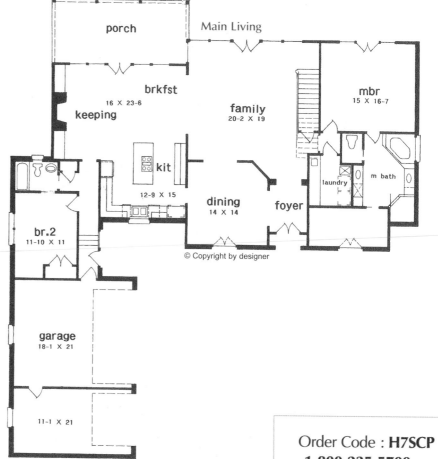

porch

Main Living

brkfst
16 X 23-6

keeping

family
20-2 X 19

mbr
15 X 16-7

kit
12-9 X 15

dining
14 X 14

foyer

laundry

m bath

br.2
11-10 X 11

garage
18-1 X 21

11-1 X 21

© Copyright by designer

2nd Level

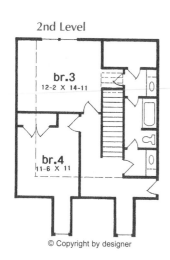

br.3
12-2 X 14-11

br.4
11-6 X 11

© Copyright by designer

64984-SC Price Code: H

Total Living Area : 3,016 sq.ft.
Main Living : 1,716 sq.ft.
2nd Level : 1,300 sq.ft.
Bedrooms : 6
Bathrooms : 4.5
Dimensions : 60'-0" x 47'-8"
Garage Type : Two-car garage
Foundation : Crawlspace

Main Living

10-8 X 11-8
11-8 X 15-0
12-8 X 15-0
16-4 X 12-0
16-0 X 15-8
12-8 X 11-6

© Copyright by designer

2-CAR GARAGE
22-4 X 20-4

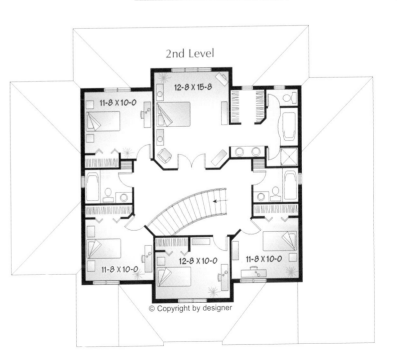

2nd Level

11-8 X 10-0
12-8 X 15-8
11-8 X 10-0
12-8 X 10-0
11-8 X 10-0

© Copyright by designer

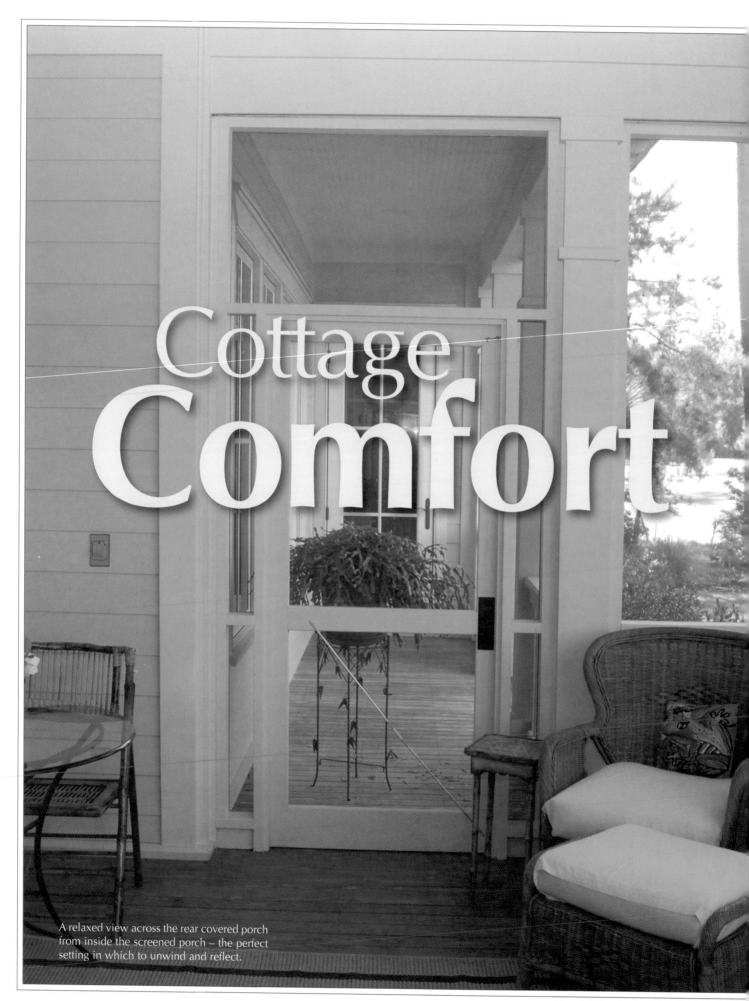

Cottage Comfort

A relaxed view across the rear covered porch from inside the screened porch – the perfect setting in which to unwind and reflect.

Photo Courtesy of The Designer

Perhaps one of the most delightful aspects of this home is it's abundance of comfortable covered porch space, front and back. Just inside the front porch, the living room and dining room join together to create an open, airy space, warmed by a fireplace and expanded by access to two covered porches to the rear. A unique feature of this design is its discreetly located study, accessed from the living room, but very private. The master suite enjoys seclusion as well, and features a luxury bath area that one would expect to find in a much larger home. A second bedroom and a bonus room above the detached garage provide additional sleeping quarters for family or overnight guests.

A backyard perspective of the home's attractive rear elevation.

LEFT and TOP: Two views of the living room. A soaring ceiling, meets overhead dormers to brighten the area with natural light. Views beyond the fireplace reveal an inviting screened porch.

ABOVE: The dining room flows openly into the living room and accesses a deep covered rear porch that expands dining options to the outdoors.

Main Living

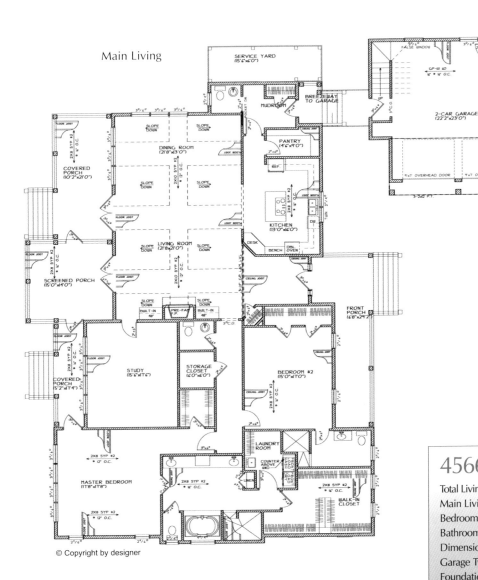

© Copyright by designer

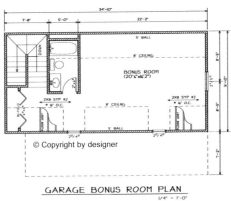

© Copyright by designer

GARAGE BONUS ROOM PLAN
1/4" = 1'-0"

45665-SC Price Code: H

Total Living Area:	3,106 sq.ft.
Main Living:	3,106 sq.ft.
Bedrooms:	2
Bathrooms:	2 Full bath (s), 2 Half (s)
Dimensions:	83'-0" x 93'-10"
Garage Type:	Two-car garage
Foundation:	Basement

Order Code : **H7SCP**
1-800-235-5700 or
www.familyhomeplans.com

94622-SC Price Code: H

Total Living Area : 3,149 sq.ft.
Main Living : 2,033 sq.ft.
2nd Level : 1,116 sq.ft.
Bedrooms : 4
Bathrooms : 3.5
Dimensions : 71'-0" x 56'-0"
Garage Type : Two-car garage
Foundation : Slab, Crawlspace

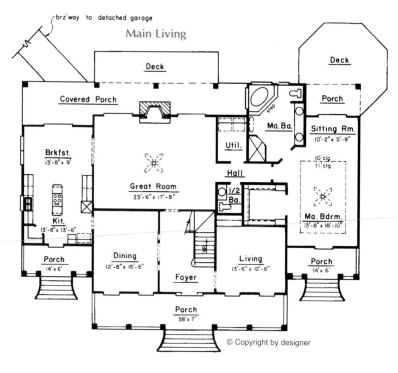

Main Living

brz'way to detached garage

Deck

Covered Porch

Deck

Porch

Brkfst.
13'-8" x 9'

Ma. Ba.

Sitting Rm.
10'-2" x 5'-9"

Util.

10' clg.
11' clg.

Great Room
23'-6" x 17'-8"

Hall

Kit.
13'-8" x 13'-6"

1/2
Ba.

Ma. Bdrm.
13'-8" x 18'-10"

Porch
14' x 6'

Dining
12'-8" x 15'-6"

Living
13'-6" x 12'-8"

Porch
14' x 6'

Foyer

Porch
38' x 7'

© Copyright by designer

2nd Level

Bdrm. 2
13'-6" x 12'

attic
storage

Dr.

Ba. 2

Ba. 3

Dr.

Balcony

railing

attic
storage

Bdrm. 3
13'-6" x 15'

open to below

Bdrm. 4
12'-8" x 13'-6"

© Copyright by designer

Order Code : **H7SCP**
1-800-235-5700 or
www.familyhomeplans.com

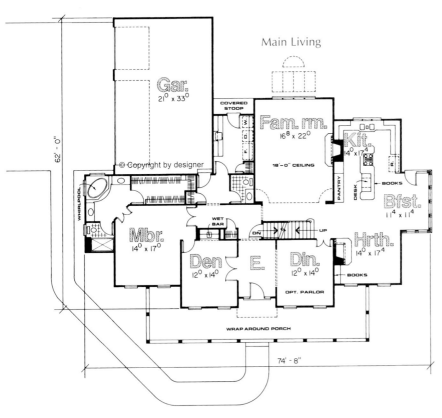

Main Living

Gar.
21⁰ x 33⁰

COVERED STOOP

Fam. rm.
16⁸ x 22⁰
18'-0" CEILING

Kit.
14⁰ x 17⁴

© Copyright by designer

PANTRY

DESK

BOOKS

Bfst.
11⁴ x 11⁴

WHIRLPOOL

WET BAR

DN

UP

R.

Mbr.
14⁰ x 17⁰

Den
12⁰ x 14⁰

E.

Din.
12⁰ x 14⁰

Hrth.
14⁰ x 17⁴

BOOKS

OPT. PARLOR

WRAP AROUND PORCH

62' - 0"

74' - 8"

99486-SC Price Code: I

Total Living Area :	3,422 sq.ft.
Main Living :	2,367 sq.ft.
2nd Level :	1,055 sq.ft.
Bedrooms :	4
Bathrooms :	3.5
Dimensions :	74'-8" x 62'-0"
Garage Type :	Three-car garage
Foundation :	Basement, Slab*, Crawlspace*

2nd Level

Br. 2
15⁸ x 12⁴

OPEN TO BELOW

UNFINISHED BONUS ROOM
14⁰ x 15³

TRAPS

BOOKS

LIN.

LIN.

DN

Br. 3
12⁰ x 14⁰
9'-0" CEILING

SHELVES

Br. 4
12⁰ x 14⁰
9'-0" CEILING

LIN.

© Copyright by designer

Order Code : **H7SCP**
1-800-235-5700 or
www.familyhomeplans.com

10768-SC Price Code: M

Total Living Area :	4,963 sq.ft.
Basement :	1,501 sq.ft.
Main Living :	2,573 sq.ft.
2nd Level :	2,390 sq.ft.
Bedrooms :	5
Bathrooms :	3.5
Dimensions :	122'-0" x 52'-6"
Garage Type :	Three-car garage
Foundation :	Basement + Crawlspace

A sprawling covered porch spans the entire length and one side of this awe inspiring design. With all five bedrooms on the upper level, the main level's layout is well-appointed for both formal and casual entertaining.

Order Code : **H7SCP**
1-800-235-5700 or
www.familyhomeplans.com

Main Living

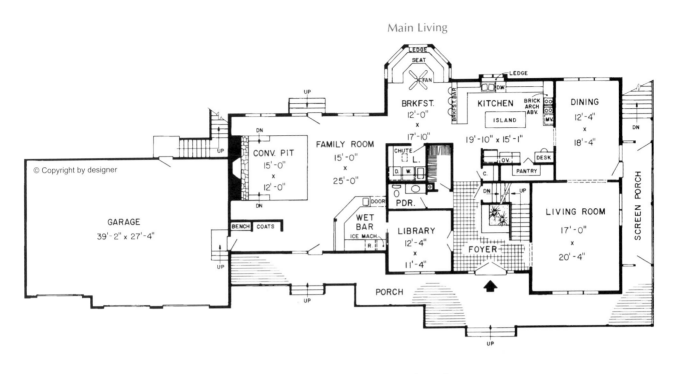

LEDGE
SEAT
FAN

LEDGE

BRKFST.
12'-0"
x
17'-10"

KITCHEN

BRICK
ARCH
ABV.

DINING
12'-4"
x
18'-4"

BRKFST. BAR

DW

ISLAND

19'-10" x 15'-1"

M.V.

UP

UP

DN

CONV. PIT
15'-0"
x
12'-0"

DN

FAMILY ROOM
15'-0"
x
25'-0"

CHUTE   L.
D.   W.

OV.

DESK

PANTRY

C.

SCREEN PORCH

DN

© Copyright by designer

GARAGE
39'-2" x 27'-4"

PDR.

DN

UP

LIVING ROOM
17'-0"
x
20'-4"

BENCH   COATS

WET
BAR
ICE MACH.
R.

DOOR

LIBRARY
12'-4"
x
11'-4"

FOYER

UP

PORCH

UP

UP

2nd Level

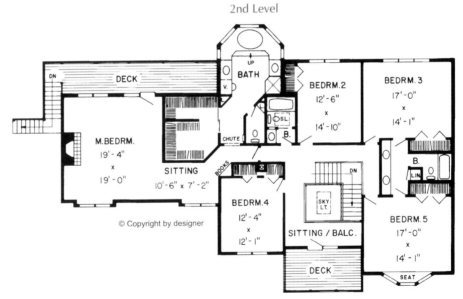

UP

BATH

V.

DN

DECK

BEDRM. 2
12'-6"
x
14'-10"

BEDRM. 3
17'-0"
x
14'-1"

SL.

B.

M. BEDRM.
19'-4"
x
19'-0"

CHUTE

BOOKS

SITTING
10'-6" x 7'-2"

B.
LIN

© Copyright by designer

BEDRM. 4
12'-4"
x
12'-1"

SKY
LT.

DN

BEDRM. 5
17'-0"
x
14'-1"

SITTING / BALC.

DECK

SEAT

This home, as shown, may differ from the original design.

94645-SC Price Code: I

Total Living Area :	3,335 sq.ft.
Main Living :	2,129 sq.ft.
2nd Level :	1,206 sq.ft.
Bedrooms :	4
Bathrooms :	4
Dimensions :	59'-4" x 64'-0"
Garage Type :	Two-car garage
Foundation :	Basement

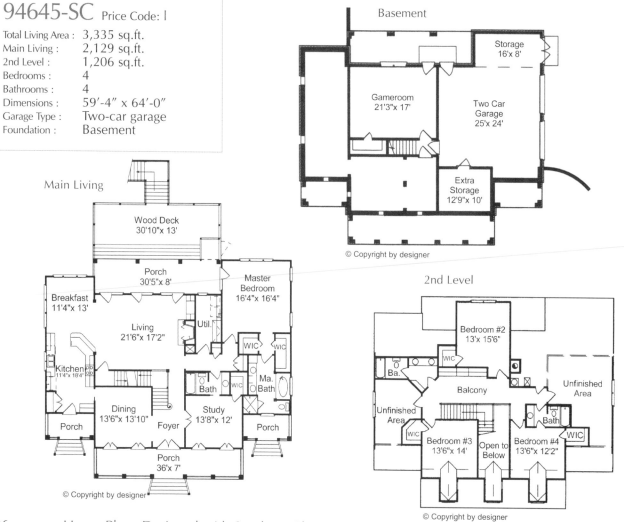

Basement

Storage
16'x 8'

Gameroom
21'3"x 17'

Two Car
Garage
25'x 24'

Extra
Storage
12'9"x 10'

© Copyright by designer

Main Living

Wood Deck
30'10"x 13'

Porch
30'5"x 8'

Master
Bedroom
16'4"x 16'4"

Breakfast
11'4"x 13'

Living
21'6"x 17'2"

Util.

WIC

WIC

Kitchen
11'4"x 18'4"

Bath

WIC

Ma.
Bath

Dining
13'6"x 13'10"

Foyer

Study
13'8"x 12'

Porch

Porch

Porch
36'x 7'

© Copyright by designer

2nd Level

Bedroom #2
13'x 15'6"

Ba.

WIC

Unfinished
Area

Balcony

Unfinished
Area

Unfinished
Area

WIC

Bath

Bedroom #3
13'6"x 14'

Open to
Below

Bedroom #4
13'6"x 12'2"

WIC

© Copyright by designer

This home, as shown, may differ from the original design.

94644-SC Price Code: G

Total Living Area :	2,898 sq.ft.
Main Living :	2,135 sq.ft.
2nd Level :	763 sq.ft.
Bedrooms :	5
Bathrooms :	3
Dimensions :	62'-6" x 70'-0"
Garage Type :	Two-car garage
Foundation :	Crawlspace

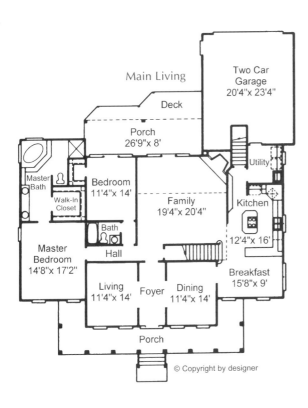

Main Living

Two Car Garage 20'4"x 23'4"

Deck

Porch 26'9"x 8'

Utility

Master Bath

Bedroom 11'4"x 14'

Family 19'4"x 20'4"

Kitchen 12'4"x 16'

Walk-In Closet

Bath

Master Bedroom 14'8"x 17'2"

Hall

Breakfast 15'8"x 9'

Living 11'4"x 14'

Foyer

Dining 11'4"x 14'

Porch

© Copyright by designer

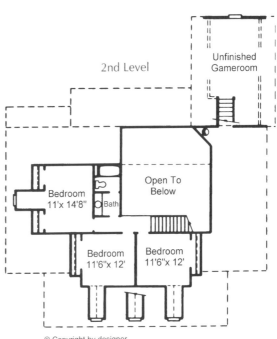

2nd Level

Unfinished Gameroom

Bedroom 11'x 14'8"

Bath

Open To Below

Bedroom 11'6"x 12'

Bedroom 11'6"x 12'

© Copyright by designer

Order Code : **H7SCP**
1-800-235-5700 or
www.familyhomeplans.com

62067-SC Price Code: M

Total Living Area :	4,978 sq.ft.
Basement :	187 sq.ft.
Main Living :	2,944 sq.ft.
2nd Level :	1,847 sq.ft.
Bedrooms :	4
Bathrooms :	5.5
Dimensions :	64'-0" x 88'-0"
Garage Type :	Two-car garage
Foundation :	Walkout Basement

An excellent choice for a sloping lot, this design presents lower level that includes a drive-under garage, expansive storage area, sprawling laundry center and storm shelter. On the main level, a sunroom brightens two adjoining secondary bedrooms.

Order Code : **H7SCP**
1-800-235-5700 or
www.familyhomeplans.com

Main Living

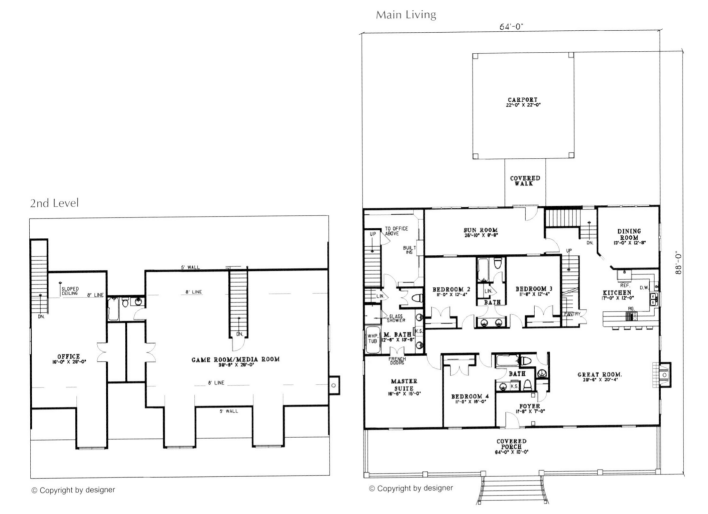

64'-0"

88'-0"

CARPORT
22'-0" X 22'-0"

COVERED WALK

SUN ROOM
26'-10" X 9'-8"

DINING ROOM
13'-0" X 12'-8"

TO OFFICE ABOVE

UP

BUILT INS

DN.

KITCHEN
17'-0" X 12'-0"

REF.

D.W.

RG.

BEDROOM 2
11'-0" X 12'-4"

LIN.

BEDROOM 3
11'-8" X 12'-4"

BATH

LIN.

PANTRY

UP

GLASS SHOWER

WHP. TUB

M. BATH
12'-6" X 13'-8"

K.S.

GREAT ROOM.
28'-6" X 20'-4"

FRENCH DOORS

MASTER SUITE
16'-6" X 15'-0"

BEDROOM 4
11'-0" X 16'-0"

BATH

K.S.

FOYER
11'-8" X 7'-0"

COVERED PORCH
64'-0" X 10'-0"

© Copyright by designer

2nd Level

SLOPED CEILING

8' LINE

5' WALL

8' LINE

8' LINE

DN.

DN.

OFFICE
16'-0" X 28'-0"

GAME ROOM/MEDIA ROOM
38'-8" X 28'-0"

8' LINE

5' WALL

© Copyright by designer

Basement

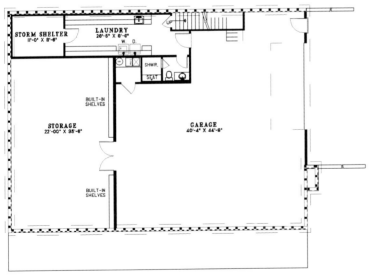

STORM SHELTER
11'-0" X 8'-6"

LAUNDRY
26'-5" X 8'-6"

W. D.

UP

SHWR.

SEAT

BUILT-IN SHELVES

STORAGE
22'-00" X 35'-6"

GARAGE
40'-4" X 44'-8"

BUILT-IN SHELVES

© Copyright by designer

61042-SC Price Code: J

Total Living Area : 3,740 sq.ft.
Main Living : 2,465 sq.ft.
2nd Level : 1,089 sq.ft.
Bedrooms : 4
Bathrooms : 4.5
Dimensions : 92'-5" x 64'-0"
Garage Type : Three-car garage
Foundation : Slab, Crawlspace

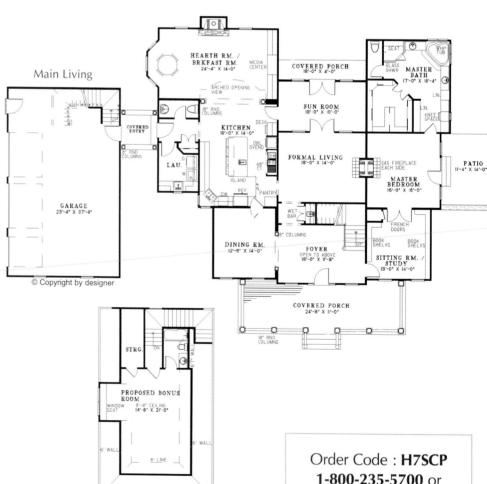

Main Living

© Copyright by designer

2nd Level

© Copyright by designer

PROPOSED BONUS ROOM
8'-0" CEILING
14'-6" X 21'-0"

Order Code : **H7SCP**
1-800-235-5700 or
www.familyhomeplans.com

‿ Home Plans Designed with Southern Charm ‿

99425-SC Price Code: H

Total Living Area : 3,072 sq.ft.
Main Living : 2,116 sq.ft.
2nd Level : 956 sq.ft.
Bedrooms : 4
Bathrooms : 3.5
Dimensions : 67'-8" x 53'-0"
Garage Type : Three-car garage
Foundation : Slab, Basement

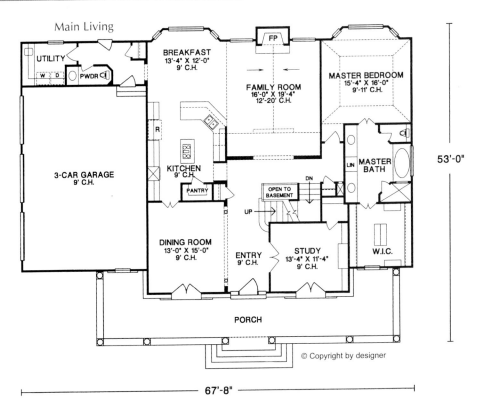

Main Living

UTILITY
W D
PWDR

BREAKFAST
13'-4" X 12'-0"
9' C.H.

FP

FAMILY ROOM
16'-0" X 19'-4"
12'-20' C.H.

MASTER BEDROOM
15'-4" X 16'-0"
9'-11' C.H.

3-CAR GARAGE
9' C.H.

R

KITCHEN
9' C.H.

PANTRY

DN

LIN

MASTER BATH

OPEN TO BASEMENT

UP

DINING ROOM
13'-0" X 15'-0"
9' C.H.

ENTRY
9' C.H.

STUDY
13'-4" X 11'-4"
9' C.H.

W.I.C.

PORCH

53'-0"

67'-8"

© Copyright by designer

2nd Level

SEAT

OPEN TO FAMILY ROOM

BEDROOM 4
13'-4" X 11'-4"
8' C.H.

BALCONY

CLO.

ATTIC

W.I.C.

BATH

W.I.C.

OPEN TO BELOW

DN

BEDROOM 2
13'-0" X 13'-4"
8' C.H.

BEDROOM 3
14'-4" X 11'-4"
8' C.H.

BATH

SEAT

SEAT

SEAT

© Copyright by designer

Order Code : **H7SCP**
1-800-235-5700 or
www.familyhomeplans.com

63360-SC Price Code: K

Total Living Area : 3,855 sq.ft.
Main Living : 2,853 sq.ft.
2nd Level : 1,002 sq.ft.
Bedrooms : 4
Bathrooms : 5
Dimensions : 79'-4" x 64'-8"
Garage Type : Three-car garage
Foundation : Slab

Main Living

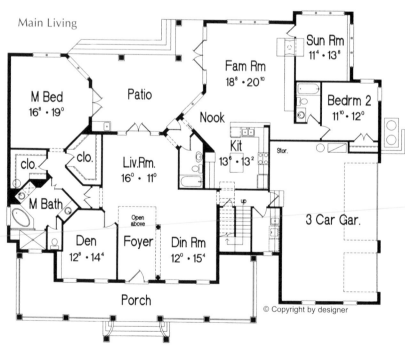

Sun Rm
11⁴ • 13⁸

Fam Rm
18⁸ • 20¹⁰

M Bed
16⁸ • 19⁰

Patio

Nook

Bedrm 2
11¹⁰ • 12⁰

clo.

clo.

Liv.Rm.
16⁰ • 11⁰

Kit
13⁸ • 13²

Stor.

clo.

M Bath

Den
12⁸ • 14⁴

Open
above

Foyer

Din Rm
12⁰ • 15⁴

up

3 Car Gar.

Porch

© Copyright by designer

2nd Level

clo.

Game Rm
23² • 14¹⁰

dn

Bedrm 4
13⁰ • 13⁵

Open to
below

Bedrm 3
13⁰ • 13²

© Copyright by designer

Order Code : H7SCP
1-800-235-5700 or
www.familyhomeplans.com

Southern Style
Front Porches

It's not clear how the front porch entered the landscape of the American South. Some historians point to the porches of West African homes, and to the possibility that the porch may have been imported by African slaves. Others point to the porticos and the piazzas of ancient Greece and Rome, and to the idea that as classical ideals became popular in architecture, the portico and piazza were merely adapted in a uniquely American way. However the porch made its way into the integral architecture of the South, it's obvious why it quickly became a cultural mainstay: the climate.

The hot and muggy conditions of the South, especially during the summer months, almost always made the outdoors more comfortable than a home's interior. Porches provided shade and places from which one might hope to catch a cool breeze. During the other nine months of the year, when the climate is more temperate, porches offered places for the middle and upper classes to spend their leisure time either swaying on a swing, reading, or sewing.

Porches may have been used to socialize with neighbors, but only on a limited scale. In the pre-war Antebellum years, few cities existed in the South. Small farms and plantations dominated the landscape, so connecting with the larger community was not always possible.

Photography © istockphoto.com

Connecting with nature though, was feasible for Southerners of the day—and fashionable. By the mid 1800s, writers and artists promoted the awe and majesty of nature as a reaction to technological advances. It's safe to say that for wealthy, aristocratic Southern families, a stately front porch was yet another status symbol, meant to impress anyone who might catch a view of it. Some families also may have hoped to give the impression that they appreciated and valued the natural surroundings, as well. Regardless of the desire for good impressions, these families—like Southern families of all means—likely succumbed to the summer's unbearable heat and humidity, escaping to their front porches in the hope of seizing any light breeze that might come along.

62104-SC Price Code: H

Total Living Area : 3,002 sq.ft.
Main Living : 1,733 sq.ft.
2nd Level : 1,269 sq.ft.
Bedrooms : 4
Bathrooms : 3
Dimensions : 50'-0" x 50'-0"
Garage Type : Two-car garage
Foundation : Slab, Crawlspace

Main Living

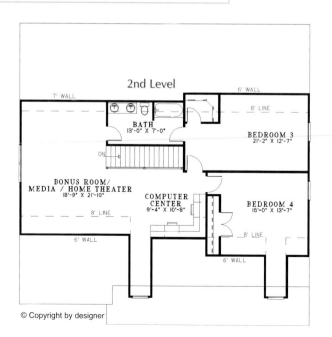

Order Code : **H7SCP**
1-800-235-5700 or
www.familyhomeplans.com

Home Plans Designed with Southern Charm

Main Living

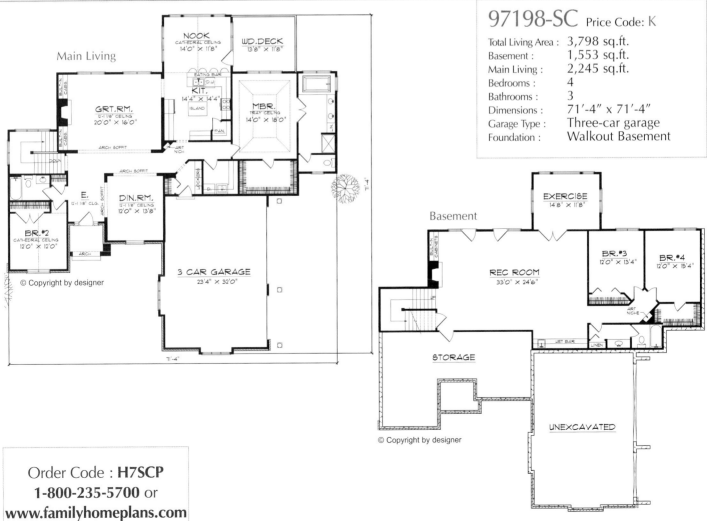

NOOK
CATHEDRAL CEILING
14'0" × 11'8"

WD. DECK
13'8" × 11'8"

EATING BAR

KIT.
14'4" × 14'4"

ISLAND

GRT. RM.
12'-1 1/8" CEILING
20'0" × 16'0"

MBR.
TRAY CEILING
14'0" × 18'0"

ARCH SOFFIT

PAN.

BUILT-IN CABS

ARCH SOFFIT

ART NICH

DOWN

E.
12'-1 1/8" CLG.

DIN. RM.
12'-1 1/8" CEILING
12'0" × 13'8"

ARCH SOFFIT

BR. #2
CATHEDRAL CEILING
12'0" × 12'0"

ARCH

3 CAR GARAGE
23'4" × 32'0"

© Copyright by designer

71'-4"

71'-4"

97198-SC Price Code: K

Total Living Area :	3,798 sq.ft.
Basement :	1,553 sq.ft.
Main Living :	2,245 sq.ft.
Bedrooms :	4
Bathrooms :	3
Dimensions :	71'-4" x 71'-4"
Garage Type :	Three-car garage
Foundation :	Walkout Basement

Basement

EXERCISE
14'8" × 11'8"

REC ROOM
33'0" × 24'6"

BUILT-IN CABINETS

BR. #3
12'0" × 13'4"

BR. #4
12'0" × 15'4"

ART NICHE

JET BAR

LINEN

STORAGE

UNEXCAVATED

© Copyright by designer

62297-SC Price Code: I

Total Living Area : 3,419 sq.ft.
Main Living : 2,607 sq.ft.
2nd Level : 812 sq.ft.
Bedrooms : 5
Bathrooms : 5
Dimensions : 72'-10" x 69'-10"
Garage Type : Three-car garage
Foundation : Basement*, Crawlspace, Slab, Walkout Basement*

Main Living

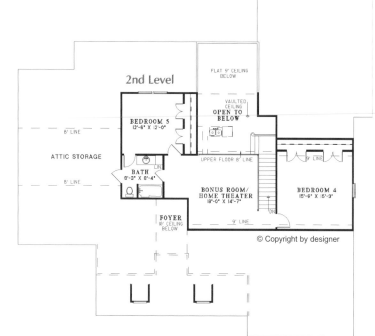

2nd Level

© Copyright by designer

Order Code : **H7SCP**
1-800-235-5700 or
www.familyhomeplans.com

62094-SC Price Code: H

Total Living Area : 3,060 sq.ft.
Main Living : 2,204 sq.ft.
2nd Level : 856 sq.ft.
Bedrooms : 3
Bathrooms : 2.5
Dimensions : 83'-4" x 70'-0"
Garage Type : Two-car garage
Foundation : Slab, Crawlspace

83'-4"

77'-0"

GARAGE
22'-0" X 29'-4"

Main Living

SEAT
GLASS
SHWR
WHP
TUB
M.BATH
17'-8" X 14'-6"

GRILLING PORCH
40'-0" X 17'-0"

8" COLUMNS

LIN.

MASTER SUITE
17'-8" X 15'-6"

LAU.
8'-4" X 9'-8"

HEARTH ROOM
15'-0" X 20'-0"

BREAKFAST
AREA
12'-2" X 10'-0"

DINING
16'-0" X 10'-0"

PANTRY

OPTIONAL
BASEMENT
STAIRS

WOOD
BOX

© Copyright by designer

D W

FRENCH
DOORS

KITCHEN
14'-6" X 10'-0"

DW

REF

MW
OVEN

UP

GREAT RM.
16'-0" X 19'-2"

BUILT-INS

STUDY
15'-0" X 9'-0"

FOYER
13'-0" X 6'-0"

7' COVERED
PORCH

8" COLUMNS

2nd Level

SLOPED CEILING
STORAGE

LOFT
17'-6" X 10'-4"

SLOPED CEILING
STORAGE

8" WALL

DN

BEDROOM 3
16'-6" X 13'-0"

BEDROOM 2
15'-0" X 13'-0"

COMPUTER
CENTER

BATH
9'-10" X
14'-2"

COMPUTER
CENTER

8" CEILING LINE

6'8" WALL

© Copyright by designer

Order Code : **H7SCP**
1-800-235-5700 or
www.familyhomeplans.com

Country
Charm

The living room's fireplace and built-in display cabinets provide an added sense of warmth to an already comfortable space.

This home, as shown, may differ from the original design.

This home, as shown, may differ from the original design.

This relaxed country-style retreat offers plenty of space to unwind, both inside and out. Eight-foot-deep covered front porches on the front and sides expand the home's living space to the outdoors. A sprawling screened porch continues the theme, with access from the living room, dining room, breakfast area and sun room. Inside the home, open interaction between the kitchen, living room and dining room creates a friendly atmosphere. The master suite is positioned for privacy at the rear of the home and is enhanced by a sunny sitting area and exercise room. Secondary sleeping quarters each have access to their own baths. The semi-detached garage even includes a separate bay for a golf cart.

Long, shaded views from within the side covered porch.

Views to the screened in porch enhance the dining room's sense of openness.

ABOVE: A view from the breakfast area into the kitchen. A large island and generous counters provide ample workspace.

LEFT: On the side of the home, a long covered porch joins a screened porch and sunroom to blur the lines between indoor and outdoor living.

Photo Courtesy of The Designer

Main Living

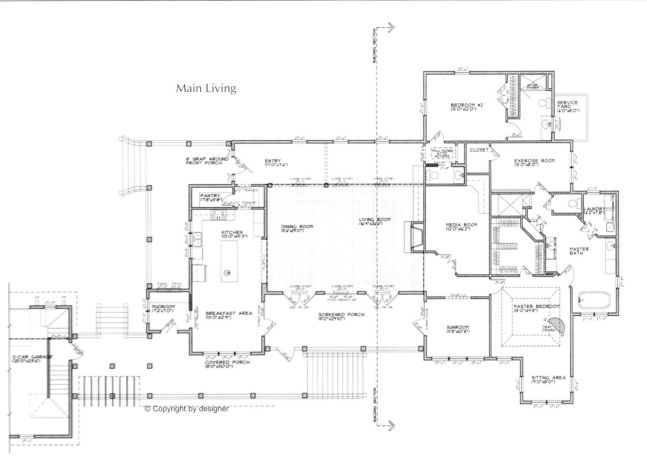

© Copyright by designer

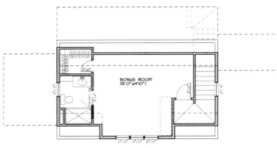

GARAGE
SECOND FLOOR PLAN

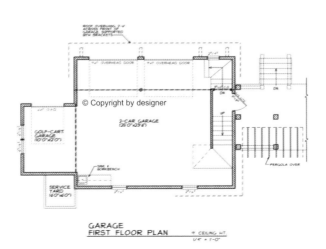

© Copyright by designer

GARAGE
FIRST FLOOR PLAN

45666-SC Price Code: H

Total Living Area:	3,092 sq.ft.
Main Living:	3,092 sq.ft.
Bedrooms:	2
Bathrooms:	2.5
Dimensions:	66'-6" x 142'-8"
Garage Type:	Two-car garage
Foundation:	Crawlspace

Order Code : **H7SCP**
1-800-235-5700 or
www.familyhomeplans.com

96881-SC Price Code: I

Total Living Area : 3,464 sq.ft.
Main Living : 1,874 sq.ft.
2nd Level : 1,590 sq.ft.
Bedrooms : 5
Bathrooms : 2.5
Dimensions : 78'-0" x 61'-0"
Garage Type : Two-car garage
Foundation : Basement, Slab,
Crawlspace

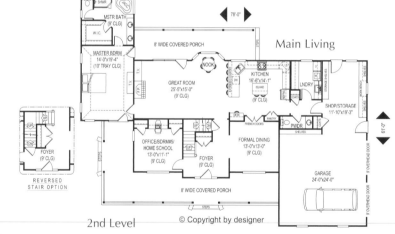

Main Living

MSTR BATH
(9' CLG)
W.I.C.

8' WIDE COVERED PORCH

MASTER BDRM
14'-0"x19'-4"
(10' TRAY CLG)

NOOK

KITCHEN
16'-8"x14'-1"
ISLAND
(9' CLG)

LNDRY

STORAGE SHELVES

SHOP/STORAGE
11'-10"x19'-3"

GREAT ROOM
25'-5"x15'-0"
(9' CLG)

FOYER
(9' CLG)

REVERSED
STAIR OPTION

OFFICE/BDRM#5/
HOME SCHOOL
13'-0"x11'-1"
(9' CLG)

FOYER
(9' CLG)

FRENCH DOORS

PANTRY

PWDR

SHELVES

FORMAL DINING
13'-0"x13'-0"
(9' CLG)

GARAGE
24'-0"x24'-0"

8' WIDE COVERED PORCH

STEPS

© Copyright by designer

2nd Level

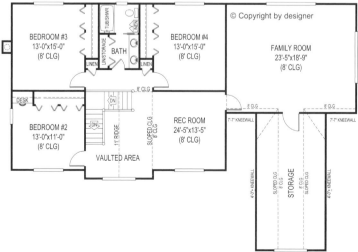

© Copyright by designer

BEDROOM #3
13'-0"x15'-0"
(8' CLG)

TUB/SHWR

LINEN

BATH

BEDROOM #4
13'-0"x15'-0"
(8' CLG)

FAMILY ROOM
23'-5"x18'-9"
(8' CLG)

DESK

BEDROOM #2
13'-0"x11'-0"
(8' CLG)

DN

11' RIDGE

SLOPED CLG
8' CLG

REC ROOM
24'-5"x13'-5"
(8' CLG)

8' CLG

8' CLG

7'-7" KNEEWALL

7'-7" KNEEWALL

VAULTED AREA

STORAGE

SLOPED CLG
8' CLG

SLOPED CLG
8' CLG

4'-0" KNEEWALL

4'-0" KNEEWALL

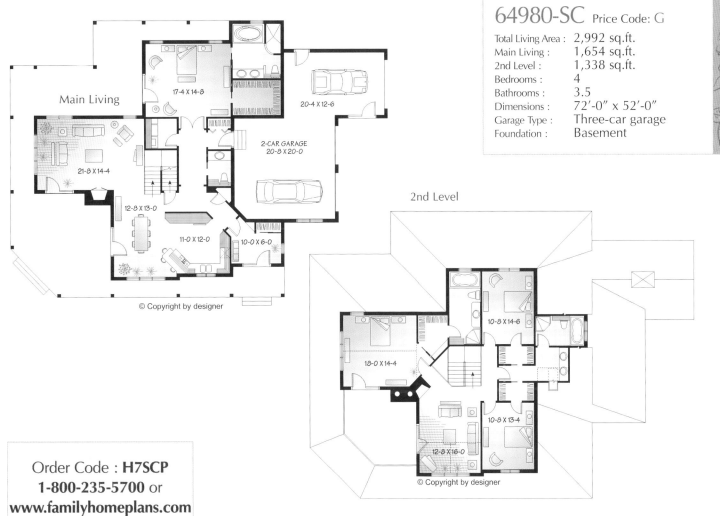

Main Living

17-4 X 14-8

20-4 12-6

2-CAR GARAGE
20-8 X 20-0

21-8 X 14-4

12-8 X 13-0

11-0 X 12-0

10-0 X 6-0

© Copyright by designer

64980-SC Price Code: G

Total Living Area :	2,992 sq.ft.
Main Living :	1,654 sq.ft.
2nd Level :	1,338 sq.ft.
Bedrooms :	4
Bathrooms :	3.5
Dimensions :	72'-0" x 52'-0"
Garage Type :	Three-car garage
Foundation :	Basement

2nd Level

10-8 X 14-6

18-0 X 14-4

10-8 X 13-4

12-8 X 16-0

© Copyright by designer

Order Code : **H7SCP**
1-800-235-5700 or
www.familyhomeplans.com

97397-SC Price Code: K

Total Living Area :	3,909 sq.ft.
Main Living :	1,854 sq.ft.
2nd Level :	2,055 sq.ft.
Bedrooms :	4
Bathrooms :	4
Dimensions :	65'-0" x 58'-0"
Garage Type :	Three-car garage
Foundation :	Walkout Basement

An enormous lower-level rec room, with fireplace and adjacent wet bar, becomes a modern-day ballroom or secluded get-away space. On the main floor, the kitchen, hearth room, dining room and great room all flow together seamlessly.

Order Code : **H7SCP**
1-800-235-5700 or
www.familyhomeplans.com

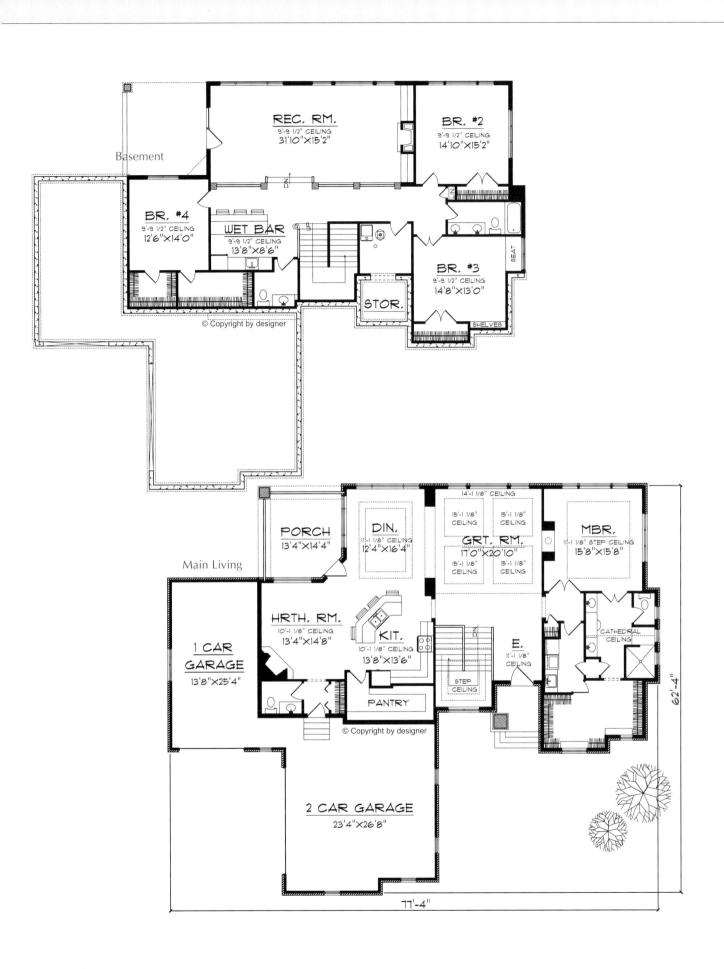

Basement

REC. RM.
9'-9 1/2" CEILING
31'10"X15'2"

BR. #2
9'-9 1/2" CEILING
14'10"X15'2"

BR. #4
9'-9 1/2" CEILING
12'6"X14'0"

WET BAR
9'-9 1/2" CEILING
13'8"X8'6"

BR. #3
9'-9 1/2" CEILING
14'8"X13'0"

STOR.

SHELVES

© Copyright by designer

Main Living

PORCH
13'4"X14'4"

DIN.
11'-1 1/8" CEILING
12'4"X16'4"

14'-1 1/8" CEILING

15'-1 1/8" CEILING

15'-1 1/8" CEILING

GRT. RM.
17'0"X20'10"

15'-1 1/8" CEILING

15'-1 1/8" CEILING

MBR.
11'-1 1/8" STEP CEILING
15'8"X15'8"

1 CAR GARAGE
13'8"X25'4"

HRTH. RM.
10'-1 1/8" CEILING
13'4"X14'8"

KIT.
10'-1 1/8" CEILING
13'8"X13'6"

E.
11'-1 1/8" CEILING

CATHEDRAL CEILING

PANTRY

STEP CEILING

© Copyright by designer

2 CAR GARAGE
23'4"X26'8"

77'-4"

62'-4"

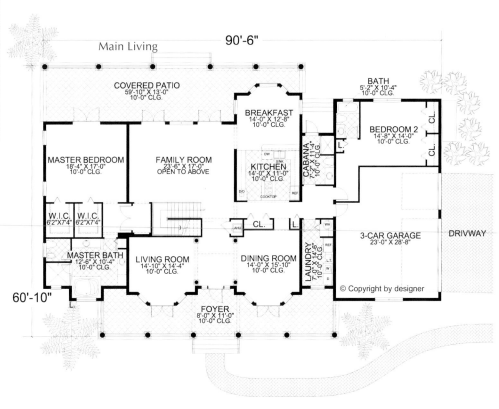

55739-SC Price Code: J

Total Living Area : 3,715 sq.ft.
Main Living : 3,026 sq.ft.
2nd Level : 689 sq.ft.
Bedrooms : 4
Bathrooms : 4
Dimensions : 81'-0" x 61'-0"
Garage Type : Two-car garage
Foundation : Slab

2nd Level

BATH
8'-0" X 7'-0"
8'-0" CLG.

W.I.C.
6' X 7'

W.I.C.
4'10"X7'

BEDROOM 3
14'-10" X 12'-0"
8'-0" CLG.

BEDROOM 4
14'-10" X 12'-0"
8'-0" CLG.

© Copyright by designer

Main Living

90'-6"

COVERED PATIO
59'-10" X 13'-0"
10'-0" CLG.

BREAKFAST
14'-0" X 12'-8"
10'-0" CLG.

BATH
5'-2" X 10'-4"
10'-0" CLG.

BEDROOM 2
14'-8" X 14'-0"
10'-0" CLG.

MASTER BEDROOM
18'-4" X 17'-0"
10'-0" CLG.

FAMILY ROOM
23'-6" X 17'-0"
OPEN TO ABOVE

KITCHEN
14'-0" X 11'-0"
10'-0" CLG.

CABANA
7'-2" X 11'-4"
10'-0" CLG.

W.I.C.
6'2"X7'4"

W.I.C.
6'2"X7'4"

MASTER BATH
12'-6" X 10'-4"
10'-0" CLG.

LIVING ROOM
14'-10" X 14'-4"
10'-0" CLG.

DINING ROOM
14'-0" X 15'-10"
10'-0" CLG.

LAUNDRY
7'-0" X 14'-6"
10'-0" CLG.

3-CAR GARAGE
23'-0" X 28'-8"

DRIVWAY

60'-10"

FOYER
8'-0" X 11'-0"
10'-0" CLG.

© Copyright by designer

Order Code : **H7SCP**
1-800-235-5700 or
www.familyhomeplans.com

96818-SC Price Code: I

Total Living Area :	3,272 sq.ft.
Main Living :	2,039 sq.ft.
2nd Level :	1,233 sq.ft.
Bedrooms :	4
Bathrooms :	4
Dimensions :	74'-2" x 49'-0"
Garage Type :	Two-car garage
Foundation :	Basement, Slab, Crawlspace

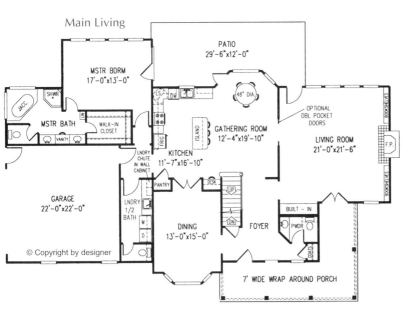

Main Living

PATIO
29'-6"x12'-0"

MSTR BDRM
17'-0"x13'-0"

JACC.   SHWR

MSTR BATH

WALK-IN CLOSET

VANITY

LNDRY CHUTE IN WALL CABINET

KITCHEN
11'-7"x16'-10"

ISLAND

48" DIA.

GATHERING ROOM
12'-4"x19'-10"

OPTIONAL DBL POCKET DOORS

LIVING ROOM
21'-0"x21'-6"

BOOKSHELVES

F.P.

GARAGE
22'-0"x22'-0"

PANTRY   DESK   UP

DN

LNDRY 1/2 BATH
W   D

DINING
13'-0"x15'-0"

FOYER

BUILT - IN

PWDR

COATS

© Copyright by designer

7' WIDE WRAP AROUND PORCH

2nd Level

60" KNEEWALL

BEDROOM #4
11'-9"x12'-6"

BATH

BEDROOM #3
12'-11"x12'-6"

WALK-IN CLOSET

WALK-IN CLOSET

36"x72"

FUTURE
21'-8"X17'-3"
(UNFINISHED)

LAUNDRY CHUTE

BATH

8'-0" CLG
SLOPED CLG

STORAGE   STORAGE   LINEN

WALK-IN CLOSET

60" KNEEWALL

BEDROOM #2
13'-0"x15'-6"

DN

REC AREA
14'-5"x14'-1"

© Copyright by designer

44083-SC · Price Code: H

Total Living Area :	3,142 sq.ft.
Main Living :	2,168 sq.ft.
2nd Level :	985 sq.ft.
Bedrooms :	4
Bathrooms :	2 Fulls, One 3/4, One 1/2
Dimensions :	90'-8" x 50'-10"
Garage Type :	Three-car garage
Foundation :	Basement, Slab*, Crawlspace*

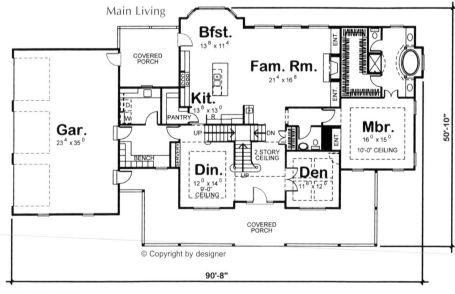

Main Living

Bfst.
13⁸ x 11⁴

COVERED PORCH

Fam. Rm.
21⁴ x 16⁸

Kit.
13⁸ x 13⁰

PANTRY

Gar.
23⁴ x 35⁰

Mbr.
16⁰ x 15⁰
10'-0" CEILING

UP

DN

2 STORY CEILING

BENCH

SERVERY

Din.
12⁰ x 14⁰
9'-0" CEILING

UP

Den
11⁸ x 12⁰

ENT.

50'-10"

COVERED PORCH

© Copyright by designer

90'-8"

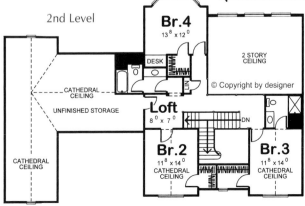

2nd Level

Br.4
13⁸ x 12⁰

DESK

2 STORY CEILING

CATHEDRAL CEILING

UNFINISHED STORAGE

© Copyright by designer

Loft
8⁰ x 7⁰

DN

CATHEDRAL CEILING

Br.2
11⁸ x 14⁰
CATHEDRAL CEILING

Br.3
11⁸ x 14⁰
CATHEDRAL CEILING

Order Code : **H7SCP**
1-800-235-5700 or
www.familyhomeplans.com

Main Living

69'-0"

37'-0"

Patio

Kit
12-0x14-10

Brkfst
12-0x12-7

Util
6-0x
12-9

D
W

R
P

Family
15-4x20-10

Dn

Garage
20-4x33-4

Dining
18-6x12-0

Entry

Up

Living
15-4x15-0

Porch depth 5-0

© Copyright by designer

87315-SC Price Code: G

Total Living Area :	2,967 sq.ft.
Main Living :	1,450 sq.ft.
2nd Level :	1,517 sq.ft.
Bedrooms :	4
Bathrooms :	3.5
Dimensions :	69'-0" x 37'-0"
Garage Type :	Three-car garage
Foundation :	Basement

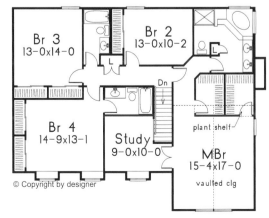

2nd Level

Br 3
13-0x14-0

L

Br 2
13-0x10-2

L

Dn

Br 4
14-9x13-1

Study
9-0x10-0

plant shelf

MBr
15-4x17-0

vaulted clg

© Copyright by designer

87400-SC Price Code: H

Total Living Area : 3,135 sq.ft.
Main Living : 3,135 sq.ft.
Bedrooms : 3
Bathrooms : 2.5
Dimensions : 108'-0" x 96'-0"
Garage Type : Three-car garage
Foundation : Crawlspace

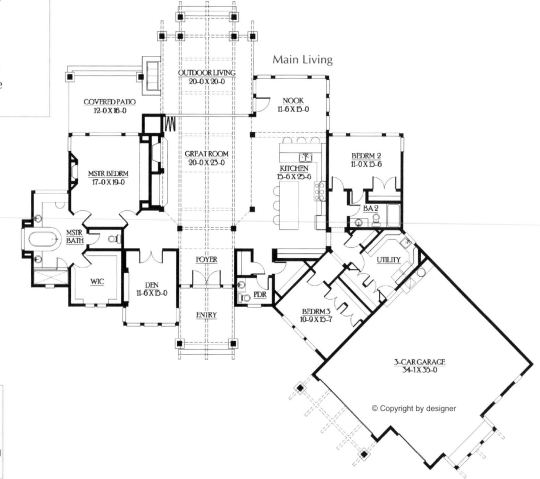

Main Living

OUTDOOR LIVING
20-0 X 20-0

COVERED PATIO
12-0 X 16-0

NOOK
11-6 X 15-0

GREAT ROOM
20-0 X 23-0

KITCHEN
15-6 X 25-6

BEDRM 2
11-0 X 15-6

MSTR BEDRM
17-0 X 19-0

BA 2

MSTR BATH

FOYER

UTILITY

WIC

DEN
11-6 X 15-0

PDR

ENTRY

BEDRM 3
10-9 X 15-7

3-CAR GARAGE
34-1 X 35-0

© Copyright by designer

Order Code : **H7SCP**
1-800-235-5700 or
www.familyhomeplans.com

Southern Style
Gas Lighting

Alongside the hallmark architectural features of Antebellum architecture was an invention that greatly contributed toward comfort in the Southern home—gas lighting. Gas lights adorned Southern homes from the height of their popularity in the 1850s through the turn of the 20th century. In 1792, Scottish engineer and inventor, William Murdoch, was the first to channel the flammability of gas for use in light fixtures. The considerable light output of gas lighting compared to oil lamps and candles quickly made it a popular option for lighting streets and factories. Gas lighting spread more slowly into residential use because of the lack of gas supply, infrastructure, and technical difficulties with the lamps. Yet, as more and more gas companies came into being, and products improved, gas lighting was common in European homes by the 1850s.

It didn't take long for gas lighting to spread to the United States. In 1817, Baltimore, Maryland was the first U.S. city to light its streets using gas. Gas light production began in the United States in the 1830s. By the 1850s local legislatures began widespread issuing of charters for local gas companies. By the turn of the 20th Century, gas lighting was the most common form of lighting for homes in the United States.

Beautifully delicate and elegant lights in Victorian, Colonial, and Classical styles characterize the light fixtures of the time. An owner's wealth and status would have determined the styles of fixtures located throughout the Southern home. Dining rooms, par-

Photo Courtesy of Carolina Lanterns

lors, and entrances—rooms where visitors were greeted—would have contained the most expensive and elaborate fixtures. Gas lamps also enhanced evening and twilight socialization, both out on the porch and inside the home, according to Jan Clouse, of Carolina Lanterns, a company specializing in reproduction gas lanterns based in Charleston, South Carolina.

Gas lighting flourished until the 1930s when electric lighting became the preferred option. Yet, gas lighting did not disappear altogether. Many neighborhoods in southern cities, such as Charleston, South Carolina and New Orleans, Louisiana, still use gas lighting to create a nostalgic effect. With its flickering flame and soft glow, gas lights create an atmosphere similar to lit candles and are appropriate anywhere people desire an authentic historical feel.

53784-SC Price Code: L

Total Living Area :	4,320 sq.ft.
Main Living :	2,630 sq.ft.
2nd Level :	1,690 sq.ft.
Bedrooms :	4
Bathrooms :	3.5
Dimensions :	80'-0" x 80'-0"
Garage Type :	Three-car garage
Foundation :	Crawlspace

This design's tasteful symmetry is enlivened by a detached single-car garage, which creates a smart arrangement for auto storage, and/or a studio/workshop. A comfortable, yet appropriately formal layout of rooms enhances this designs versatility for family living and entertaining.

Order Code : **H7SCP**
1-800-235-5700 or
www.familyhomeplans.com

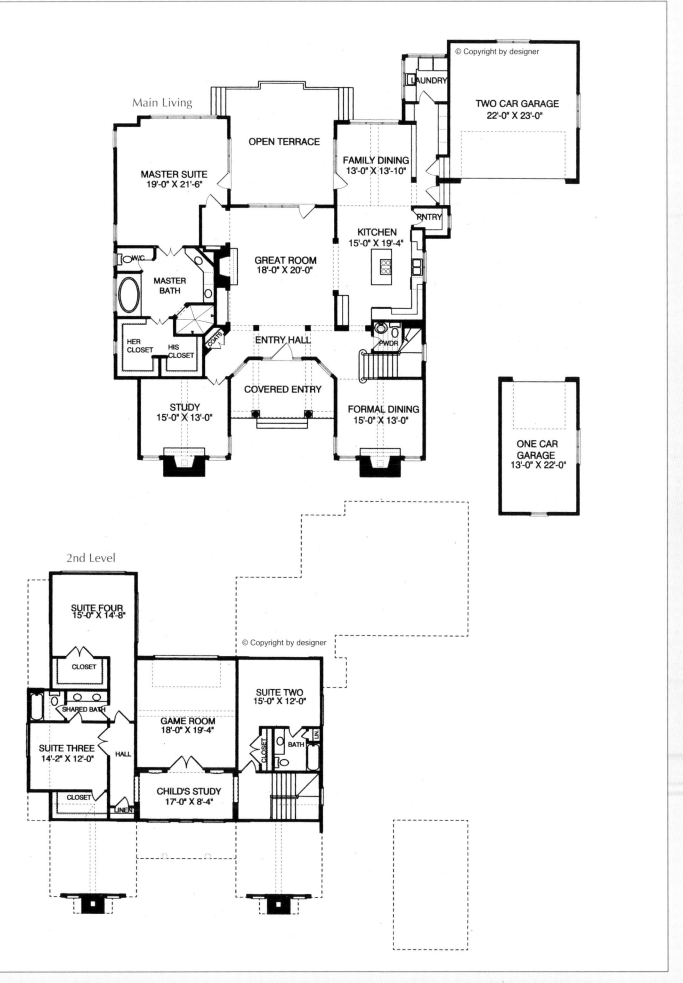

Main Living

MASTER SUITE
19'-0" X 21'-6"

OPEN TERRACE

FAMILY DINING
13'-0" X 13'-10"

© Copyright by designer

TWO CAR GARAGE
22'-0" X 23'-0"

LAUNDRY

W/C

MASTER
BATH

GREAT ROOM
18'-0" X 20'-0"

KITCHEN
15'-0" X 19'-4"

RNTRY

HER
CLOSET

HIS
CLOSET

COATS

ENTRY HALL

PWDR

STUDY
15'-0" X 13'-0"

COVERED ENTRY

FORMAL DINING
15'-0" X 13'-0"

ONE CAR
GARAGE
13'-0" X 22'-0"

2nd Level

SUITE FOUR
15'-0" X 14'-8"

CLOSET

© Copyright by designer

SUITE TWO
15'-0" X 12'-0"

SHARED BATH

GAME ROOM
18'-0" X 19'-4"

SUITE THREE
14'-2" X 12'-0"

HALL

CLOSET

BATH

LIN

CLOSET

CHILD'S STUDY
17'-0" X 8'-4"

LINEN

50053-SC Price Code: F

Total Living Area :	2,524 sq.ft.
Main Living :	1,722 sq.ft.
2nd Level :	802 sq.ft.
Bedrooms :	4
Bathrooms :	2.5
Dimensions :	56'-8" x 55'-6"
Garage Type :	Two-car garage
Foundation :	Basement

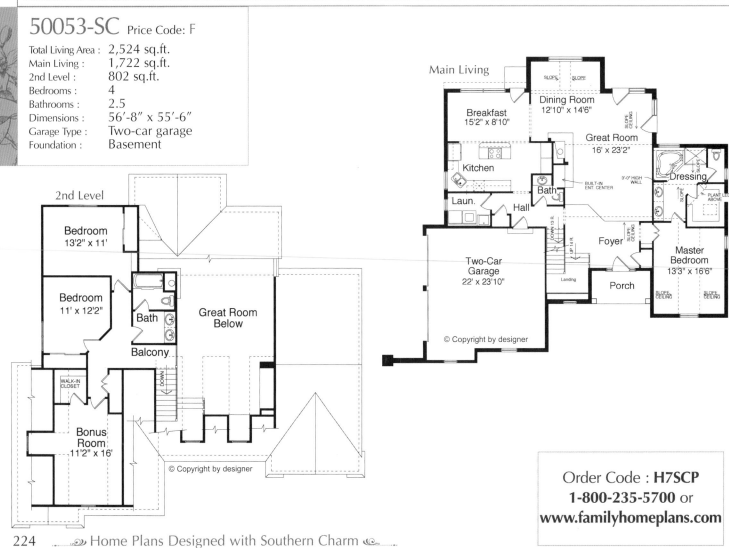

2nd Level

Bedroom 13'2" x 11'

Bedroom 11' x 12'2"

Bath

Great Room Below

Balcony

WALK-IN CLOSET

DOWN

Bonus Room 11'2" x 16'

© Copyright by designer

Main Living

Dining Room 12'10" x 14'6"

Breakfast 15'2" x 8'10"

SLOPE SLOPE

SLOPE CEILING

Great Room 16' x 23'2"

Kitchen

BUILT-IN ENT. CENTER

3'-0" HIGH WALL

Dressing

Bath

SLOPE

PLANT LEDGE ABOVE

Laun.

Hall

DOWN 13 R.

UP 14 R.

Foyer

SLOPE CEILING

Master Bedroom 13'3" x 16'6"

Two-Car Garage 22' x 23'10"

Landing

Porch

SLOPE CEILING

SLOPE CEILING

© Copyright by designer

87314-SC Price Code: H

Total Living Area : 3,138 sq.ft.
Main Living : 1,958 sq.ft.
2nd Level : 1,180 sq.ft.
Bedrooms : 4
Bathrooms : 3.5
Dimensions : 54'-0" x 57'-4"
Garage Type : Two-car garage
Foundation : Basement

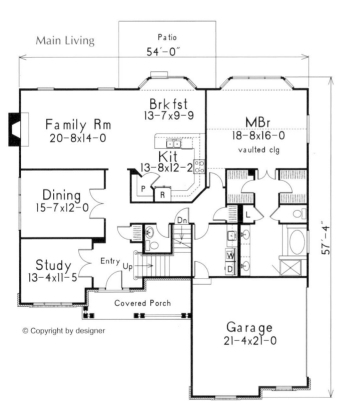

Main Living

Patio
54'-0"

Family Rm
20-8x14-0

Brkfst
13-7x9-9

MBr
18-8x16-0
vaulted clg

Kit
13-8x12-2

Dining
15-7x12-0

P   R

Dn

Study
13-4x11-5

Entry   Up

Covered Porch

Garage
21-4x21-0

57'-4"

© Copyright by designer

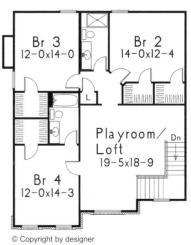

2nd Level

Br 3
12-0x14-0

Br 2
14-0x12-4

L

Playroom/
Loft
19-5x18-9

Dn

Br 4
12-0x14-3

© Copyright by designer

24800-SC Price Code: M

Total Living Area :	4,836 sq.ft.
Basement :	1,584 sq.ft.
Main Living :	1,615 sq.ft.
2nd Level :	1,637 sq.ft.
Bedrooms :	5
Bathrooms :	3
Dimensions :	74'-0" x 40'-0"
Garage Type :	Three-car garage
Foundation :	Basement

This design is charmingly Victorian, yet more than

accommodating to current-day lifestyles. Main living spaces flow seamlessly from one to another, while a sensible area just inside the garage provides space to intercept backpacks, jackets and muddy shoes.

Order Code : **H7SCP**
1-800-235-5700 or
www.familyhomeplans.com

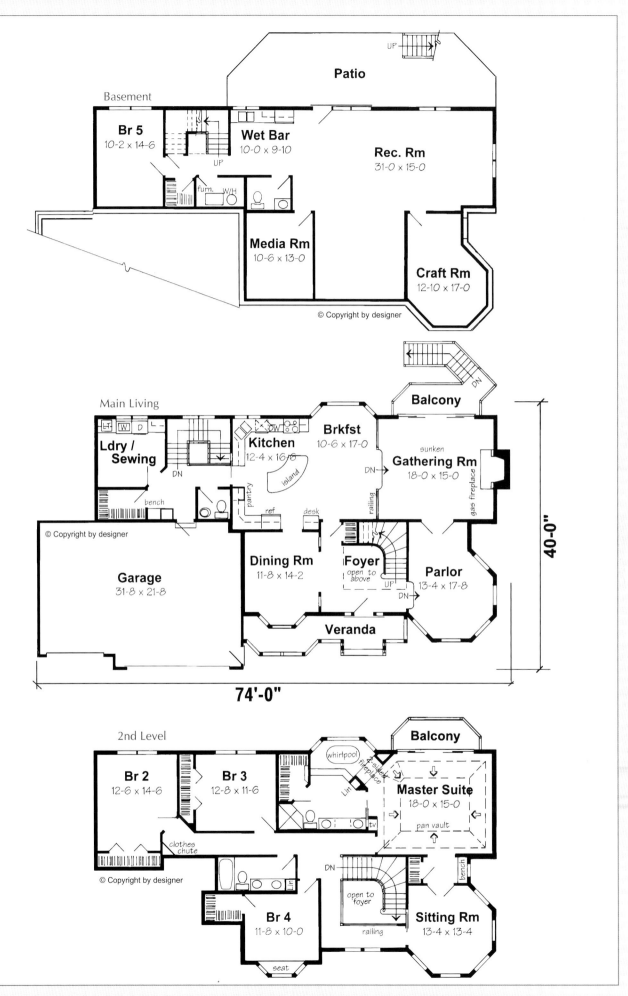

Patio

Basement

Br 5
10-2 x 14-6

UP

Wet Bar
10-0 x 9-10

furn.   W/H

Rec. Rm
31-0 x 15-0

Media Rm
10-6 x 13-0

Craft Rm
12-10 x 17-0

© Copyright by designer

DN

Main Living

Ldry / Sewing

W   D

DN

bench

© Copyright by designer

Kitchen
12-4 x 16-6

island

Brkfst
10-6 x 17-0

Balcony

sunken

Gathering Rm
18-0 x 15-0

DN

gas fireplace

pantry

ref   desk

railing

Dining Rm
11-8 x 14-2

Foyer
open to above

UP

DN

Parlor
13-4 x 17-8

Garage
31-8 x 21-8

Veranda

40'-0"

74'-0"

2nd Level

Br 2
12-6 x 14-6

Br 3
12-8 x 11-6

whirlpool

fireplace

Lin

Balcony

Master Suite
18-0 x 15-0

pan vault

clothes chute

© Copyright by designer

tv

Br 4
11-8 x 10-0

DN

open to foyer

railing

bench

Sitting Rm
13-4 x 13-4

seat

63077-SC Price Code: M

Total Living Area :	4,725 sq.ft.
Main Living :	2,963 sq.ft.
2nd Level :	1,762 sq.ft.
Bedrooms :	4
Bathrooms :	4
Dimensions :	77'-0" x 100'-10"
Garage Type :	Three-car garage
Foundation :	Slab

Authentic Victorian details define the character of this charming design. Just inside, an octagonal music room greets guests. Opposite the music room, a two-story library is appointed to impress with its spiral staircase and upper-level study.

Order Code : **H7SCP**
1-800-235-5700 or
www.familyhomeplans.com

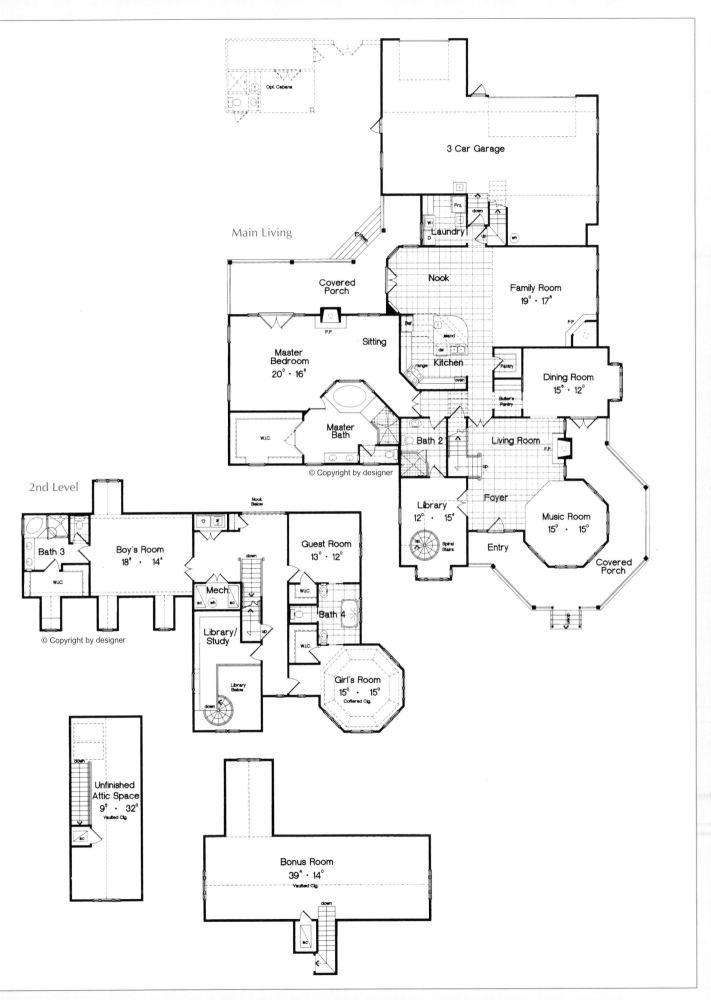

Opt. Cabana

3 Car Garage

Main Living

Laundry

Nook

Family Room
19⁰ · 17⁸

Covered
Porch

F.P.

Sitting

Kitchen

Island

range

oven

Pantry

Butler's Pantry

Dining Room
15⁸ · 12⁰

Master
Bedroom
20⁰ · 16⁸

Master
Bath

W.I.C.

Bath 2

Living Room

F.P.

© Copyright by designer

Foyer

Library
12⁰ · 15⁴

Music Room
15⁰ · 15⁰

Spiral
Stairs

Entry

Covered
Porch

2nd Level

Bath 3

W.I.C.

Boy's Room
18⁸ · 14⁴

Nook
Below

Mech

Guest Room
13⁰ · 12⁰

W.I.C.

Bath 4

W.I.C.

© Copyright by designer

Library/
Study

Library
Below

down

Girl's Room
15⁰ · 15⁰
Coffered Clg.

down

Unfinished
Attic Space
9⁰ · 32⁰
Vaulted Clg.

sc

Bonus Room
39⁴ · 14⁰
Vaulted Clg.

down

sc

Other Favorites from Garlinghouse

America's First and Oldest Publisher of Home Plan Books.

BUILDERS' FIRST-CHOICE HOME PLANS

A specially selected collection of 200 home designs favored by homebuilders from coast to coast. Special features include helpful information on Selecting a Builder, Choosing a Neighborhood, High-Performance Windows, Energy-Efficient Doors and Being Well Insulated. A special presentation features plans for popular backyard projects such as decks, sheds, garages, gazebos, arbors, playhouses, porches, additions and more.

$12.95 US $14.95 CAN

THE BEST OF COOLHOUSEPLANS.COM

COOLhouseplans.com is one of the most popular home plan sites on the Internet. This book offers the time-saving benefit of a pre-selection of the web site's best-selling home designs from North America's top residential architects and designers. Full-color presentations of 275 thoughtful floor plans and enticing elevations are enhanced by helpful "COOL Tips" to help you better understand special design features.

$12.95 US $14.95 CAN

THE BEST BABY BOOMER HOME PLANS

Baby Boomers seeking peace and quiet from their lively teenagers will appreciate this book as much as empty-nesters who wish to enjoy day-to-day living on one, comfortable level. 300 home plans feature a main floor location for the master suite. In addition, illustrated highlights offer practical insights, such as Choosing a Building Site, Recognizing Well-Designed Floor Plan Layouts, Designing for Privacy, and much more.

$12.95 US $14.95 CAN

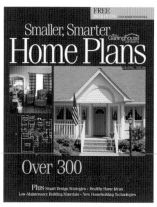

SMALLER, SMARTER HOME PLANS

With today's limitations on available building sites, this book offers over 300 space-saving designs that don't sacrifice on style or functionality. Discover insights on the makings of a healthy home, as well as the latest advance-ments in homebuilding materials and technologies. A valuable resource for homebuyers considering an "in-fill" lot, or for anyone wanting a beautiful, yet smaller home of less than 2,500 sq. ft.

$12.95 US $14.95 CAN

TO ORDER CALL 1.800.235.5700

the Garlinghouse company

HELPING TO BUILD DREAMS SINCE 1907

Discover more home plan books from Garlinghouse by visiting us online at **www.familyhomeplans.com**.

IMPORTANT INFORMATION
to make your dream come true

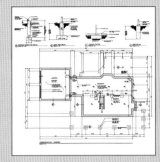

Foundation Plan

These plans will accurately show the dimensions of the footprint of your home, including load-bearing points and beam placement if applicable. The foundation style will vary from plan to plan. (Please note: There may be an additional charge for optional foundation plan. Please call for details.)

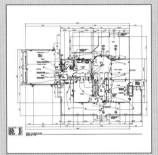

Detailed Floor Plans

The floor plans of your home accurately depict the dimensions of the positioning of the walls, doors, windows, stairs, and permanent fixtures. They will show you the relationship and dimensions of rooms, closets, and traffic patterns. The schematic of the electrical layout may be included in the plan.

Roof Plan

The information necessary to construct the roof will be included with your home plans. Some plans will reference roof trusses, while many others contain schematic framing plans. These framing plans will indicate the lumber sizes necessary for the rafters and ridgeboards based on the designated roof loads.

Typical Wall Section

This section will address insulation, roof components, and interior and exterior wall finishes. Your plans will be designed with either 2x4 or 2x6 exterior walls, but if you wish, most professional contractors can easily adapt the plans to the wall thickness you require.

Exterior Elevations

These fronts, rear, and side views of the home include information pertaining to the exterior finish materials, roof pitches, and exterior height dimensions.

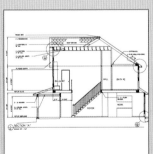

Typical Cross Section

A cut-away cross section through the entire home shows your building contractor the exact correlation of construction components at all levels of the house. It will help to clarify the load bearing points from the roof all the way down to the basement. Available for most plans.

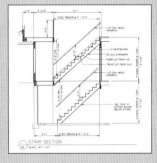

Stair Details

If the design you have chosen includes stairs, the plans will show the information that you need in order to build them-either through a stair cross section or on the floor plans.

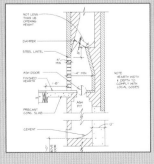

Fireplace Details

If the home you have chosen includes a fireplace, a fireplace detail will show typical methods of constructing the firebox, hearth, and flue chase for masonry units, or a wood frame chase for zero-clearance units. Available for most plans.

Cabinet Plans

These plans, or in some cases elevations, will detail the layout of the kitchen and bathroom cabinets at a larger scale. Available for most plans.

Options & Extras

Reversed Home Plans

Need your plan flipped end-for end? Simply order your plan "reversed" and you'll receive one full set of mirror-image plans (with the writing backwards) as a master guide for you and your builder. The remaining sets in your order will come as originally designed, so the dimensions and notes are easily read. Reversed plans are only available with multiple set orders. Some plans are available in an easy-to-read "Right-Reading Reverse" format. Call 800-235-5700 for Right-Reading Reverse availability. Mirror Reverse $50 Charge. Right-Reading Reverse $135 Charge.

Remember to Order Your Materials List

For obtaining faster, more accurate bids, materials lists give the quantity, dimensions and specifications for the major materials needed to build your home. Materials Lists are available for all home plans except as otherwise indicated, but can only be ordered with a set of home plans. Electrical, plumbing and HVAC specifications are not included. **Call 800-235-5700 for pricing.**

State Seals for Construction Prints

Many of our home plan construction drawings can be sealed by an architect that is registered in most states. Although an architect's seal will not guarantee approval of your home plan blueprints, a seal is sometimes required by your state or local building department in order to get a buil-ding permit. Please talk to your local building officials, before you order your blueprints, to determine if a seal is needed in your area. You will need to provide the county and state of your building site when ordering an architect's seal on your blueprints. Please allow at least an additional five to fifteen working days to process your order. Call 800-235-5700 for details.

State Energy Certificates

A few states require that an energy certificate be prepared for your new home, to their specifications, before a building permit can be issued. Your local building official can tell you if one is required in your state. Please note: energy certificates are only available on orders for construction prints with an architect's state seal. Call 800-235-5700 for more details, or to order.

Specifications & Contract Form

You will receive this form free of charge with your home plan order. The form is designed to be filled in by you or your contractor, noting the exact materials to be used in the construction of your new home. Once signed by you and your contractor it will provide you with peace of mind throughout the construction process.

Questions?

Call our customer service department 1-800-235-5700.

Detail Plans

Information on Construction Techniques—NOT PLAN SPECIFIC

PLEASE NOTE: These detail plans are not specific to any one home plan and should be used ONLY as a general reference guide.

$\$19.95$ per set (includes postage) ($47.95 for all three)

Because local codes and requirements vary greatly, we recommend that you obtain drawings and bids from licensed contractors to do your mechanical plans. However, if you want to know more about techniques—and deal more confidently with subcontractors—we offer these remarkably useful detail sheets. These detail sheets will aid in your understanding of these technical subjects.

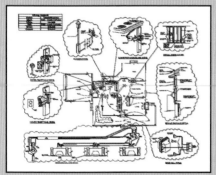 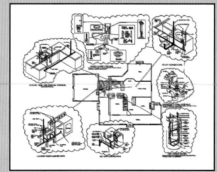 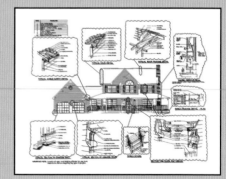

Residential Electrical Details

Eight sheets detailing distribution panel layout with outlet and switch schematics, circuit breaker and wiring installation methods and ground fault interrupter specifications. Conforms to requirements of National Electrical Code. Color coded with a glossary of terms.

Residential Plumbing Details

Eight sheets detailing plumbing hook-ups for toilets, sinkes, washers, sump pumps and septic system construction. Conforms to requirements of National Plumbing Code. Color coded with a glossary of terms and quick index.

Residential Construction Details

Ten sheets detailing foundation options (poured concrete basement, concrete block, or monolithic concrete slab). Shows all aspects of floor, wall and roof framing. Provides details for roof dormers, overhangs, chimneys and skylights. Conforms to requirements of Uniform Building Code or BOCA code. Includes a glossary of terms and quick index.

Modifying
Your Design Easily

BEFORE

How to Modify Your Garlinghouse Home Plan

Simple modifications to your dream home, including minor non-structural changes and material substitutions, can be made by you and your builder with the consent of your local building official, by marking the changes directly on your blueprints. However, if you are considering making significant changes to your chosen design, we recommend that you use the services of the Garlinghouse staff. We will help take your ideas and turn them into a reality, just the way you want.

Here's our procedure:

Call 800-235-5700 and order your modification estimate. **The fee for this estimate is $50**. We will review your plan changes and provide you with an estimate to draft your specific modifications before you purchase the vellums. **PLEASE NOTE:** A vellum must be purchased to modify a home plan design. After you receive your estimate, **if you decide to have Garlinghouse do the changes, the $50 estimate fee will be deducted from the cost of your modifications**. If, however, you chose to use a different service, the $50 estimate fee is non-refundable. (Note: Personal checks cannot be accepted for the estimate.)

A 75% deposit is required before we begin making the actual modifications to your plans.

Once the design changes have been completed to your vellum plan, a representative will call to inform you that your modified vellum plan is complete and will be shipped as soon as the final payment has been made. **For additional information, call us at 800-235-5700**. Please refer to the Modification Pricing Guide for estimated modification costs.

Reproducible Vellums for Modification Ease

If you decide not to use Garlinghouse for your modifications, we recommend that you follow our same procedure of purchasing vellums. You then have the option of using the services of the original designer of the plan, a local professional designer, or an architect to make the modifications.

With a vellum copy of our plans, a design professional can alter the drawings just the way you want, then you can print as many copies of the modified plans as you need to build your house. And, since you have already started with our complete detailed plans, the cost of those expensive professional services will be significantly less than starting from scratch.

Modification Pricing Guide

Prices for changes will vary depending on the number of modifications requested, the house size, quality of original plan, format provided and method of design used by the original designer. Typically, modifications cost around $1500, excluding the price of the (hand-drawn or computer generated) vellum.
Please contact us to get your $50 estimate at: 800-235-5700

AFTER

Ignoring Copyrights Laws Can Be A $100,000 Mistake

⊘ What You Can't Do

U.S. copyright laws allow for statutory penalties of up to $100,000 per incident for copyright infringement involving any of the copyrighted plans found in this publication. The law can be confusing. So, for your own protection, take the time to understand what you can and cannot do when it comes to home plans.

⊘ You Cannot Duplicate Home Plans

Purchasing a set of blueprints and making additional sets by reproducing the original is illegal. If you need more than one set of a particular home plan, you must purchase them.

⊘ You Cannot Copy Any Part of a Home Plan to Create Another

Creating your own plan by copying even part of a home design found in this publication without permission is called "creating a derivative work" and is illegal.

⊘ You Cannot Build a Home Without a License

You must have a specific permission or a license to build a home from a copyrighted design, even if the finished home has been changed from the original plan. It is illegal to build one of the homes found in this publication without a license.

"How do we build this house with the features we really want - and stay within our budget?"

"All the bells and whistles." Know what they're going to cost before you build, with BuildQuote™. Unlike any other construction cost estimating system, BuildQuote™ allows you to compare the costs of various building material choices on the same house plan. BuildQuote™ is easy to use and puts you in control of construction costs by calculating how your choices in flooring, siding, roofing and more, will affect the final cost to build.

At $29.99, BuildQuote™ is one of the wisest investments you can make before you build.

Learn more at www.garlinghouse.com
With BuildQuote™, your cost is your choice.

BuildQuote™ is a licensed trademark of RSMeans.

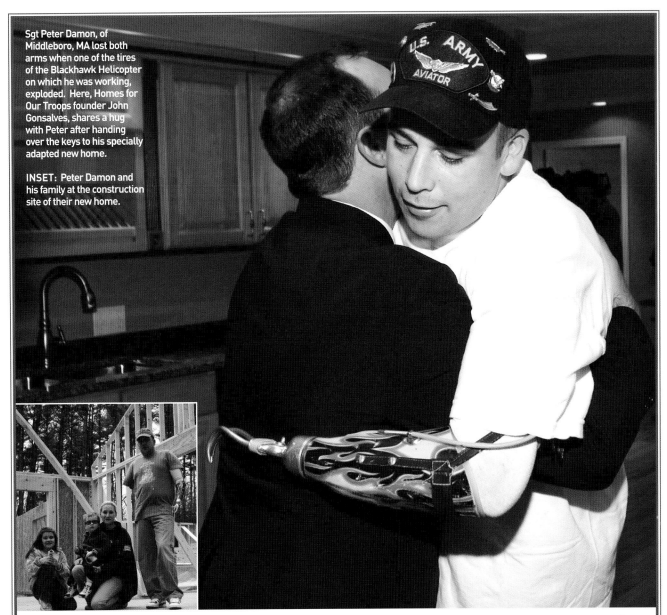

Sgt Peter Damon, of Middleboro, MA lost both arms when one of the tires of the Blackhawk Helicopter on which he was working, exploded. Here, Homes for Our Troops founder John Gonsalves, shares a hug with Peter after handing over the keys to his specially adapted new home.

INSET: Peter Damon and his family at the construction site of their new home.

THANK A HERO

Most of us will never know the harsh realities of war. But there are those among us - veterans of combat - who understand its horrors all too well. They have bravely risked their lives in the heat of battle, only to return home to their families bearing unimaginable wounds. Often, these life-altering injuries require extensive modifications to their homes, just to allow for day-to-day living.

Homes for Our Troops is a non-partisan, non-profit organization that builds and renovates homes for war veterans who have lost limbs, are blind, deaf, or paralyzed; or have other severe injuries sustained while serving our country.

To date, Homes for Our Troops has constructed dozens of homes for wounded veterans - homes suited to their difficult physical needs. All of this has been accomplished though the help of volunteers on job sites, as well as through monetary donations from concerned individuals, businesses and a variety of organizations.

The Garlinghouse Company is committed to supporting the mission of Homes for Our Troops. We invite you to provide your support as well. To learn more about Homes for Our Troops and to discover ways in which you can make a positive difference in the lives of these wounded veterans, visit www.homesforourtroops.org.

Order Form

Price Level	1 Set	4 Sets	8 Sets	Vellums	PDF Files*	CADD Files*	Material List*	Add. Sets
A	$ 485.00	$ 555.00	$ 595.00	$ 735.00	$ 735.00	$ 1,235.00	$ 60.00	$ 50.00
B	$ 515.00	$ 585.00	$ 625.00	$ 765.00	$ 765.00	$ 1,265.00	$ 60.00	$ 50.00
C	$ 545.00	$ 615.00	$ 655.00	$ 795.00	$ 795.00	$ 1,295.00	$ 70.00	$ 50.00
D	$ 575.00	$ 645.00	$ 685.00	$ 825.00	$ 825.00	$ 1,325.00	$ 70.00	$ 50.00
E	$ 605.00	$ 675.00	$ 715.00	$ 855.00	$ 855.00	$ 1,355.00	$ 70.00	$ 50.00
F	$ 635.00	$ 705.00	$ 745.00	$ 885.00	$ 885.00	$ 1,385.00	$ 70.00	$ 50.00
G	$ 665.00	$ 735.00	$ 775.00	$ 915.00	$ 915.00	$ 1,415.00	$ 70.00	$ 50.00
H	$ 695.00	$ 765.00	$ 805.00	$ 945.00	$ 945.00	$ 1,445.00	$ 80.00	$ 50.00
I	$ 725.00	$ 795.00	$ 835.00	$ 975.00	$ 975.00	$ 1,475.00	$ 80.00	$ 50.00
J	$ 755.00	$ 825.00	$ 865.00	$ 1,005.00	$ 1,005.00	$ 1,505.00	$ 80.00	$ 50.00
K	$ 785.00	$ 855.00	$ 895.00	$ 1,035.00	$ 1,035.00	$ 1,535.00	$ 80.00	$ 50.00
L	$ 845.00	$ 915.00	$ 955.00	$ 1,095.00	$ 1,095.00	$ 1,595.00	$ 90.00	$ 50.00

*not all plans offer CAD files, PDF Files, & Materials List.

To Place an Order

To order your home plans or ask questions about a plan call **toll free 1-800-235-5700**
To order your plan on-line using our secure server, visit:
www.familyhomeplans.com

Order Code No. **H7SCP**

____Set(s) of blueprints for plan # _____ $ _____

____Vellum for plan # _____ $ _____

____PDF files for plan # _____ $ _____

____CADD files for plan # _____ $ _____

____Foundation _____ $ _____

____* Call for pricing on alternate foundations ____ $ _____

____Additional set(s) (Not available for 1 set-study set) _____ $ _____

____Mirror Image Reverse _____ $ _____

____Right Reading Reverse _____ $ _____

____Materials list for plan # _____ $ _____

____Detail Plans (Not plan specific) @ $19.95 each - All 3 @ $ 47.95

____❑ Construction ❑ Plumbing ❑ Electrical ____ $ _____

____Shipping _____ $ _____

____Subtotal_____ $ _____

____Sales Tax (VA and SC residents add 5%. Not required for other states.) $ _____

TOTAL AMOUNT ENCLOSED _____ $ _____

Shipping

Home Plan Shipping

US Orders: Ground $25
2nd $40
Overnight $50

CANADA: Expedited $80

International: 3-4 Weeks $100

Project Plan Shipping

Ground $10
2nd $20
Overnight $30

Expedited $60

***Plan orders will ship out the following business day.

Credit Card Information

Charge To: ❑ Mastercard ❑ Visa ❑ American Express ❑ Discover

Card # | | | | | | | | | | | | | | | | | | |

Signature _____ Exp. ____/____

Name: _____

Street: _____

City: _____

State: _____ Zip Code: _____

Daytime Phone: _____

Email Address: _____

Send your check, money order, or credit card information to:
(No C.O.D.'s Please) *Prices subject to change without notice.*

Please submit all **UNITED STATES & OTHER NATIONS** orders to:
The Garlinghouse Company
Attn: Order Fulfillment Dept.
4125 Lafayette Center Drive, Suite 100
Chantilly, VA 20151
CALL: (800) 235-5700 FAX: (703) 222-9705

Payment must be made in U.S. funds. Foreign Mail Orders: Certified bank checks in U.S. funds only
TERMS OF SALE FOR HOME PLANS: All home plans sold through this publication are copyright protected. Reproduction of these home plans, either in whole or in part, including any direct copying and/or preparation of derivative works thereof, for any reason without the prior written permission of The Garlinghouse Co., is strictly prohibited. The purchase of a set of home plans in no way transfers any copyright or other ownership interest in it to the buyer except for a limited license to use that set of home plans for the construction of one, and only one, dwelling unit. The purchase of additional sets of that home plan at a reduced price from the original set or as a part of a multiple-set package does not entitle the buyer with a license to construct more than one dwelling unit.

Blueprint Order Information

Before ordering, please read all ordering information.

For Our **USA** Customers:
Order Toll Free: 1-800-235-5700
or FAX your Credit Card order to 1-703-222-9705
All foreign residents (except Canada) call 1-703-547-4154

For Our **CANADIAN** Customers:
Order Toll Free: 1-800-235-5700 ext. 5

To Place an Order
To order your home plans or to ask a questions about a plan
1-800-235-5700

Customer Service
Questions on existing orders? **1-800-895-3715**

Please have ready: 1. Your credit card number 2. The plan number 3. The order code number

Order Code No. **H7SCP**

How Many Sets of Plans Will You Need?
The Standard 8-Set Construction Package
Our experience shows that you'll speed up every step of construction and avoid costly building errors by ordering enough sets to go around. Each tradesperson wants a set—the general contractor and all subcontractors: foundation, electrical, plumbing, heating/air conditioning, and framers. Don't forget your lending institution, building department, and, of course, a set for yourself. *** Recommended For Construction ***

To Reorder, Call 800-235-5700
If you find after your initial purchase that you require additional sets of plans, a materials list, or other items, you may purchase them from us at special reorder prices (please call for pricing details) provided that you reorder within six months of your original order date. There is a $28 reorder processing fee that is charged on all reorders. For more information on reordering plans, please contact our Sales Department.

An Important Note About Building Code Requirements
All plans are drawn to conform to one or more of the industry's major national building standards. However, due to the variety of local building regulations, your plan may need to be modified to comply with local requirements—snow loads, energy loads, seismic zones, etc. Do check them fully and consult your local building officials. A few states require that all building plans used be drawn by an architect registered in that state. While having your plans reviewed and stamped by such an architect may be prudent, laws requiring non-conforming plans like ours to be completely redrawn forces you to unnecessarily pay very large fees. If your state has such a law, we strongly recommend you contact your state representative to protest. The rendering, floor plans, and technical information contained within this publication are not guaranteed to be totally accurate. Consequently, no information from this publication should be used either as a guide to constructing a home or for estimating the cost of building a home. Complete blueprints must be purchased for such purposes.

Customer Service/Exchanges Call 800-895-3715
If for some reason you have a question about your existing order, please call 800-895-3715. Your plans are custom printed especially for you once you place your order. For that reason we cannot accept any returns. If for some reason you find that the plan you have purchased from us does not meet your needs, then you may exchange that plan for any other plan in our collection. We allow you 30 days from your original invoice date to make an exchange. At the time of the exchange, you will be charged a processing fee of 30% of the total amount of your original order, plus original shipping costs, plus the difference in price between the plans (if applicable), plus the cost to ship the new plans to you. Call our Customer Service Department for more information. Please Note: Reproducible Vellums can only be exchanged if they are unopened.

Important Shipping Information
Please refer to the shipping charts on the order form for service availability for your specific plan number. Our delivery service must have a street address or Rural Route Box number—never a post office box. (PLEASE NOTE: Supplying a P.O. Box number will only will delay the shipping of your order.) Use a work address if no one is home during the day. Orders being shipped to APO or FPO must go via First Class Mail. Please include the proper postage. For our International Customers, only Certified bank checks and money orders are accepted and must be payable in U.S. currency. For speed, we ship international orders Air Parcel Post. Please refer to the chart for the correct shipping cost.

Important Canadian Shipping Information
To our friends in Canada, we have a plan design affiliate in Penticton, BC. This relationship will help you avoid the delays and charges associated with shipments from the United States. Moreover, our affiliate is familiar with the building requirements in your community and country. We prefer payments in U.S. currency.

Design, Build & Decorate

Your New Home on Your Table
Don't let the frustration of complicated home design software get between you and your dream. Visualize and test your ideas using our proven design systems.

3-D Home Kit
* $34.95
(plus $9.95 shipping)
"Build" Your New Home
Construct a three-dimensional scale model home of up to 3,000 square feet. (For larger homes, order an extra kit.) A complete assortment of cardboard building materials—from brick, stone, clapboards, roofing and decking to windows, doors, skylights, stairs, bathroom fixtures, kitchen cabinets and more. Includes Floor Plan Grid, interior walls, special Scaled Ruler and Roof Slope Calculator, professional design notes and complete model building instructions.

Home Quick Planner
* $24.95
(plus $9.95 shipping)
Design and Decorate Your New Home
Go ahead! Knock down walls and move cabinets, bathroom fixtures, furnture, windows and doors—even whole rooms. 700 pre-cut, reusable peel-and-stick furniture, fixture and architectural symbols. Includes 1/4-in. scale Floor Plan Grid, stairs, outlets, switches, lights, plus design ideas.

To order, call 1-800-235-5700

Plan Index

One Story Home Plans

PLAN #	SQ.FT.	PAGE #
45667	2525	176
82117	3003	101
97511	3032	183
61052	3059	89
45666	3092	208
45665	3106	188
87400	3135	220
63219	3183	36
55836	3276	182
66241	3281	97
44064	3365	96
66239	3417	105
66234	3428	84
63260	3430	180
63162	3436	175
66088	3510	102
96884	3594	69
73104	3600	94, 95
65912	3623	60
53710	3687	145
97198	3798	205
44084	3823	90
44068	3887	100
97397	3909	214, 215
87401	4195	66, 67
66240	4599	118, 119
97714	5937	92, 93
73030	6223	86, 87
97157	6311	98, 99

Two Story Home Plans

PLAN #	SQ.FT.	PAGE #
92623	2653	59
87315	2967	219
62012	3060	30
62256	3130	31
87305	3144	42
87304	3216	35
99437	3235	34
65472	3251	55
72030	3265	133
72049	3270	120
97704	3296	15
97717	3311	22
55730	3323	184
50020	3366	14
72031	3385	125
87316	3420	43
92671	3445	18, 19
44085	3662	165
98251	3688	25
98281	3698	128
10778	3746	47
94937	3806	148
24800	4836	226, 227
10768	4963	194, 195

Two Story Home Plans with Master Bedroom on Main Level

PLAN #	SQ.FT.	PAGE #	PLAN #	SQ.FT.	PAGE #	PLAN #	SQ.FT.	PAGE #
50053	2524	224	53705	3467	164	61025	4155	12, 13
94644	2898	197	97459	3473	27	53734	4170	126, 127
76129	2934	65	97163	3489	114	66237	4182	138, 139
64980	2992	213	65910	3499	24	65240	4204	70, 71
62104	3002	204	63023	3557	174	24978	4207	48, 49
64984	3016	187	96883	3570	169	50108	4222	17
97525	3029	186	53798	3609	149	99440	4228	58
62094	3060	207	72016	3620	140	65614	4242	38, 39
99425	3072	201	93182	3650	104	97166	4247	106, 107
53719	3091	158	97515	3658	185	53748	4320	222, 223
65650	3096	137	53708	3669	154	61049	4532	82, 83
99177	3109	108	63024	3680	109	53775	4547	172, 173
24969	3122	54	72059	3691	136	53776	4574	52, 53
87314	3138	225	73068	3697	78	96885	4626	150, 151
44083	3142	218	55739	3715	216	68359	4629	142, 143
94622	3149	192	73243	3716	115	97756	4652	72, 73
72029	3159	132	97162	3728	85	63077	4725	228, 229
73027	3256	170	61042	3740	200	53743	4934	166, 167
97169	3259	116	92237	3783	50	62067	4978	198, 199
96818	3272	217	53768	3798	171	96882	5003	56, 57
66242	3273	144	50127	3816	110	44086	5010	44, 45
65908	3284	40	69008	3850	46	50154	5072	76, 77
73176	3332	155	63360	3855	202	53744	5087	146, 147
92219	3335	37	67845	3863	64	73406	5139	80, 81
94645	3335	196	99402	3904	79	96886	5183	160, 161
68186	3335	122, 123	10670	3935	88	65615	5474	28, 29
66243	3355	124	24803	3947	68	97358	5752	156, 157
87302	3368	91	99462	3950	51	50062	6209	8, 9
62297	3419	206	62020	3955	26	66236	6274	134, 135
99486	3422	193	82126	3978	16	63082	6462	130, 131
66238	3428	121	53802	4004	162, 163	68361	7004	152, 153
57302	3430	168	63073	4094	20, 21			
76131	3448	181	63166	4106	32, 33			
96881	3464	212	99408	4139	62, 63			